JUNIOR CERTIFICATE

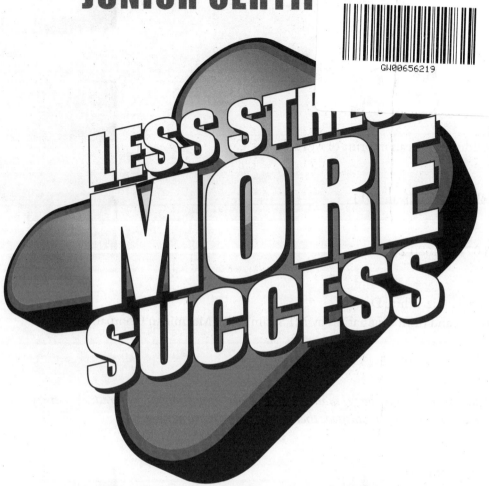

LESS STRESS MORE SUCCESS

Business Studies Revision

John F. O'Sullivan

Gill Education
Hume Avenue
Park West
Dublin 12
www.gilleducation.ie

Gill Education is an imprint of M.H. Gill & Co.

978 07171 4680 2

Design by Liz White Designs
Artwork and print origination by MPS Limited, a Macmillan Company

The paper used in this book is made from the wood pulp of managed forests. For every tree felled, at least one tree is planted, thereby renewing natural resources.

For permission to reproduce photographs, the author and publisher gratefully acknowledge the following:

© Alamy: 38, 130R; Courtesy of An Post: 131; Courtesy of Australian Wool Innovation Limited: 27B; Courtesy of Eircom: 130L; Courtesy of Excellence Ireland Quality Association: 27C; Courtesy of Guaranteed Irish: 27T; Courtesy of The Irish Congress of Trade Unions: 151; Courtesy of The National Consumer Agency: 30; Courtesy of The Ombudsman: 31.

The authors and publisher have made every effort to trace all copyright holders, but if any has been inadvertently overlooked we would be pleased to make the necessary arrangement at the first opportunity.

CONTENTS

Preface

The aim of this book is to provide students with a comprehensive summary of the Junior Certificate Business Studies course, **both Ordinary and Higher Level**.

- All chapters updated to reflect **recent** business developments.
- It contains more than **fifty fully-worked solutions** to exam questions.
- **Past examination papers** are fully **analysed** with reference to specific questions outlined.
- The start of the book contains advice on how to approach the **examination**, **exam format** with specific information on description of **questions**, **marks** per question and **time allocation** is included.

I hope that this book will be of major assistance when revising business studies in the months prior to the Junior Certificate examination.

John F. O'Sullivan BComm HDE
Business Studies Department
St Peter's Community School
Passage West
Co. Cork

This book is dedicated to Claire, Breffni, Shane, Cillian and Jennifer.

Examination Format, Advice, Guidelines

Ordinary Level

Examination format

One paper – 400 marks – 2½ hours

Section A – 20 short questions covering the entire syllabus at 5 marks each = 100 marks.

Answer **ALL** questions.

Section B – 8 questions, **ANSWER 5** questions at 60 marks each = 300 marks.

Examination timing

Reading time	10 minutes
Section A	25 minutes
Section B	23 minutes per question

Examination advice

Section A **(100 marks)**

- Section A is compulsory; all 20 short questions must be answered in the **Examination booklet**.
- These short questions can be taken from any part of the syllabus.
- Remember:
  (a) Short correct answers are required.
  (b) Where one tick (✔) is required, tick only ONCE.
  (c) Roughwork and calculations must be shown.
  (d) Calculators may be used – but show workings clearly.
- Section A questions will be a mixture of calculations, matching terms and explanations, completing sentences/documents, true/false questions, balancing an account.

Section B **(300 marks)**

Section B will contain 8 questions. Students must answer any **5** questions.

Section B will be answered in the **Examination Booklet**.

Questions in Section B may be taken from the following areas:

- Household Budget
- Final Accounts – Business
- Final Accounts – Service Firm
- Letter Writing
- Banking
- Employment and Wages
- Business Documents

- Petty Cash/Analysed Cash Book
- Club Accounts
- Farm Accounts
- Forms of Business Ownership
- Delivery/Transport
- Borrowing
- Marketing/Sales Promotion/Advertising
- Insurance
- Economics, National Budgeting
- Inflation, Foreign Trade
- Chain of Production/Channels of Distribution
- Information Technology
- Consumer/Letter of Complaint

exam focus
Tick each one off after you have revised it.

Analysis of past examination papers

Section B – Ordinary Level

	2010	2009	2008	2007	2006	2005	2004	2003	2002	2001	2000
Household Budget	1	1	1	1	1	1	1	1	1	1	1
Final Accounts – Business	2	2	2	2	2	2		2	2	2	
Final Accounts – Service							2				2
Letter Writing	3	3	3	3	3	3	3	3	3	3	3
Banking			4	4			4	4		4	4
Employment and Wages	4			7	4	4			4	7	
Business Documents	5	5	5	5	5	5	5	5	5	5	5
Petty Cash/Analysed Cash Book			6		6	6			6	6	
Club Accounts	6			6			6				6
Farm Accounts		6					6				
Forms of Business Ownership		4			7	8			7		
Delivery/Transport		7	7	8		7			8		
Borrowing								8			7
Marketing/Sales Promotion							7				
Insurance	7							7			
Economics, National Budgeting, Foreign Trade, Production	8	8	8		8		8			8	
Information Technology											8

Higher Level

Note: Material that is to be studied only by those taking Higher level is indicated in the text.

Examination format

Two papers – 400 marks

Paper I	240 marks	21/2 hours

Section A

20 short questions covering the entire syllabus at 4 marks each = 80 marks

Answer ALL questions.

Remember to include Section A in your Answer Book.

Section B

6 Questions given.

Answer any **4** questions at 40 marks each = 160 marks

Paper II	160 marks	2 hours

6 Questions given.

Answer any **4** questions at 40 marks each = 160 marks

Examination timing

Paper I	2½ hours
Reading Time	5 minutes
Section A	45 minutes approx.
Section B	25 minutes for each question
Paper II	2 hours
Reading Time	4 minutes
Questions	29 minutes for each question

Examination advice

Paper I Section A **(80 marks)**

- All **20** questions must be answered on the question paper.
- Allow approximately 45 minutes for Section A.
- These questions can be chosen from any part of the syllabus.
- Remember to **return completed Section A with your answer book.**
- Remember:
  (a) Short correct answers are required.
  (b) Where one tick (✔) is required tick only ONCE.
  (c) Roughwork and calculations must be shown.
  (d) Calculators may be used – but show workings clearly.

- Section A questions will be a mixture of:
  - calculations
  - matching terms and explanations
  - multiple choice
  - double-entry bookkeeping
  - completing business documents
  - control accounts
  - currencies, etc.

Paper I Section B **(160 marks)**

Answer **4 Questions** from 6 at 40 marks each.

Students must apply their knowledge of the course to Household, Personal and Social situations.

Questions in **Section B** may be taken from the following areas:

- Household Budgeting
- Club Accounts
- Economics, National Budgeting, Trade
- Money/Banking/Borrowing
- Consumer
- Insurance
- People at Work
- Information Technology

Tick off each one when you have revised it.

Analysis of past examination papers

Paper I, Section B – Higher Level

	2010	2009	2008	2007	2006	2005	2004	2003	2002	2001	2000
Household Budget	1	1	1	1	1	1	1	1	1	1	1
Club Accounts	2	2	2	2	2	2	2	3	5	5	4
Economics, National Budgeting, Trade	3	3	3	3	3	6	3	4	6	4	3
Money/Banking/ Borrowing	6	4	4	5	6	4	5	2	2	3	2
Consumer	4		5	4		5		5	3		5
Insurance		5			5		4			2	
People at Work	5	6	6	6	4	3	6	6	4		6
Information Technology										6	

Paper II **(160 marks)**

Answer **4** out of 6 questions.

Students must apply their knowledge of the course to business situations.

Questions in Paper II may be taken from the following:

- Books First Entry, Ledger, Trial Balance
- Business Documents
- At Work
- Marketing
- Insurance
- Final Accounts
- Banking, Finance, Cash Flow Forecast
- Delivery Systems
- Forms of Business
- Ratio Analysis
- Analysed Cash Book – Monitoring Overheads

Tick each one off when you have revised it.

Analysis of past examination papers

Paper II – Higher Level

	2010	2009	2008	2007	2006	2005	2004	2003	2002	2001	2000
Books First Entry, Ledger, Trial Balance	1	1	1	1	1	1	1	1	1	1	1
Business Documents	2	2	2	2	2	2	2	2	5	2	2
At Work			3		3			3		5	
Marketing			3	5	6		3			3	
Insurance	3					3					4
Final Accounts	4	4	4	4	4	4	4	4	2	4	3
Banking, Finance, Cash Flow Forecast	6			3		5	5	6	4		5
Delivery Systems	5		5		5			5		6	
Forms of Business		6				6			3		
Ratio Analysis		5		6					6		
Analysed Cash Book – Monitoring Overheads			6				6				6

SECTION 1
The Business of Living

Budgeting

The Consumer

Financial Services for the Consumer

1 Income

To be able to:

- Identify sources of income
- Estimate or calculate income
- Interpret a wages slip
- File and record income

A. Income

Income is money we receive.

B. Regular income

Regular income is received each week or month, e.g. wages, salary, unemployment benefit.

C. Additional income

Additional income is received occasionally, e.g. overtime, bonus, commission.

D. Benefit in kind

It is a non-financial reward in lieu of money which workers may receive, e.g. subsidised meals, company car.

E. Sources of income

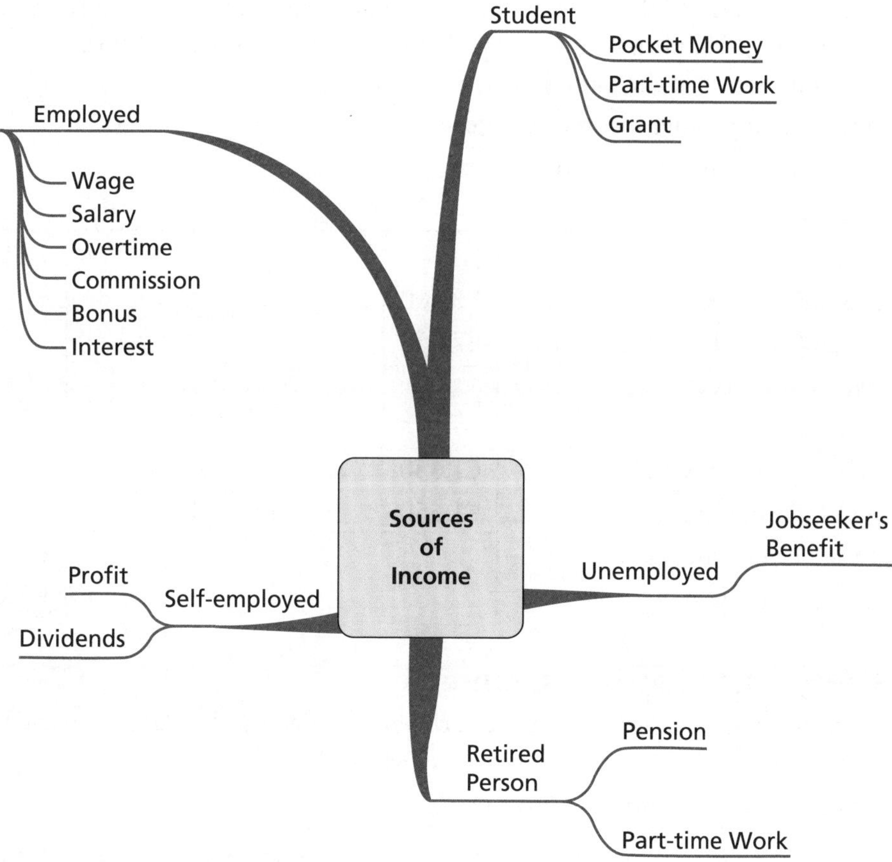

F. Gross wage (Gross pay)

Gross wage = basic pay + overtime + commission + bonus

G. Net wage (Net pay)

Net wage = gross pay − deductions

H. Deductions

There are two types of deduction: statutory deductions and non-statutory deductions.

I. Statutory deductions

The three statutory deductions are **PAYE**, **PRSI** and **Universal Social Charge (USC)**.

1. PAYE (Pay as you earn)

This is **income tax**: every employee is liable to pay income tax, which is calculated using the **'Tax Credits' system** as follows:

(1) The employee is taxed on the full amount of their income, that is, income multiplied by the appropriate rate(s) of tax.

(2) Employee's tax credit is deducted from tax liability to give net amount of income tax due.

Example – Tax Computation

John is single and earns €50,000 a year. He has single-person tax credit of €1,650 and a PAYE credit of €1,650. He pays tax on the first €32,800 at the rate of 20% and on the remainder of his salary at the rate of 41%.

Calculate: (i) John's net income tax due.
(ii) His net income for the year.

Solution

Wages/Salary			€50,000
Tax: €32,800 at 20%	€6,560		
Tax: €17,200 at 41%	€7,052		
Gross income tax		€13,612	
Less tax credit			
Single-person tax credit	€1,650		
PAYE tax credit	€1,650	(€3,300)	
Net income tax due			€10,312
Net income for year			€39,688

2. PRSI (Pay-related social insurance)

This is a contribution toward a **social welfare benefit** that may be claimed in the future, i.e. jobseeker's benefit, illness benefit and state pension.

PRSI is charged as a percentage of gross pay.

What income tax is used for	What PRSI is used for
It helps to pay for state services:	It provides the following benefits:
Gardaí	Jobseeker's benefit
Army	Maternity benefit
Health services	State pension
Public services	Illness benefit
	Deserted wife's benefit
	Widow's pension
	Dental/Optical benefit

3. Universal social charge (USC)

A tax payable on gross income from all sources.

J. Non-statutory deductions

These are deductions that the employee requests to be taken from his/her gross pay, e.g. union fees, Health Insurance (VHI, Quinn Healthcare, Hibernian Health), pension (superannuation), car insurance, savings. The employer deducts these at source and passes them on to the relevant organisation.

K. Summary

Gross pay = Basic pay + Overtime + Bonus + Commission
Net pay = Gross pay − Total deductions

This is a payslip question.

Grace McKenna is employed as an Accounting Technician in Rockwell Oil Company Ltd. Her normal working week is 36 hours. If she works any longer, she gets overtime pay at time and a half.

Grace's wage slip for 8 January 2011 was:

Employee: Grace McKenna		**Week 1**	**8th January 2010**	
PAY	€	DEDUCTIONS	€	Rockwell Oil Company Ltd
BASIC	432.00	PAYE	90.00	
OVERTIME	18.00	PRSI	9.60	
		USC	18.40	NET PAY
GROSS PAY	€450.00	TOTAL DEDUCTIONS	€118.00	€332.00

(A) (i) What is Grace McKenna's basic pay per hour? (5)

(ii) How many hours overtime did she work in Week 1? (5)

(B) The following week Grace worked 40 hours. Her PAYE was €100.80, her PRSI was €10.00 and her Universal Social Charge was €22.18. There was no change in her basic pay. Using this information, complete her wage slip for Week 2 dated 15 January 2011. (20)

Suggested solution

(A)	**(i)** Grace McKenna's Basic Pay Per Hour	€12 (5)	Workings: $\frac{€432\ (1)}{36\ (1)} = €12$
	(ii) Number of hours overtime worked	1 Hour (5)	Workings: 12 (1) × 1.5 (1) = 18

(B) Grace's wage slip 15th January 2010.

Employee	**Grace McKenna**		**Week 2**	**Date: 15/01/09 (1)**
PAY	€	DEDUCTIONS	€	Rockwell Oil Company Ltd
BASIC	432.00 (3)	PAYE	100.80 (2)	
OVERTIME	72.00 (4)	PRSI	10.00 (2)	
		USC	22.18 (2)	NET PAY
GROSS PAY	504.00 (2)	TOTAL DEDUCTIONS	132.98 (2)	371.02 (2)

ROUGH WORK;	Gross Pay	Deductions	Net Pay	
Basic	36 hours × €12 = €432	Paye 100.80	Gross Pay	504.00
O/T	4 hours × €18 = € 72	Prsi + 10.00	Deductions	−132.98
		USC + 22.18		
	€504	€132.98		€371.02

See:

Ordinary Level
Section A
2005 Q7
2003 Q7

Higher Level
Paper I Section A
2008 Q6
2007 Q2

2 Expenditure

To be able to:

- List major items of household expenditure
- Classify expenditure under appropriate headings
- Prepare simple expenditure estimates
- Check bills/invoices/delivery notes
- File and record expenditure

A. Types of expenditure

1. Fixed expenditure

A **fixed amount** must be paid out on a **fixed date**.

2. Irregular expenditure

Amount varies and/or the **payment date varies**.

3. Discretionary expenditure

Spending on **unnecessary items** and undertaken only if one has surplus cash. Expenditure that could be done without.

B. Examples of household expenditure

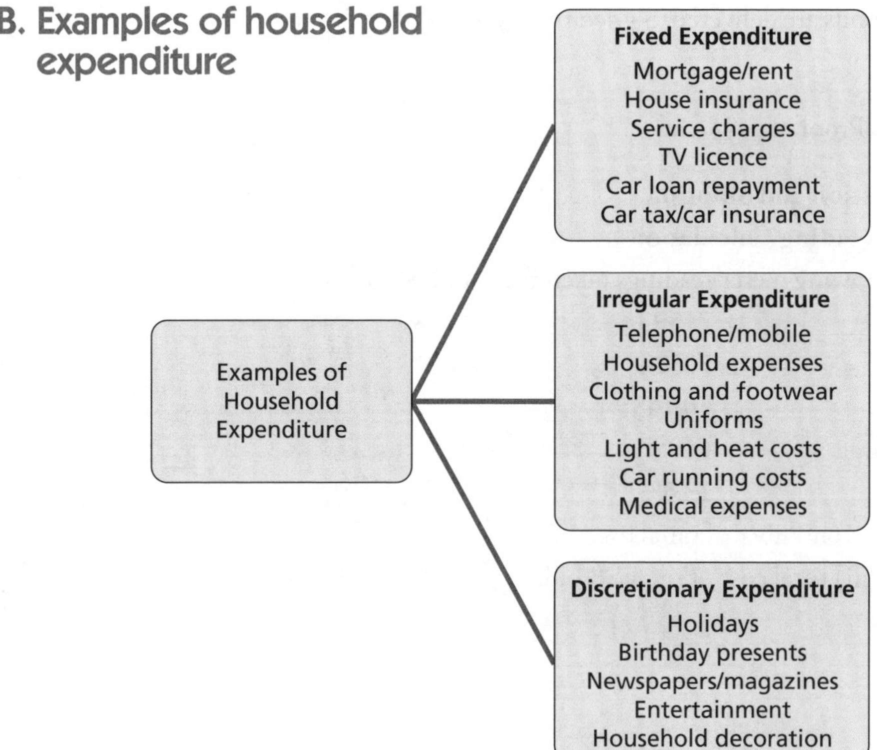

C. Filing expenditure records

Electricity bills, telephone bills and all other invoices, delivery notes and receipts should be carefully filed in a safe place so that they can be easily and quickly located when required.

D. Checking bills – invoices – delivery notes

All bills should be checked for accuracy before you pay them.

1. Electricity bill

This bill is made up of General Domestic (charge per unit used), Standing Charge (rental for service and meters) and Value Added Tax.

2. Telephone bill

A **landline telephone bill** is made up of residence line rental, equipment rental, call charges and value added tax (VAT).

A mobile phone bill is made up of a monthly service charge, call charges and value added tax (VAT).

3. Invoice

Sent by seller to buyer when goods are bought on credit. Shows quantity, description, unit price, VAT and total cost.

4. Delivery note

Sent when goods are delivered. Signed by buyer. Proof of delivery.

5. Receipt

List of items. Proof of payment.

Sample Question and Solution

ESB Meter Reading Calculation

Study the following meter readings taken from an ESB bill.

Present	71593
Previous	70524
Cost per unit	€0.1455
Standing charge	€19.49
VAT	13.5%

Calculate (i) number of units used

(ii) total cost of the ESB bill.

Solution

(i) Number of units used:

$$71593 - 70524 = 1069$$

(ii) Total of the ESB bill

Cost of electricity 1069 × €0.1455	€155.54
Standing charge	€ 19.49
	€175.03
VAT @ 13.5% on €175.03	€ 23.63
Total due	€198.66

You must be able to calculate the cost of a household bill, e.g. ESB bill, from the information given.

See:

Ordinary Level
Section A
2009 Q5
2009 Q6
2009 Q7
2007 Q9
2006 Q11

Higher Level
Paper I
Section A
2005 Q16
2004 Q17

3 The Budget

To be able to:

- Match income and expenditure
- Set priorities in expenditure
- Identify shortfalls in income
- Prepare personal/household budget
- Analyse critically personal/household spending
- Classify and record income and expenditure
- Compare the budget with the actual expenditure
- Prepare a Budget Comparison Statement

A. Budget

A budget is a financial plan which forecasts future income, expenditure and savings. We must estimate or guess what these figures will be.

B. Reasons why a household would prepare a budget

(1) To make sure that the family will have **enough to cover future expenditure**.

(2) To ensure that they will **live within their means**.

(3) To see which months they may have to arrange **borrowings**.

(4) To see which months they will have a **surplus** or **deficit**, so that they can plan for the future.

(5) To identify the amount to be spent on **different areas**, e.g. car, house.

(6) To identify areas of expenditure that they could **cut back** on.

C. Planning a budget

(1) Estimate future income – include overtime, etc. and allow for expected pay increases/pay decreases.

(2) Estimate future expenditure – allow for increased costs, i.e. cost of living, and for possible future expenditure, e.g. holidays.

(3) **Compare estimated income with estimated expenditure.**
If estimated income > estimated expenditure → **surplus** (savings).
If estimated income < estimated expenditure → **deficit** (shortage).
If estimated income = estimated expenditure → **breakeven.**

(4) **Net cash = Total income − Total expenditure.**

(5) **Opening cash** is 'the amount of cash that the family have at the start of the month'.

(6) **Closing cash** is found by **'adding net cash to the opening cash'** and is the amount of cash that the family **expects** to have at the end of the month.

(7) **Closing cash of one month will be the opening cash of the next month.**

Planning a Budget

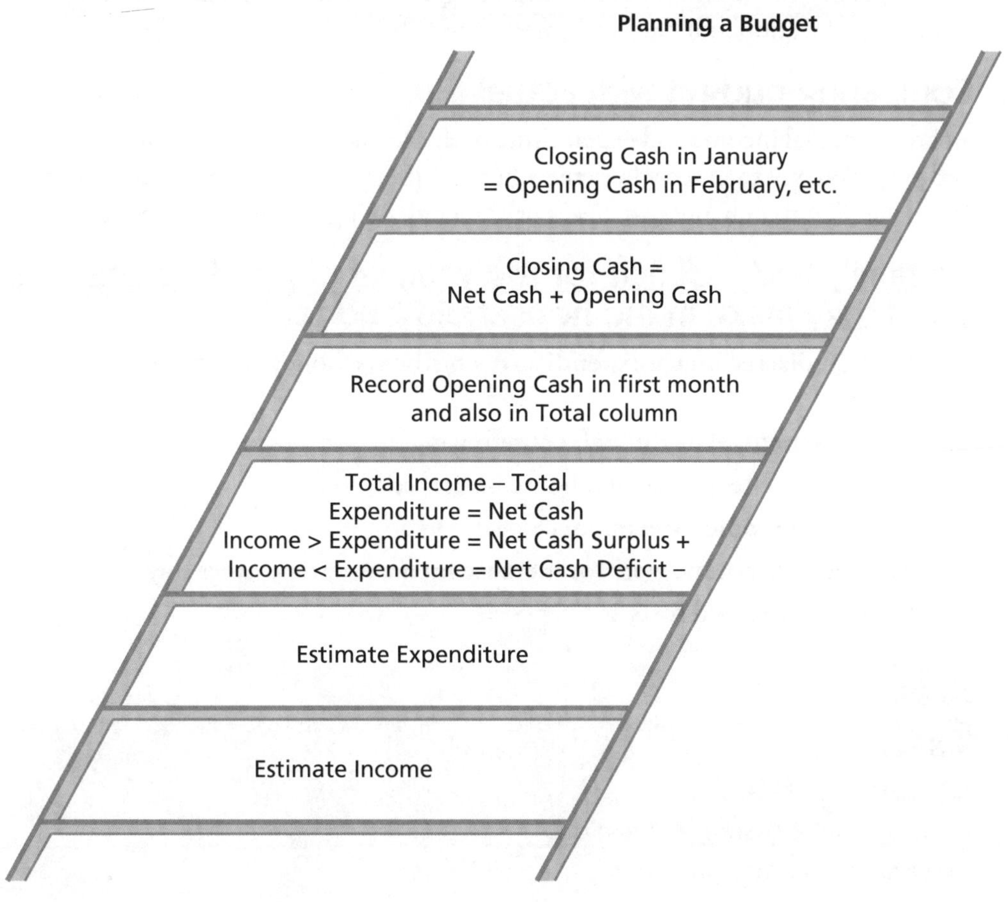
Closing Cash in January
= Opening Cash in February, etc.
Closing Cash =
Net Cash + Opening Cash
Record Opening Cash in first month
and also in Total column
Total Income – Total
Expenditure = Net Cash
Income > Expenditure = Net Cash Surplus +
Income < Expenditure = Net Cash Deficit –
Estimate Expenditure
Estimate Income

D. Current expenditure and capital expenditure, accruals and savings

(1) **Current expenditure** is spending on items necessary to run the house and family **on a daily basis**, e.g. food, entertainment, clothing, petrol.

(2) **Capital expenditure** is spending on items that will last a **long period of time**, e.g. house, car, television, video, cooker.

(3) **Accruals**
These are services that we do not pay for at the time of use, e.g. electricity, telephone. When we get the bill we pay the amount owed.

(4) **Planning Savings**
This is putting money aside for the future, e.g. to buy a house or car, to finance children's education, holidays and emergencies.

E. Comparing budget with actual

Compare the actual income and expenditure with the budgeted income and expenditure. You will then see where the actual is different from the budgeted and be able to make whatever changes are necessary when drawing up the next budget.

F. If a family had a deficit for the year, what possible changes could they make in the household budget?

(1) **Cut back on discretionary expenditure** – birthdays, holidays, entertainment, presents, etc.

(2) **Reduce household costs** through better buying.

(3) Shop around for **cheaper** car and house insurance.

(4) Consider **selling some investments**.

(5) Do overtime or part-time work, or **increase income** in some other way.

(6) **Cut back** on household costs and car costs.

Ordinary Level

This is a Household Budget question.

Answer all parts of this question:

The following is a budget for the Kerins household for four months from July to October. Opening Cash in Hand is €594.

Planned Income

- Liam Kerins earns €2,880 net per month and expects to receive a holiday bonus of €600 net in August.
- Martina Kerins earns €2,340 net per month and expects to receive an increase of €300 net in October.
- Child Benefit is expected to be €540 per month.

Planned Expenditure

- House **mortgage** of €900 per month will **increase** by €120 per month from 1 August.
- The Kerins household pays a **health insurance** premium of €180 per month. This premium will **increase** by €30 per month from 1 September.
- **House insurance** premium of €720 **per year** will be **payable monthly** from 1 July.
- **Education** costs will be as follows: French Language course fees will cost €960 in July, school uniforms will cost €1,020 in August, and school books and school tours will cost €700 in September. School bus ticket will cost €80 in September.
- **Telephone bills** for the landline are expected to be €150 in July and €168 in September. In addition bills for mobile phones and broadband will cost the household €108 per month.
- Household expenses are €1,440 per month except in August, when they will be €600 **less**.
- The Kerins household uses **public transport** to travel to work. Liam's train ticket will cost €198 per month and Martina's Dart ticket costs €114 per month.
- **Household bills** for light and heat are expected to be €120 in August and €92 in October while heating oil will cost €100 in October.
- **Entertainmen**t will cost €660 per month except in September when it will be an **extra** €300 due to a wedding.
- The Kerins have booked a **holiday** costing €3,600. They must pay a deposit of €960 in July and the balance in August.
- **Birthday presents** will cost €600 in September and €840 in October.

(A) Complete the blank Household Budget form (using all the above figures). (50)

(B) Explain what 'House Mortgage' means. (5)

(C) The Kerins family intends to paint the living room in November at a cost of €900. State whether this expenditure will be fixed, irregular, or discretionary. (5)

(60 marks)

Suggested solution and marking scheme

(A)

Kerins Household	July	Aug	Sept	Oct	Total
Planned Income	€	€	€	€	€
Liam Kerins – Salary	2,880(½)	3,480(½)	2,880(½)	2,880(½)	12,120(½)
Martina Kerins – Salary	2,340(½)	2,340(½)	2,340(½)	2,640(½)	9,660(½)
Child Benefit	540(½)	540(½)	540(½)	540(½)	2,160(½)
A. TOTAL INCOME	5,760(½)	6,360(½)	5,760(½)	6,060(½)	23,940(½)
Planned Expenditure					
Fixed					
House mortgage	900(½)	1,020(½)	1,020(½)	1,020(½)	3,960(½)
Health insurance	180(½)	180(½)	210(½)	210(½)	780(½)
House insurance	60(½)	60(½)	60(½)	60(½)	240(½)
SUBTOTAL	1,140(½)	1,260(½)	1,290(½)	1,290(½)	4,980(½)
Irregular					
Education costs	960(½)	1,020(½)	780(½)		2,760(½)
Telephone costs	258(½)	108(½)	276(½)	108(½)	750(½)
Household expenses	1,440(½)	840(½)	1,440(½)	1,440(½)	5,160(½)
Transport costs	312(½)	312(½)	312(½)	312(½)	1,248(½)
Light and heat		120(½)		192(½)	312(½)
SUBTOTAL	2,970(½)	2,400(½)	2,808(½)	2,052(½)	10,230(½)
Discretionary					
Entertainment costs	660(½)	660(½)	960(½)	660(½)	2,940(½)
Holiday costs	960(½)	2,640(½)			3,600(½)
Birthday costs			600(½)	840(½)	1,440(½)
SUBTOTAL	1,620(½)	3,300(½)	1,560(½)	1,500(½)	7,980(½)
B. Total Expenditure	5,730(½)	6,960(½)	5,658(½)	4,842(½)	23,190(½)
Net Cash (A–B)	30(½)	(600)(½)	102(½)	1,218(½)	750(½)
Opening Cash	594(½)	624(½)	24(½)	126(½)	594(½)
Closing Cash	624	24	126	1,344(½)	1,344(½)

(B) House Mortgage: **A long-term** (2) **Loan** (1) for a house. **The deeds of the house are held by the lender until the loan (and interest) is repaid in full.** (2) If the borrower defaults, the lender may reclaim the house and sell it.

(C) Spending €900 Painting: **Discretionary** (5)

HL

Higher Level

Type I Partially Completed Budget

This is a Household Budget question.

Answer all parts of this question.

This question involves a partially completed budget form for three months. You are required to complete this form by filling in the figures for the remainder of the year as well as the Total for the Year column.

(A) At the end of the question is a partially completed budget form for the Watson household. You are required to complete this form by filling in the figures for the 'Estimate April to December' column and the 'Total for Year' column. The following information should be taken into account.

- Ernst expects to get promoted to a management position in July and this will **increase his salary** by 30% from 1 July.
- Virginia expects to earn an extra €420 from overtime in October and will get a Christmas bonus of €600 in December.
- The Watson household expects to get a **tax refund** of €2,400 in July.
- The **car loan** will be fully paid off after the August payment.
- The **mortgage** will increase by €32 per month from 1 June.
- **House insurance** is payable monthly and will decrease by 20% from 1 June.
- **Landline telephone** costs will be €120 every second month from 1 May and mobile phone costs are estimated to be €84 per month from 1 April.
- **Household costs** will remain the same except for the month of July when they will decrease by 50% as they plan to go on holiday.
- **Car running** costs are expected to remain the same each month.
- **ESB** for the 12 months (January – December) is expected to be €1,020.
- The household expect to spend €180 on **birthdays** in May and €540 in October.
- Ernst and Virginia plan to go on **holiday** in July which will cost €3,000. The balance must be paid in June.
- There is no further household decoration planned. **(30 marks)**

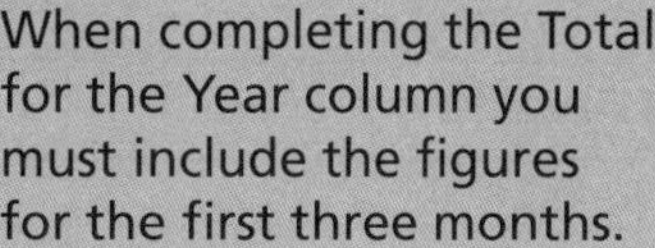

When completing the Total for the Year column you must include the figures for the first three months.

Suggested solution and marking scheme

(A) Planned Budget for the Watson Household

Income	Jan	Feb	March	Total Jan–Mar	Estimate Apr–Dec	Total for year Jan–Dec
Ernst Watson Salary	1,080	1,080	1,080	3,240	11,664(1)	14,904(1)
Virginia Watson Salary	900	900	900	2,700	9,120(1)	11,820(1)
Tax Refund					2,400(1)	2,400(1)
TOTAL INCOME	1,980	1,980	1,980	5,940	23,184	29,124
Planned Expenditure						
Fixed						
Car Loan	360	360	360	1,080	1,800(1)	2,880(1)
Mortgage	660	660	660	1,980	6,164(1)	8,144(1)
House insurance	30	30	30	90	228(1)	318(1)
SUBTOTAL	1,050	1,050	1,050	3,150	8,192	11,342
Irregular						
Telephone costs	180	84	264	528	1,236(1)	1,764(1)
Household costs	480	480	480	1,440	4,080(1)	5,520(1)
Car running costs	72	72	72	216	648(1)	864(1)
Light and heat	108	96	72	276	744(1)	1,020(1)
SUBTOTAL	840	732	888	2,460	6,708	9,168
Discretionary						
Birthdays		60		60	720(1)	780(1)
Household Decoration			2,400	2,400		2,400
Holidays			600	600	2,400(1)	3,000(1)
SUBTOTAL		60	3,000	3,060	3,120	6,180
TOTAL EXPENDITURE	1,890	1,842	4,938	8,670	18,020	26,690
Net Cash	90	138	(2,958)	(2,730)	5,164(1)	2,434(1)
Opening Cash	192	282	420	192	(2,538)(1)	192(1)
Closing Cash	282	420	(2,538)	(2,538)	2,626(1)	2,626(1)

Marking Scheme – Household Budget

Estimate April–Dec = 15 figures @ 1 mark each **15 marks**

Total for year Jan–Dec = 15 figures @ 1 mark each **15 marks**

Excluding totals of Income, Expenditure, all subtotals and household decoration

HL

Type II Original Budget and Revised Budget

This is a Household Budget question.

Answer ALL sections.

This question involves an original budget and a revised budget where household circumstances have changed.

(A) At the end of the question is an original Budget and a revised Budget form for the O'Mahony family from July to September. After preparing the Budget for July to September Mr O'Mahony was informed that he would be getting a promotion in his job. This would result in an increase in the family income starting in July. The O'Mahony family decided to revise their Budget in view of the changed circumstances.

You are required to complete the revised Budget form, taking the following into account:

- Mr O'Mahony's **annual salary** will be €28,560 net payable monthly.
- Ms O'Mahony decided to go job sharing which would result in a 30% **reduction in her net salary** from the beginning of July.
- The O'Mahony family decided to buy a **second car** by getting another loan. The total cost of this new loan including interest will be €12,000 repayable monthly over 4 years beginning in August.
- The **insurance** on the **new car** will cost €450 for the year payable in full in July.
- **Household costs** will be reduced by €80 per month immediately.
- **Car running costs** will increase by 40% per month beginning in July.
- They decided to take a **holiday** in July at a cost of €1,600.
- They intend to postpone the **house decorating** until November.
- All other income and expenses are to remain the same.

(30 marks)

(B) Answer the following questions.

(i) In the original Budget name a month in which planned income is greater than planned expenditure.

(ii) Comment on the O'Mahony's finances before July.

(iii) Is their revised budget a good one for their new circumstances? Give reasons for your answer.

(10)

(40 marks)

Source: Junior Certificate Higher Level

Suggested solution and marking scheme

(A)

	ORIGINAL BUDGET				REVISED BUDGET				
	JULY	AUG	SEPT	TOTAL	JULY	AUG	SEPT	TOTAL	
INCOME									
Mr O'Mahony Salary	1,700	1,700	1,700	5,100	2,380	2,380	2,380	7,140(1)	
Ms O'Mahony Salary	800	800	800	2,400	560	560	560	1,680(1)	
Child Benefit	40	40	40	120	40	40	40	120(1)	
Total Income	2,540	2,540	2,540	7,620	2,980(1)	2,980(1)	2,980(1)	8,940(1)	7 marks
EXPENDITURE									
Fixed									
House Mortgage	500	500	500	1,500	500	500	500	1,500(1)	
Car Loan	230	230	230	690	230	480	480	1,190(1)	
Car Insurance		510		510	450	510		960(1)	
House Insurance			190	190			190	190(1)	
Subtotal	730	1,240	920	2,890	1,180	1,490	1,170	3,840(1)	5 marks
Irregular									
Household Costs	920	920	920	2,760	840	840	840	2,520(1)	
Car Running Costs	115	115	115	345	161	161	161	483(1)	
Light & Heat		60		60		60		60(1)	
Telephone	75		75	150	75		75	150(1)	
Subtotal	1,110	1,095	1,110	3,315	1,076	1,061	1,076	3,213(1)	5 marks
Discretionary									
Holidays					1,600			1,600(1)	
Entertainment	200	200	200	600	200	200	200	600(1)	
Birthdays & Presents	40		40	80	40		40	80	
Household Decoration		175		175					
Subtotal	240	375	240	855	1,840	200	240	2,280(1)	3 marks
Total Expenditure	2,080	2,710	2,270	7,060	4,096(1)	2,751(1)	2,486(1)	9,333(1)	4 marks
Net Cash	460	−170	270	560	(1,116)	229	494	(393)	
Opening Cash	−100	360	190	−100	(100)(1)	(1,216)(1)	(987)(1)	(100)(1)	4 marks
Closing Cash	360	190	460	460	(1,216)(1)	(987)	(493)	(493)(1)	2 marks

(B)

(i) July or September. (2)

(ii) They owed 100. (1)

(iii) No. (1)

- They intend to overspend by €393.
- Net Cash disimproved from surplus 560 to deficit 393.
- Had to borrow on all 3 months.
- Discretionary expenditure increased too much, i.e. holidays.

One reason at 3 marks

OR

- Yes. (1)
- Had a surplus in August and September.
- Overdraft is declining each month.
- Had a holiday and a new car yet overdraft only €493.

One reason at 3 marks

Type III Budget Comparison Statement

This question involves a Budget Comparison Statement requiring students to compare budgeted and actual income/expenditure and complete the 'difference' column. Make sure to put in the plus (+) and minus (−) signs, otherwise marks will be lost. An example is provided on page 20.

Budget Comparison Statement

This is a Household budget question.

Answer all parts of this question.

When the Burke household checked their analysed Cash Book at the end of December they discovered that their actual income and expenditure for the 12 months differed from the budgeted figures (contained in the Budget Comparison statement at the end of question) due to the following:

- The **salaries** of the Burke household increased by 4%.
- There are two children in the household. The monthly **child benefit** increased by €20 per child from 1 September.
- The actual **interest** received for the year was €180.
- The Burke household received €400 from the **sale of old furniture**.
- **Mortgage payments** increased by €15 per month from 1 March.
- The Burke household have a no claims bonus, so their **car insurance** was 15% less than budgeted.
- The **house insurance** was €325 for the year.
- **Household costs** were 7.5% greater than budgeted.
- **Car costs** were €375 greater than budgeted.
- **Clothing and footwear** costs were €300 less than budgeted.
- **Light and heat** costs were 6% less than budgeted.
- **Medical expenses** of €2,500 were incurred due to a serious illness to one of the children.
- **Entertainment** costs averaged €100 per month except for the three months of June, July and December, which averaged €170.
- Due to a **wedding**, presents cost an additional €190.
- **Holidays** were cancelled due to child's illness.

Using the Budget Comparison Statement at end of question enter the appropriate figures into the **'Actual'** column.

Show the differences between the **'Actual'** and **'Budget'** figures by completing the column marked **'Difference'**. Use a **plus** or **minus** sign in front of each figure in that column.

Note: Use **'plus'** sign if **'Actual'** is GREATER than the **'Budget'** figure.
Use **'minus'** sign if **'Actual'** is LESS than the **'Budget'** figure.

Example:

	Budget	Actual	Difference
	260	200	−60
	470	490	+20
Total	730	690	−40

(22 marks)

Suggested solution and marking scheme

Budget Comparison Statement for the Burke household for the year.

INCOME	Budget Jan–Dec €	Actual €	Difference €
Salaries	21,000	21,840(½)	+840(½)
Child Benefit	720	880(½)	+160(½)
Interest	250	180(½)	−70(½)
Other		400(½)	+400(½)
TOTAL INCOME	21,970	23,300	+1,330(1)
EXPENDITURE			
Fixed			
Mortgage	4,080	4,230(½)	+150(½)
Car insurance	560	476(½)	−84(½)
House Insurance	235	325(½)	+90(½)
Subtotal	4,875	5,031	+156(1)
Irregular			
Household costs	7,800	8,385(½)	+585(½)
Car costs	1,550	1,925(½)	+375(½)
Clothing and footwear costs	2,000	1,700(½)	−300(½)
Light and heat costs	1,600	1,504(½)	−96(½)
Medical expenses	400	2,500(½)	+2,100(½)
Subtotal	13,350	16,014	+2,664(1)
Discretionary			
Entertainment costs	1,560	1,410(½)	−150(½)
Presents	300	490(½)	+190(½)
Holidays	1,800		−1,800(½)
Subtotal	3,660	1,900	−1,760(½)
TOTAL EXPENDITURE	21,885	22,945	+1,060(1)
Net Cash	85	355(½)	+270(½)
Opening Cash	1,400	1,400(1)	
Closing Cash	1,485	1,755(1)	

Marking Scheme: 32 figures × ½ mark = 16 marks
6 figures × 1 mark = 6 marks **(22 marks)**

Note: Do not complete the shaded boxes.

See:

Ordinary Level
Section A
2008 Q17
2006 Q1

Ordinary Level
Section B
2009 Q1
2008 Q1
2007 Q1
2006 Q1
2005 Q1

Higher Level
Paper I
Section B

Partially Completed Budget
2006 Q1
2003 Q1
2002 Q1

Original Budget and Revised Budget
2007 Q1
2004 Q1

Budget Comparison Statement
2009 Q1
2008 Q1
2005 Q1
2001 Q1

4 Household Accounts

To be able to:

- Prepare an Analysed Cash Book

A. Analysed Cash Book

Used to record actual income and expenditure of the household.

In the Analysed Cash Book we have two columns on each side, one for Cash and one for Bank.

An Analysed Cash Book is laid out as follows:

Debit Receipts (Money in) ANALYSED CASH BOOK Credit Payments (Money out)

Date	Details	Cash	Bank	Date	Details	Cheque Nos.	Cash	Bank	Analysis Columns

Explanation

(1) The debit side (left side) records opening cash and money coming in/received.

(2) The credit side (right side) records money owed to the bank and money going out/paid out.

B. Rule for analysed cash book

DEBIT: MONEY RECEIVED

CREDIT: MONEY PAID

C. Balancing analysed cash book

- Balance only Cash and Bank columns.
- Add both columns.
- Find difference = balance.
- Put balance on smaller side.
- Total both sides.
- Bring down balance (B/d) on opposite side.
- Bank DR → asset – money in bank.
  CR → overdraft
- Total analysis columns.

D. Contra entry

Affects both sides of Cash Book.

(1) Lodged Cash in Bank → Money into Bank → Debit
Money out of Cash → Credit

TYPES

(2) Withdrew from Bank → Money out of Bank → Credit
Money into Cash → Debit

E. 'Did household budget live within its means?'

Every household should try to live within its means for the week/month. However, this isn't always possible. To answer this question you find **total income** for the period and compare it with **total expenditure** for the period. If income was greater than expenditure – the family lived within its means. If expenditure was greater than income – the family did not live within its means.

This is a Household Account Question.

The Scanlon family keeps a record of all financial transactions in an Analysed Cash Book. On 1 March they had €215 in the bank.

During March they had the following bank transactions:

		€
March 2	Purchased paint for house by cheque (No. 32).	78
March 3	Lodged wages cheque.	1,347
March 4	Withdrew cash by ATM for groceries.	68
March 6	Paid for coat by cheque (No. 33).	89
March 9	Paid for car service by cheque (No. 34).	35
March 10	Lodged children's allowance.	60
March 13	Paid for medicine by cheque (No. 35).	32
March 16	Paid house insurance by cheque (No. 36).	167
March 18	Withdrew cash by ATM for groceries.	75
March 21	Bought petrol by cheque (No. 37).	49
March 25	Purchased shoes by cheque (No. 38).	56
March 27	Paid membership fee to Golf Club by cheque (No. 39).	450

(A) Enter the above figures in the Analysed Cash Book and balance it. Use the following money column headings:

Debit (Receipts) side: Total, Wages, Child Benefit, Other.

Credit (Payments) side: Total, Groceries, House, Shoes and Clothes, Car, Other.

(20 marks)

Suggested solution

(A)

Analysed Cash Book

Date (½)	Details (½)	Total	Wages	Child Benefit	Others	Date (½)	Details (½)	Cheq. No. (½)	Total	Groc.	House-hold	Shoes/ Clothes	Car	Others
Mar 1	Balance	215 (½)				Mar 2	Paint	32	78 (½)		78 (½)			
Mar 3	Wages	1,347 (½)	1,347 (½)			Mar 4	Groceries	ATM	68 (½)	68 (½)				
Mar 10	Child All.	60 (½)		60 (½)		Mar 6	Coat	33	89 (½)			89 (½)		
						Mar 9	Car Service	34	35 (½)				35 (½)	
						Mar 13	Medicine	35	32 (½)					32 (½)
						Mar 16	House Ins.	36	167 (½)		167 (½)			
						Mar 18	Groceries	ATM	75 (½)	75 (½)				
						Mar 21	Petrol	37	49 (½)				49 (½)	
						Mar 25	Shoes	38	56 (½)			56 (½)		
						Mar 27	Golf Club	39	450 (½)					450 (½)
			1,347 (½)	60 (½)					1,099 (½)	143 (½)	245 (½)	145 (½)	84 (½)	482 (½)
		1,622												
Mar 13	Balance	523 (½)												

Marking scheme:
Date column 2 × ½ = 1 mark
Details column 2 × ½ = 1 mark
Cheque no. column ½ mark
35 figures × ½ mark = 17½ marks
20 marks

See:
Higher Level
Paper I
Section B
2000 Q1A

The Consumer

Introduction to the concept of being a good consumer, consumer rights and consumer protection.

5 The Informed Consumer

To understand the following:

- The informed consumer
- The qualities of a good consumer
- A loss leader
- A price war
- How to calculate unit price
- How to order goods/services, receipts and credit notes
- Bar codes
- Symbols on goods

A. Consumer

A consumer is a person who buys goods and services, e.g. food, clothes, cars, entertainment, newspapers, etc.

B. The informed consumer

(1) Is aware of legal rights under consumer law.
(2) Is aware of organisations that protect him/her.
(3) Is able to make a valid complaint.
(4) Does not buy impulsively.
(5) Makes enquiries, shops around, checks prices to get value for money.
(6) Prepares a budget and sticks to it.
(7) Keeps receipts.
(8) Keeps the guarantee.
(9) Checks for value/quality.

C. Ordering goods and services

(1) **By letter** – keep a copy of the order-letter for future reference.

(2) **By telephone** – keep a written record and get the name of the person who took the order.

(3) **Personal call** – find out the exact cost, and view the goods.

D. Paying for goods

When you order the goods, you may be asked to pay a deposit – a small payment that is part of the purchase price and is made to ensure that the customer will return to collect the goods and pay the balance due.

E. Receipts

When you pay for the goods, you should receive a receipt – this is written proof that payment was made, and it may be required if there are any problems with the goods at a later date.

F. Symbols on goods

Guaranteed Irish – symbol of quality – operated by Guaranteed Irish

Approved Quality Symbol – used on products that have reached a high standard

G. Bar code

- Series of parallel lines, thirteen digits.
- Shows country of origin, product number, company number, check digit.
- Records price – receipt is produced.
- Stock record reduced by one.

H. Unit price

Unit pricing, i.e. per kg/litre, allows the consumer to find the best value. Consumers can calculate the unit price by dividing price by quantity.

$$\text{Unit Price} = \text{Price} \div \text{Quantity}$$

(i) Calculate the unit price for each of the following boxes of cereal.

Size	Price	Weight	Unit Price
Small	€1.58	400 g	
Medium	€2.70	750 g	
Large	€3.90	1 kg	

(ii) Which size represents the best value for money?

Suggested solutions

Workings

(i)

Unit Price = Price ÷ Quantity

Small	€1.58 ÷ 400	= 0.395 cent per gram
Medium	€2.70 ÷ 750	= 0.36 cent per gram
Large	€3.90 ÷ 1000	= 1.39 cent per gram.

(ii) Which size represents best value for money – MEDIUM

See:

Ordinary Level
Section A
2009 Q9
2008 Q13
2004 Q8
2001 Q15
2000 Q6

Higher Level
Paper I
Section A
2007 Q19

6 Consumer Rights and Protection

To be able to:

- Apply legislation
- Identify Consumer Protection Agencies

A. Why do consumers need protection?

To ensure that the standards of goods and services available to the public are reasonable and acceptable.

B. How is the consumer protected?

- The government protects the consumer by passing **laws**.
- **Agencies** have been set up to inform and protect individual consumers.

C. Laws

What are my rights when buying goods?

When you buy goods or services, you enter into a **contract** with the seller. You pay your money, and in return the seller is obliged to provide goods and services that meet certain conditions.

Sale of Goods and Supply of Services Act 1980

This sets out the conditions with which goods and services must comply, which are as follows:

(1) Goods should be:

- of **merchantable quality**.
- **fit for their purpose**.
- **as described**.

If goods are bought by **sample**, they should correspond with the sample.

(2) Suppliers of services should:

(a) Have the **necessary skill** to provide the service, e.g. car mechanic.

(b) Provide the service with **proper care and diligence**.

(c) Ensure that **materials and parts** used in the service will be of **merchantable quality**.

(3) It is the **seller** who is responsible for putting things right. The compensation may be:

- refund
- repair
- replacement.

You must learn the provisions of the Sale of Goods and Supply of Services Act 1980 and the Consumer Protection Act 2007.

(4) A **guarantee** is a bonus in addition to your normal legal rights. If you have a valid complaint, it may be easier to claim under the guarantee. A guarantee is where the manufacturer/supplier undertakes to repair or replace any defective part without charge during the period of the guarantee.

(5) **Illegal Shop Notices:**

NO MONEY REFUNDED
CREDIT NOTES ONLY
NO LIABILITY ACCEPTED FOR FAULTY GOODS
GOODS WILL NOT BE EXCHANGED

These notices are **illegal** and should not be displayed. You are not bound to accept a credit note. If your complaint is valid, you can refuse all offers of a credit note and insist on a cash refund.

Consumer Protection Act 2007

The main elements of the Consumer Protection Act 2007 are:

(1) **It established the National Consumer Agency**, whose main functions are to:

- Promote and protect the interests and welfare of consumers.
- Enforce consumer law.
- Encourage compliance with Consumer Laws.
- Investigate suspected offences under Consumer Laws.

national **consumer** agency
gníomhaireacht náisiúnta **tomhaltóirí**
putting **consumers** first

(2) **Consumer Protection. It deals with misleading claims about goods, services and prices.** In particular the Act:

- Protects consumers from misleading advertisements and requires that the information in advertisements is fair and accurate.
- It is illegal for an adviser or business to make false or misleading claims about goods, services or prices.

(3) **Misleading Practices, Aggressive Practices**

The Act prohibits traders from engaging in **misleading practices** and **aggressive practices** which may result in consumers purchasing products because of misleading advertising, misleading information, harassment, unfair pressure or threatening behaviour by the trader. These practices are prohibited by the Act.

EU legislation on labelling and price

Food labels – what the labels should show

(1) Name of food.
(2) List of ingredients in descending order of weight.
(3) Quantity.
(4) 'Best before date' for almost all food.
(5) Storage conditions or conditions of use.
(6) Name and address of manufacturer or seller.

(7) Particulars of place of origin.

(8) Instructions for use where necessary.

Pricing of food

(1) All foodstuffs must display a **selling price**.

(2) Food sold in bulk or loose must display a **unit price**.

D. Agencies that protect the consumer

1. Consumer Association of Ireland

(a) Set up to protect the interests of consumers in Ireland.

(b) It provides information and advice to members about goods, services and consumer law, and publishes an information magazine, *Consumer Choice.*

(c) It helps consumers to solve complaints.

2. Office of the Ombudsman

(a) **The Ombudsman**

The main duty of the Ombudsman is to investigate complaints made by members of the public about how they have been treated by public bodies in Ireland.

Financial Services Ombudsman

People can make a complaint if they are unhappy with the services provided by any of the following bodies:

- Government Departments
- Health Boards
- Local Authorities
- An Post (the post office)

(b) **The Financial Services Ombudsman**

The Financial Services Ombudsman deals independently with unresolved complaints from consumers about their individual dealings with all financial services providers. The Ombudsman is therefore the arbitrator of unresolved disputes and is impartial. This arbitration is provided as a free service to the complainant.

The following financial service providers may be **subject to investigation** by the Ombudsman:

- Banks
- Credit Unions
- Building Societies
- Mortgage, Insurance and other Credit intermediaries
- Insurance Companies

3. Trade associations

Most retailers and suppliers of services are members of Trade Associations that set down standards, e.g. Irish Travel Agents Association (ITAA), Society of Irish Motor Industry (SIMI).

You must be able to outline the role of Consumer Protection Agencies.

Consumers can complain to the relevant association if standards are not being met.

4. Advertising Standards Authority

(a) Promotes better standards of advertising.
(b) Ensures advertisements are decent and fair.
(c) They will investigate complaints from the public who find an advertisement to be untruthful. The ASAI may get the firm to withdraw or alter the advertisement.

5. Small claims court

- If a consumer has a claim against a trader for faulty goods/services up to **€2,000**, he/she can have the claim processed in the Small Claims Court.
- It is **quick and cheap**, as no solicitors are required.
- The court is managed by an official called the **registrar**.
- The claimant must pay a fee of **€15**, which is refundable if he/she wins the case.
- **The claimant must have made every effort to settle the dispute with the seller before appealing to the court.**

6. Media

Television and radio programmes, as well as newspapers and magazines, provide useful information to consumers. Here are some examples:

- *Prime Time*
- *Business News*
- *Consumer Choice*
- *Which*? magazine

7. National Standards Authority of Ireland

Monitors the safety standards of products sold in Ireland.

8. Financial Regulator

Financial documents should be clear. The Financial Regulator promotes consumers' interests by regulating financial services firms in Ireland.

exam Q

See:

Ordinary Level	**Higher Level**	**Higher Level**
Section A	Paper I	Paper I Section B
2007 Q12	Section A	2007 Q4
2006 Q2	2001 Q1	2005 Q4 c d
2005 Q15		2002 Q5 a c
2002 Q2		2002 Q3
2001 Q7		2000 Q5

7 Consumer Complaints

Caveat Emptor – Let the Buyer Beware

aims To be able to:
- Identify causes for complaint
- Present oral or written complaints
- File and record details
- Carry out simple research into consumer products
- Write a letter of complaint

A. Genuine complaints

If goods are not of merchantable quality, or not as described, or not fit for their purpose, you then have a valid complaint and are entitled to some remedy, such as a **cash refund**, **replacement** or **repair**.

B. Non-valid complaint

A complaint is not valid, and the consumer has no rights, if:

(1) You **change your mind** about the goods after buying them.

(2) A fault arises due to **misuse**.

(3) A fault was **pointed out at the time of purchase**.

Making a complaint

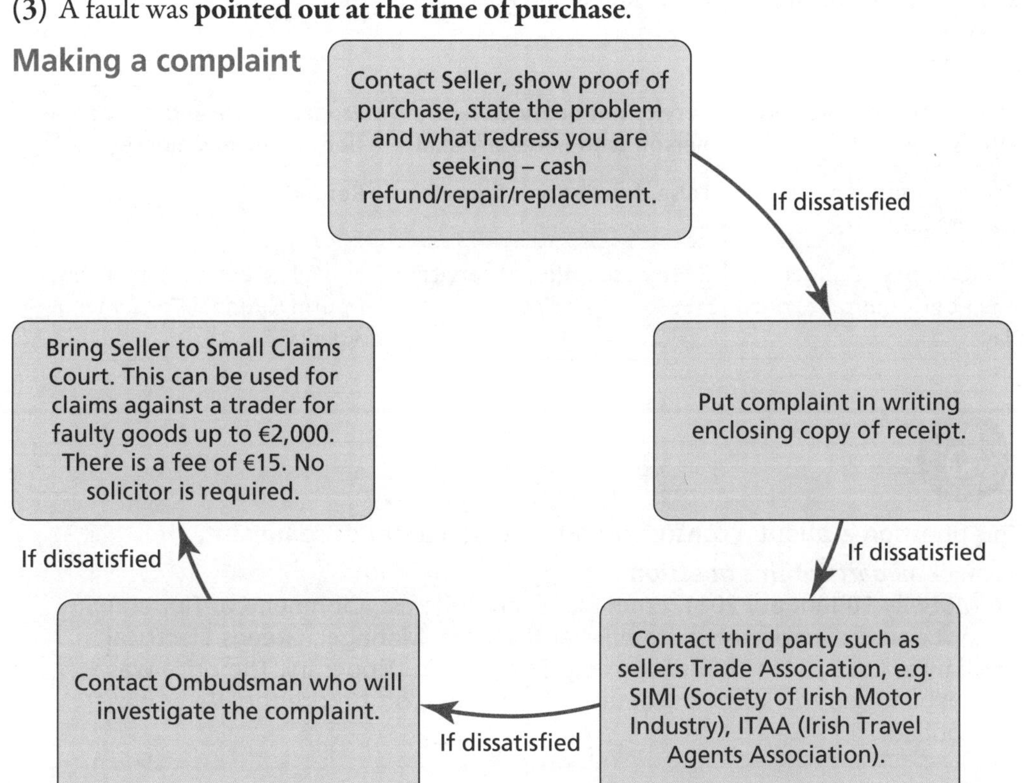

Contact Seller, show proof of purchase, state the problem and what redress you are seeking – cash refund/repair/replacement.
If dissatisfied
Put complaint in writing enclosing copy of receipt.
If dissatisfied
Contact third party such as sellers Trade Association, e.g. SIMI (Society of Irish Motor Industry), ITAA (Irish Travel Agents Association).
If dissatisfied
Contact Ombudsman who will investigate the complaint.
If dissatisfied
Bring Seller to Small Claims Court. This can be used for claims against a trader for faulty goods up to €2,000. There is a fee of €15. No solicitor is required.

C. Compensation

A consumer who has a valid complaint may be entitled to:

(1) Full **cash refund**.

(2) Replacement of the goods.

(3) Repair – where problem is of a minor nature.

What about a credit note?

A consumer may be offered a credit note instead of a cash refund. This allows him/her to buy something else in the same shop to the value of the credit note. **You are not bound to accept a credit note.**

What about a repair?

A repair may be an acceptable solution if the problem is of a minor nature.

D. Examples of consumer complaints

Complaint	Problem	Consumer rights
New car battery will not start car	Battery not of **merchantable quality**	Replacement or refund
Stain remover does not remove stain	Stain remover **not fit for purpose**	Replacement or refund
Shoe polish described as black on box but navy when applied	Polish **not as described**	Replacement
Lawnmower breaks down after service	**Service not provided by person with necessary skill**	Proper service and compensation for inconvenience
Car described as never crashed but it was	**False description of goods**	Refund
Photographs developed in one hour – but takes one day	**False description of services**	No rights, but consumer should inform National Consumer Agency

This question is about a consumer and writing a letter of complaint.

Answer all parts of this question.

On Monday 10 January 2011, Emma Shorten, Hillcrest, Clonmel, Co. Tipperary, bought a new electric kettle from Peter Richards, Manager, Greens Electrical Appliances Ltd., 20 North Main Street, Clonmel, Co. Tipperary. The price was €79. When used the kettle automatically switched off before the water was fully boiled.

On Wednesday 12 January 2011, Emma wrote to the shop manager stating that she bought the kettle in the shop and that it was faulty. She explained the fault, she said she would bring it back to the shop together with the receipt. She also stated what her rights were under consumer Law.

(A) Write the letter that Emma Shorten sent to Peter Richards on 12 January 2011. (40)

(B) Name **TWO** agencies that Emma could contact if she was not satisfied with the response received from Greens Electrical Appliances Ltd. In **each** case write **one** sentence to explain how the agency could help Emma. (12)

(C) List the **TWO** main laws that protect consumers. (8)

(60 marks)

You must be able to write a letter of complaint.

Suggested solution

(A) LETTER OF COMPLAINT

Hillcrest
Clonmel (2)
Co. Tipperary

12 January 2011 (2)

Mr Peter Richards
Manager
Greens Electrical appliances Ltd
20 North Main Street
Clonmel
Co. Tipperary (2)

Re: Complaint about Electric Kettle (1)

Dear Mr Richards (2)

I am writing to you in connection with a new electric kettle I bought in your shop on 10/01/2011. (4)

When used the kettle automatically switched off before the water was fully boiled. The kettle is clearly unfit for its purpose. (4)

I will be bringing it back to your shop together with my receipt. (4)

I hope it can be **repaired**, if not I will be looking for **a replacement** kettle or a full **refund**. These are my legal entitlements. (8)

I look forward to seeing you shortly.

Yours faithfully (2)

Emma Shorten (2)

3 marks for presentation and neatness

(4 marks English) as follows:

- **1 mark Paragraphs**
- **1 mark Punctuation**
- **1 mark Spellings**
- **1 mark Grammar**

Marking scheme – Letter of complaint

Letter Format:	**(20 marks)**
2 marks each for two addresses, date, salutation, close (yours___), signature (six items @ 2 marks each)	**12 marks**
1 mark for reference	**1 mark**
4 marks for English (paragraphs, punctuation, grammar, spelling)	**4 marks**
3 marks for presentation/neatness	**3 marks**
	20 marks
Letter Content:	**(20 marks)**
Where she bought the electric kettle	**4 marks**
Explanation of problem	**4 marks**
Future plan	**4 marks**
Two consumer rights mentioned 4 + 4	**8 marks**
	20 marks
	(Total 40 marks)

(B) EXAMPLES OF AGENCIES WHICH PROTECT CONSUMERS

- **National Consumer Agency**
  - Represents the voice of consumers
  - Enforces consumer legislation
  - Increases awareness of consumer issues
- **Small Claims Court**
  - Deals with consumer claims up to €2,000
  - It is quick and cheap, as no solicitors are required
- **Consumer Association of Ireland**
  - Set up to protect the interests of consumers in Ireland
  - Provides information and advice to members about goods, services and consumer law
  - Publishes an information magazine 'Consumer Choice'
  - Helps consumers to solve complaints.
- **Trade Association**
  - Set standards for their own members which ensure that consumers will get the best possible service.
  - Consumers can complain to the relevant association if standards are not being met.
- **National Standards Authority of Ireland (NSAI)**
  - Sets standards for safety and quality of goods and services which consumers buy.

Marking Scheme – Agencies which protect the consumer

Two agencies @ 3 marks each		**6 marks**
Two explanatory sentences @ 3 marks each	**6 marks**	**12 marks**

(C) List the two main laws that protect consumers.

1. Sale of Goods (2) and Supply of Services Act (2) 1980.
2. Consumer (2) Protection Act (2) 2007.

Marking Scheme – Laws that protect consumers

2 Consumer Laws @ 4 marks each **8 marks**

Total (60 marks)

See:

Ordinary Level	**Higher Level**	**Higher Level**
Section B	Paper I	Paper I
2008 Q3	Section A	Section B
2003 Q3	2006 Q16	2008 Q5

Introduction to money, banking services, personal borrowing, savings and insurance.

8 Money and Banking

To be able to:

- Identify different types of money
- Open and operate an account
- Recommend a method of payment
- Complete a cheque and other bank documents
- Interpret a statement
- Cross a cheque in an appropriate manner
- Show how a cheque might be negotiated
- Recommend a suitable financial institution
- Prepare a bank reconciliation statement
- Calculate interest on deposits and borrowings

1. Forms of money

A. Barter

Before money was introduced, people had a system of barter or **exchanging** one product for another.

B. Money

The problems with barter led to the introduction of money, which had a standard value. Gold and silver were chosen and minted into coins.

C. Paper money

People gave their gold and silver to a goldsmith for safe-keeping. The goldsmith gave the person a receipt. These receipts were then used to buy goods and services. The person in possession of these receipts returned to the goldsmith and collected the gold.

D. Forms of money today

(1) **Notes and coins** (Euro and Cent)

(2) **Cheques**

(3) **Plastic cards** – Credit cards, Laser cards, smart cards, ATM cards, store cards, charge cards.

E. The euro

The euro is the currency of **seventeen** European Union countries namely Belgium, Cyprus, Estonia, Germany, Greece, Spain, France, Ireland, Italy, Malta, Luxembourg, the Netherlands, Austria, Portugal, Finland, Slovakia and Slovenia. Euro notes and coins have been in circulation since January 2002.

Benefits of the euro

There are a number of clear benefits to having a single European currency.

(1) **Practical benefits for citizens** – tourism has increased, as citizens can travel more easily with the Euro. No currency conversion is required for travel within the Euro zone.

(2) **Price comparisons** – all goods and services are priced in Euros.

(3) **Reduced business costs** – there are no bank charges on foreign currency transactions.

2. Saving

A. Saving

Saving means not spending

Reasons for saving

(1) To put money aside for emergencies.

(2) To earn interest on money saved.

(3) To put a deposit on a house.

(4) To buy expensive items, like a car.

(5) To pay for children's education.

(6) To go on holiday.

B. Investing

Investing means making your savings work so that they will earn interest.

Why invest your savings?

(1) To earn interest.

(2) For safety reasons.

C. Factors to be considered before deciding where to invest

The wise investor will consider the following:

(1) **Safety** – will savings be safe?

(2) **Interest** – will savings earn interest?

(3) **Liquidity** – will it be easy to withdraw savings?

(4) **Tax** – will the investor have to pay Deposit Interest Retention Tax (DIRT)?
(5) **Future benefits** – mortgage/loan.
(6) **Convenience** – suitable opening hours.

D. Financial institutions for investing your savings

1. Commercial bank

Deposit account

- **Interest** is paid and is subject to **Deposit Interest Retention Tax** (DIRT).
- Money is **safe** and can be **withdrawn on demand**.

2. Building society

Deposit account

- A competitive interest rate is paid on deposits.
- Interest is subject to **DIRT**.
- **Savings record** – you can apply for a mortgage (House Loan).
- Many branches around the country with convenient opening hours.

3. Credit union

Savings account

- Interest on savings comes in the form of a dividend.
- Members can obtain loans at reasonable rates of interest.
- Local and convenient.

4. An Post

All savings invested with An Post are very safe. They are state-guaranteed.

(a) **Deposit account**

- **Interest** is paid on deposits.
- Interest is subject to **DIRT**.
- Withdrawals can be made at any branch of An Post.

(b) **Instalment saving**

- Save a **fixed amount** every month for twelve months.
- The money is then **left on deposit** for a period of one to five years.
- Guaranteed minimum rate of interest **after five years**.
- Interest is **tax-free**.

(c) **Savings certificates**

- Guaranteed minimum return after five years and six months.
- Interest is **tax-free**.

(d) **Savings bonds**

- Guaranteed minimum return after three years.
- Interest is **tax-free**.

5. Stocks and shares

People could invest their savings in **shares in companies**. The investor would:

- Get a **dividend**.
- Make a **capital gain** if share price increases.

6. Insurance companies

- A person could save by taking out an **endowment policy**.

E. Calculating interest on a deposit account

Interest on a deposit account is calculated on a simple interest or compound interest basis.

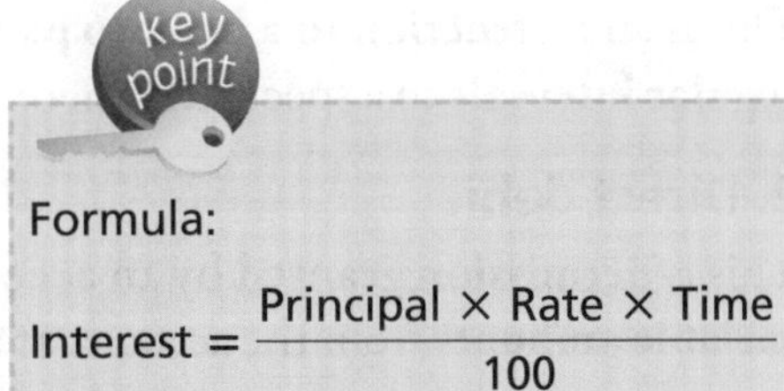

Formula:

$$\text{Interest} = \frac{\text{Principal} \times \text{Rate} \times \text{Time}}{100}$$

1. Simple interest

The interest is calculated on a fixed principal over a period of time.

2. Compound interest

The interest earned in one year is added on to the principal, and the next year interest is calculated on this new principal.

> CAR (Compound Annual Rate) is used to compare various deposits and investments in financial institutions.

F. Deposit interest retention tax (DIRT)

(1) A **tax on interest** earned in a Deposit Account.

(2) It is **deducted at 25%** rate by the financial institution and sent to the Revenue Commissioners.

Example

Gross interest earned	€400
Less DIRT 25%	€100
Interest received	€300

3. Money transmission

Money transmission is transferring money from one person to another.

Methods of transferring money within Ireland:

A. Cash – registered mail

Notes may be sent through the post, but the letter should be registered to ensure its safe transfer.

B. Cheque payments

1. Cheques

A person with a current account can make payments by cheque.

2. Bank draft

A bank draft is a cheque drawn by a bank on its own bank account. Very safe.

C. Direct bank payments

1. Standing order

This is an **instruction to a bank to pay** a **fixed amount** from the account at **fixed regular intervals** to a specified firm or creditor, e.g. rent, mortgage.

2. Direct debit

This is **permission granted by an account-holder to a creditor** to **withdraw fixed or variable amounts** from the account **at any time**, e.g. an ESB bill.

3. Credit transfer (Bank Giro)

This is a way of **transferring money directly** into another person's or firm's bank account.

4. Pay path

An electronic method for **transferring wages from employers to the bank account of their employees**. It is a safe, convenient and time-saving method of paying wages.

D. Card payments

1. Automated teller machine (ATM) – cash dispensers

(**a**) Customer is given an ATM card and a personal identification number, PIN.
(**b**) Customer goes to ATM at any bank, inserts card in machine, keys in PIN.
(**c**) Customer can lodge, withdraw, check the account balance, order a statement, order a cheque book, pay a bill.

2. Credit card

- Buying goods now but paying later.
- The credit card company pays the seller.
- The cardholder receives a **monthly** statement from the credit card company.
- If the cardholder **clears his/her** account each month, **no interest** or extra charges are payable. If the account is not fully cleared, a high rate of interest applies on the outstanding balance.
- Government stamp duty applies.
- Examples are MasterCard and Visa.

3. Charge card

- Buying goods now but paying later.
- **Account must be settled when statement arrives.**
- Fee is paid to card provider for use.
- Examples are American Express and Diners Club.

4. Store card/fuel card

- Department stores and oil companies give their customers store/fuel cards.
- Customers are given a credit limit.
- Examples include Esso, Shell, Texaco, Brown Thomas, and Marks & Spencer.

5. Laser card/debit card

- Operates from a Current Account.
- The Laser Card is swiped in the seller's terminal or card reader.
- The amount is entered (with cashback if required).
- The buyer enters PIN number or signature.
- The amount of the purchase is instantly transferred from the buyer's account to the seller's account by electronic means.
- A receipt is printed for the customer.
- The cardholder may use it to withdraw cash.

E. An Post – sending money home or abroad

An Post offers a variety of secure methods for sending money nationally and internationally. A person can send money nationally by postal money order and internationally by Eurogiro, Sterling Draft and Western Union.

1. Sending money nationally

Postal money order

You can pay bills, shop by mail order, donate to charity and send monetary gifts by post. Just go to your local post office to carry out the transaction.

2. Sending money internationally

(a) Eurogiro

Suitable if you are sending money to Europe. You transfer the money into the currency of the receiving country. It is paid to the recipient in cash or lodged into a bank account. It is cost-effective, and the service is carried out at most post offices. Transfers are usually completed within four working days.

(b) Sterling draft service

Suitable for making Sterling Draft payments to many countries worldwide. The Sterling Draft is lodged to the recipient's bank account.

(c) Western Union money transfer

Suitable if you need to send money quickly. Recipients pick up their money in local currency in minutes. Global coverage – no bank account is required. The recipient picks up the money at a local Western Union branch. The service is carried out at selected post offices nationwide.

F. Foreign exchange

1. Bank draft – foreign draft

A bank draft can also be purchased and made out in a foreign currency, e.g. US dollars. This is a very acceptable way of making foreign payments.

2. Traveller's cheques

(a) Cheques are pre-printed in various amounts in the currency required.
(b) Paid for and signed by the buyer in the presence of a bank official when purchased.
(c) Signed again when being cashed/used in the presence of the seller of the goods or services. Passport required to check the signatures.

3. Credit cards

MasterCard and Visa can be used as a means of paying for goods and services abroad.

4. Laser card

A laser card with Cirrus facility enables a person to withdraw cash from ATM machines displaying the Cirrus symbol worldwide.

This is a Banking Question. Answer (A) and (B).

(A) State a method of payment provided by Banks, which you would recommend, in **each** case below.

(i) A tenant wishes to pay rent monthly, directly from her own bank current account to the landlord's bank account.

Answer: *Standing Order.*

(ii) A student, who does not have a bank account, wishes to pay exam fees directly into the bank account of the Department of Education and Skills.

Answer: *Credit Transfer.*

(iii) A student wishes to send sterling to a London publisher for a book.

Answer: *Sterling Bank Draft.*

(iv) Mrs O'Connell wants to have her telephone bill paid in future directly by her bank from her current account.

Answer: *Direct Debit.* (24)

(B) Eithne Dunne, Ahamore, Castlecomer, Co. Kilkenny, has a current account No. 42367898 at the Castlecomer branch of the Bank of Ireland.

On 20 May 2014 Eithne visited her bank with €40 notes and €10 coins to send, by credit transfer, to her niece, Maura O'Gorman.

Maura O'Gorman keeps her account, No. 10864219, with the Allied Irish Banks Ltd, Rathmines branch, Dublin.

Assuming you are Eithne Dunne, complete fully the Credit Transfer form from the information supplied. (16)

Solution

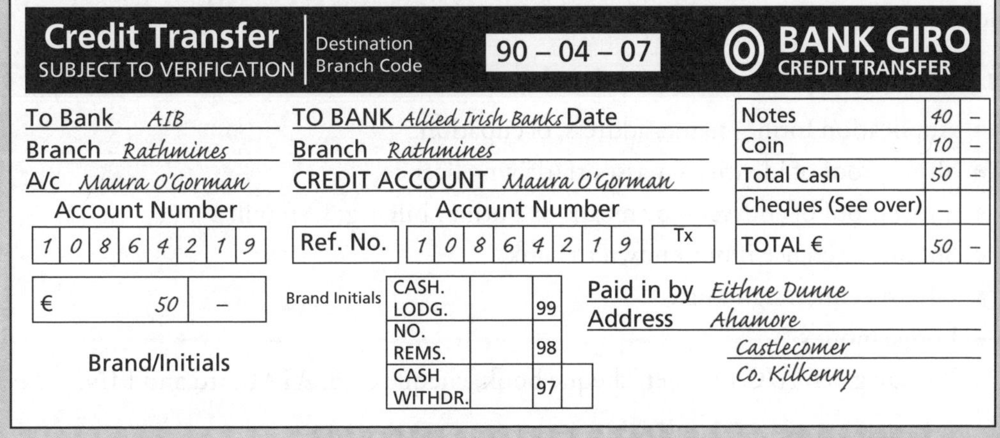

Credit Transfer SUBJECT TO VERIFICATION | Destination Branch Code 90 – 04 – 07 | BANK GIRO CREDIT TRANSFER

To Bank *AIB*
Branch *Rathmines*
A/c *Maura O'Gorman*
Account Number: *1 0 8 6 4 2 1 9*

TO BANK *Allied Irish Banks* Date
Branch *Rathmines*
CREDIT ACCOUNT *Maura O'Gorman*
Account Number: Ref. No. *1 0 8 6 4 2 1 9* Tx

Notes	*40*	–
Coin	*10*	–
Total Cash	*50*	–
Cheques (See over)	–	
TOTAL €	*50*	–

€ *50* –

Brand/Initials

Brand Initials

CASH. LODG.		99
NO. REMS.		98
CASH WITHDR.		97

Paid in by *Eithne Dunne*
Address *Ahamore*
Castlecomer
Co. Kilkenny

Source: Junior Certificate Higher Level. **(40 marks)**

4. Bank accounts

A. Legal requirements that must be satisfied when opening a bank account

- Proof of the source of the money if it's a large amount.
- Identification by means of a **passport** or **driving licence**.
- Proof of age.
- Proof of address by means of a **utility bill**.
- PPS number.

B. Deposit account

Money invested earns interest and can be withdrawn on demand at any bank.

C. How to open a deposit account

- Application form – name, address, occupation.
- Show proof of identity – passport/driving licence/utility bill, e.g. ESB bill.
- Show proof of address – utility bill, e.g. ESB bill.
- Given Deposit Book and ATM card.

D. Lodging money to a deposit account

- Complete lodgment slip.
- Present slip, cash and deposit book to cashier – balance will be updated and account credited.

E. Withdrawing money from a deposit account

- Complete **withdrawal slip**.

F. Current account

If you want to use a cheque book to make payments you must open a Current Account. Money in a Current Account does not earn interest.

G. How to open a current account

- Application form – name, address, occupation.
- Show proof of identity – passport/driving licence.
- Show proof of address – by means of a utility bill, e.g. ESB bill.
- Submit reference if not known to bank.
- Give specimen signature.
- Lodge money.
- You are given A/C number, cheque book, cheque card, ATM card and PIN.

H. Advantages of having a current account

Account holders:

- May withdraw money at any time using ATM, cheque book or Laser.
- May get an overdraft or loan.
- Can arrange to have payments made by standing order or direct debit.
- Can avail of credit transfers.
- Can pay bills by Laser card in shops etc., all over the country.
- Can benefit from PayPath.
- Can have Internet and telephone banking.

I. Lodging money to a current account

- Lodgment slip, **OR**
- ATM lodgment, **OR**
- Credit Transfer.

Note: Cheques etc. are accepted subject to examination and verification and are transmitted for collection at the customer's risk. Although credited to the account when paid in, they should not be drawn against until cleared. Customers should keep details of cheques lodged.

LODGMENT RECORD Subject to verification — **LODGMENT** — **Bank of Ireland**

Name(s) *John Ryan*

Account Number

8	7	1	6	5	2	3	8

€ 710 –

Please specify Account: Current ☑ Savings ☐ Other ☐

Note: Cheques, etc. are accepted subject to examination and verification and are transmitted for collection at the customer's risk. Though credited to account when paid in they should not be drawn against until cleared. Customers should keep details of cheques lodged.

Thank you for banking with us.

Please specify Account: **Current** ☑ **Savings** ☐ **Other** ☐

Name(s) *John Ryan*

Address *24 Main Street Cork*

Date *24/9/16*

Paid in by *John Ryan*

Brand/Initials

FOR BANK USE

SERIAL NUMBER	9	0	4	8	3	2

Customer's Account Number

8	7	1	6	5	2	3	8

Tx

Notes	200	–
Coin	50	–
Total Cash	250	–
Cheque Total	460	–
Total €	710	–

J. Withdrawing money from a current account

- Withdrawal slip at bank counter, **OR**
- Write a cheque, **OR**
- ATM withdrawal **OR**
- Standing order or direct debit, **OR**
- Laser card/Debit card

Practice completing lodgment and withdrawal slips.

WITHDRAWAL RECORD — **WITHDRAWAL** — **Bank of Ireland**

Name(s) *John Ryan*
24 Main St., Cork

Account Number

8	7	1	6	5	2	3	8

€ 200 –

Please specify Account: **Current** ☑ **Savings** ☐ **Other** ☐..........

....

Thank you for banking with us.

Please specify Account: **Current** ☑ **Savings** ☐ **Other** ☐

Received the sum of (words) *Two hundred Euro*

Date *15/10/16*

Name of Account Holder(s) *John Ryan*

Signature(s) *John Ryan*

JOINT SAVINGS ACCOUNT
I certify that all parties in the Account are alive at this date.
Signed:

Brand/Initials

SERIAL NUMBER

9	0	4	8	3	2

Address *24 Main St Cork*

Customer's Account Number

8	7	1	6	5	2	3	8

Tx

€ 200 –

K. Bank overdraft

(1) Bank overdraft is where a person withdraws more money than the amount held in the account with prior permission of the bank.
(2) An agreed limit is set by bank.
(3) Interest is charged on overdrawn amounts on a daily basis.
(4) An overdraft can be repaid at any time in variable amounts and should be cleared for 30 days each year.

L. Conditions that must be met before a current account can be overdrawn

(1) Established customer/banking history/savings record.
(2) Creditworthy/good credit rating.
(3) Is able to repay/secure employment/regular income/wage/salary.
(4) Agrees to keep within the overdraft limit.
(5) The account must be cleared of the agreed overdraft limit within the time specified or within one year.

Differences between a current account and a deposit account

- Cheque books are given to current account holders **but not** to deposit account holders.
- Current accounts usually don't earn interest **while** deposit accounts do earn it.
- Overdrafts may be given on a current account and **none** with a deposit account.
- Regular payments can be made by standing order and direct debit from a current account only.
- A deposit account holder may receive a book for recording lodgments and withdrawals.
- Current account is used for day-to-day use while a deposit account is used for savings.

M. Preparation of bank account

All Current Account customers should keep their own personal bank accounts to record:

(1) **Opening Balance.**
(2) **Lodgments** to the account.
(3) **Withdrawals** or **payments** made from the account.
(4) **Closing Balance.**

Ordinary level students can use either format. Higher level students must be able to use **both** formats.

Bank account – Format

The bank account can be laid out using a **T Account Ledger** format or in the **continuous balancing ledger format**.

N. Bank statement

Current account holders receive regular bank statements. It is a copy of the customer's account from the **bank's point of view**. It shows transactions known to the bank.

A bank statement shows:

(1) Opening balance – Balance column.
(2) Lodgments into the account – Credit column.
(3) Payments from the account – Debit column.
(4) Closing balance in the account on a particular date.

O. Comparing bank account and bank statements

When you receive a bank statement, the final figure shows what the bank says you have in your account. This figure may be different from the figure in your own personal bank account.

Reasons for difference

(1) **Cheques written – not yet cashed.**

(2) **Lodgments made – but not shown on statement.**

(3) **Certain items** will appear in the **bank statement** that the **account holder will not know about until the statement arrives**, e.g. standing orders, direct debits, current account fees, interest charged, government duty on cheque books, credit transfers into the account.

When the balance shown in the bank statement does not agree with the balance in the customer's own bank account, **a bank reconciliation statement** must be prepared.

How to reconcile the two balances

1. Correct or update the bank account

Look at bank statement and at bank account. **Identify items known to bank.**

Credit bank account with items that were taken out of the account, e.g. bank interest, standing orders, direct debits, current account fees, government duty on cheque books.

Debit the bank account with items that went into the account, e.g. credit transfers, salary paid direct to account.

The bank account is now correct.

2. Prepare a bank reconciliation statement

Start with balance as per bank statement.

Add lodgments not credited.

Subtract cheques not presented for payment.

Your answer will be balance as per corrected bank account.

Example: Bank A/C – Bank Statement – Bank Reconciliation Statement

(a) Bank Account is prepared by the customer.

DR + Bank A/C CR –

			€			Ch. No.	€
1/1/16	Balance	B/d	500✓	1/1/16	Rowan	Ch. 1	400✓
1/1/16	Osborne		500✓	1/1/16	Wages		100✗
1/1/16	Kershaw		10✗	1/1/16	Holmes	Ch. 2	400✓
				1/1/16	Balance C/d		110
			1,010				1,010
1/1/16	Balance	B/d	110				
					(Customer has €110 in bank)		

(b) Bank Statement is prepared by Bank

Bank Statement		–	+	
Date	**Details**	**Debit €**	**Credit €**	**Balance €**
1/1/16	Balance			500 ✓
1/1/16	Cheque No. 1	400 ✓		100
1/1/16	Lodgment		500 ✓	600
1/1/16	Bank Charges	20 ✗		580
1/1/16	Cheque No. 2	400 ✓		180

According to the bank the customer has €180 in bank.

(c) Corrected Bank Account

Items that are in the Bank Statement but not in Bank A/C.

Corrected Bank A/C							
			€				€
1/1/16	Balance	B/d	110	1/1/16	Bank Charges		20
				1/1/16	Balance	C/d	90
			110				110
1/1/16	Balance	B/d	90				

(d) Bank Reconciliation Statement (To reconcile the difference)

	€
Balance as per Bank Statement	180
Add Lodgment not Credited – Kershaw (DR in bank not in bank statement)	10
	190
Less Cheque not Presented – Wages (CR in bank not in bank statement)	100
Balance as per Bank Account	90

P. Reasons why a bank reconciliation statement is prepared

(1) To identify any errors in the bank's records.

(2) To identify any errors or omissions in the customer's records.

(3) To identify:

- Cheques drawn but not presented
- Lodgments not credited
- Bank charges/interest charges

(4) To see the correct balance in the account.
(5) To clarify if the updated cash book is in agreement with the bank statement.

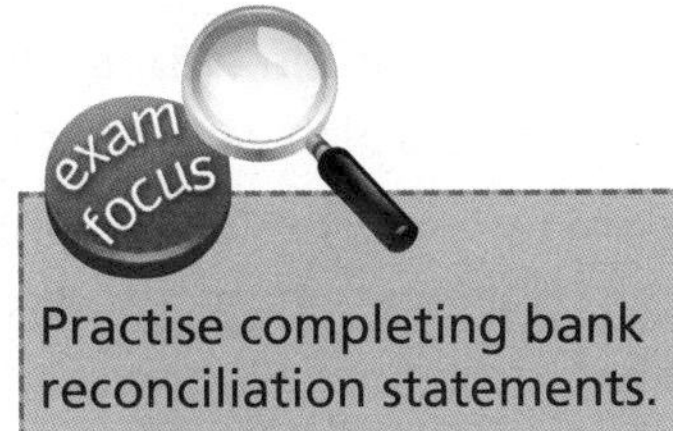

Practise completing bank reconciliation statements.

This is a Banking question.

Answer all parts of this question:

Sandra Thomas opened a bank account in Bank of Ireland on 01/01/2011 and lodged €480 to the account. The following are her transactions for the month of March.

2011		€
04/03/11	Purchased groceries by Cheque no. 101	48
05/03/11	Withdrew by ATM	36
07/03/11	Lodged to her account	300
09/03/11	Purchased rail tickets by Cheque no. 102	30
11/03/11	Purchased cosmetics by Cheque no. 103	84
19/03/11	Purchased clothes by Cheque no. 104	54
30/03/11	Lodged to her account	240

(A) Write up Sandra's own records of her bank transactions for March 2011 and show her closing balance. (10)

(B) Compare Sandra's own records with the bank statement she received (below).
  (i) Make whatever adjustments are necessary to Sandra's own records.
  (ii) Prepare a Bank Reconciliation Statement. (15)

BANK STATEMENT NO. 8 31 March 2011

Date	Detail	Debit €	Credit €	Balance €
2010				
March 1	Lodgment		480	480
March 5	ATM	36		444
March 6	Cheque No. 101	48		396
March 7	Lodgment		300	696
March 9	S/O	240		456
March 12	C/T		120	576
March 16	Cheque No. 103	84		492
March 19	ATM	36		456

(C) (i) Outline **two** reasons why a Bank Reconciliation statement is prepared.
(ii) Explain what is meant by C/T on March 12.
(iii) Explain the difference between Direct Debit and Standing Order.
(iv) State **two** differences between a Current Account and Deposit Account. (15)
(40 marks)

Suggested solution and marking scheme

(A) (B) (i) SANDRA THOMAS OWN RECORDS

Dr Bank Account Cr

Date	Details	€	Date	Details	€
01/03/11	Lodged	480(1)	04/03/11	Purchases Cheque No. 101	48(1)
07/03/11	Lodged	300(1)	05/03/11	ATM	36(1)
30/03/11	Lodged	240(1)	09/03/11	Rail tickets Cheque No. 102	30(1)
			11/03/11	Cosmetics Cheque No. 103	84(1)
			19/03/11	ATM	36(1)
			26/03/11	Clothes Cheque No. 104	54(1)
			31/03/11	Balance	732(1)
		1,020			1,020
31/03/11	Balance	732(1)		SO	240(1)
	CT	120(1)		Balance	612(1)
		852			852
	Balance	612			

(10 marks) (for the first section, totalling 1,020)

(4) (for the second section, totalling 852)

(ii) Bank Reconciliation statement at 31 March 2011

	€	€
Balance as per bank Statement (1)		456(1)
Add Lodgment not credited (1)		240(1)
		696(1)
Less Cheques drawn not presented (1)		
Cheque No. 102	30(1)	
Cheque No. 104	54(1)	84(1)
Balance as per Cash Book (1)		612(1)

(11)

(C) (i) Reasons why a Bank Reconciliation Statement is prepared

1. To identify any errors or omissions in the customer's records/cash book.
2. To identify any errors in the Bank's Records/Bank Statement.
3. To identify cheques drawn and not presented.
4. To identify lodgments not credited.
5. To clarify if the updated cash book is in agreement with the Bank Statement.
6. To identify Bank Charges/Interest Charges/Standing Orders/Direct Debits/Credit Transfer.
7. To see the Balance left in the account.

2 reasons @ 2 marks each **4 marks**

(ii) Explain what is meant by C/T on March 12.
Credit Transfer – This is a way of transferring money directly(1) into another person's or firm's bank account. (1) It is also known as Bank Giro. **2 marks**

(iii) Difference between a Direct Debit and Standing Order.

Direct Debit – **Permission granted** by the account holder to a creditor/firm to withdraw **fixed or variable** amounts from the account **at any time**.

Standing order – **An Instruction to a Bank** to pay a **fixed amount** from the account at **regular intervals** to a specified firm/creditor.

1 difference @ 3 marks **3 marks**

(iv) Difference between a Current Account and a Deposit Account

1. Interest – a deposit account **earns interest**, whereas a current account generally receives **no interest** but interest is charged on overdrawn balances.
2. Access – with a current account money can be withdrawn by **cheque/ATM/laser card/withdrawal slip** whereas with a deposit account money can be **withdrawn by ATM or withdrawal slip on a visit to the bank.**
3. Cheque Books – **cheques** can be used to withdraw money **with current accounts**. There are **no cheque books** issued with deposit accounts.
4. Overdraft: **Current account holders may** be allowed to **overdraw their current account**. Deposit account holders can **only withdraw funds they have on deposit.**

2 differences @ 3 marks each **6 marks**

(40 marks)

5. Cheques

A. Definition of a cheque

A cheque is a written instruction from the holder of a current account to his/her bank to pay a stated sum of money out of the holder's account to the person named in the cheque or to the bearer.

B. Parties to a cheque

(1) **Drawer** – Person who writes the cheque.

(2) **Drawee** – Bank where drawer holds his account.

(3) **Payee** – Person to whom the cheque is payable.

C. Cheque

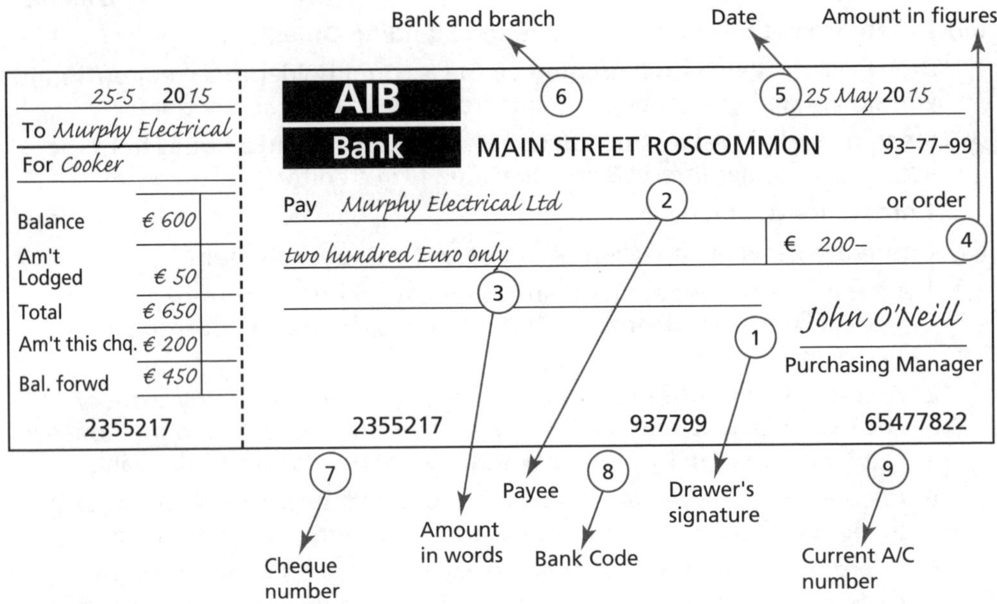

D. Counterfoil of cheque (stub)

The purpose of the counterfoil is to record the amount of the cheque, the name of the person paid and the date that the cheque was written. The amount left in the account after the cheque is also recorded. The account holder uses completed counterfoils to write up his own bank records.

E. Rules for completing a cheque

- Keep words close together.
- Keep figures close to € sign.
- Complete stub.
- Initial corrections.
- Cross cheque.

exam focus

Practise writing cheques.

F. Cheque card/banker's card

(1) An identity card given to creditworthy current account holders.

(2) Guarantees cheque up to a certain limit.

(3) Many banks now have a combined ATM/cheque card and photograph.

(4) Cheques can be cashed at outlets where you are not personally known.

(5) Details of the card include card number, expiry date and cardholder's signature.

Steps to be followed when accepting a personal cheque with a cheque card.

(i) The cheque must be signed in the presence of the Payee/Seller.

(ii) The Drawer's signature must match that on the card.

(iii) The cheque book code number must match that on the card.

(iv) The card must not be out of date.

(v) Write the card number on the back of the cheque.

(vi) The amount of the cheque must be for less than the cheque card limit.

G. Crossing a cheque

Draw two parallel lines across the face of the cheque. This makes the cheque safe, as it must be paid into the bank account of the payee.

Types of crossing

(1) General Crossing

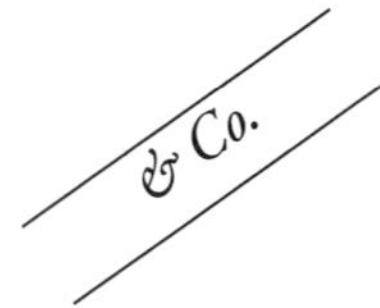

One with the words 'and Company' between two parallel lines on the face of the cheque. It has to be lodged to a bank account and can't be cashed at the counter.

(2) Special Crossing

A/c payee only

One with 'Account Payee only' written on its face. Cheque can be paid only into payee account.

H. Endorsing/negotiating a cheque

The payee signs the back of the cheque and passes it on to a third party.

I. Different types of cheque

(1) Stale cheque – one which is not presented for payment within six months of the date on it. The bank refuses to cash it as it's out of date.

(2) Postdated cheque – is one with a future date on it and is not valid until then.

(3) Antedated cheque – has a date before the date of issue.

(4) **Blank cheque** – vital information is missing.

(5) **Dishonoured cheques** – cheques which the bank refuses to cash. The cheques will be returned to the payee marked R/D – Refer to Drawer.

J. Why banks refuse to cash a cheque

(1) If the cheque is stale.

(2) If drawer dies or becomes bankrupt.

(3) If drawer has not enough money in the account.

(4) If amount in words does not match figures.

(5) If forgery is suspected.

(6) If signature does not match specimen signature.

(7) If cheque is not signed.

K. Cashing a cheque

When you receive a cheque you can:

(1) Lodge it in your bank account.

(2) Endorse it and give it to someone else.

(3) Cash it in a shop where you are known.

6. Other banking services

A. Term loan

(1) Given for a fixed term, usually from two to seven years.

(2) Given for a specific purpose.

(3) Repaid in fixed monthly instalments.

(4) Must be negotiated with the bank manager.

B. Mortgages – house loans

Banks give house loans. The deeds of the premises will be given as collateral – security. Costs involved in House Purchase include – solicitor's fees, stamp duty, administration fees, registration fees, surveyor's fees.

C. Strongroom facilities

For storage of valuables and jewellery, or deeds of premises.

D. Purchase and sale of shares

Banks provide the facility for purchasing and selling shares in companies quoted on the stock exchange.

E. Advice

Banks provide income tax, life assurance and financial advice to individuals, the farming community and business community.

F. Telephone and Internet banking

Customers can access a range of services twenty-four hours a day, including checking accounts, paying bills, money transmission, applying for loans, ordering foreign currency.

G. Night safe

A facility where money can be lodged in the bank after banking hours through a chute located in the bank wall; a numbered leather wallet and key are provided. The account is credited the following day.

H. Foreign exchange

All banks provide a foreign exchange service. This is the exchanging of one currency for another.

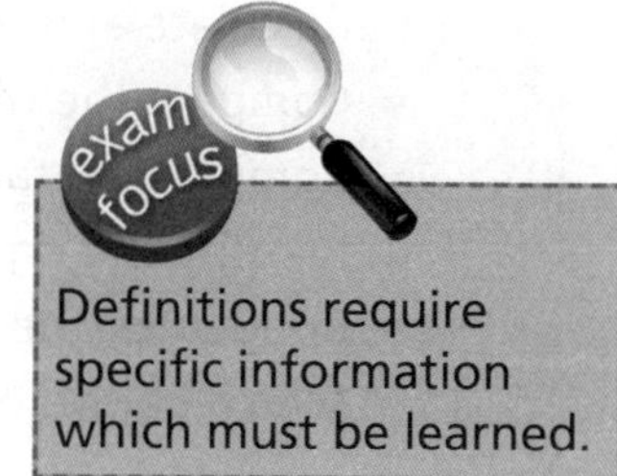

exam focus
Definitions require specific information which must be learned.

7. Irish financial agencies

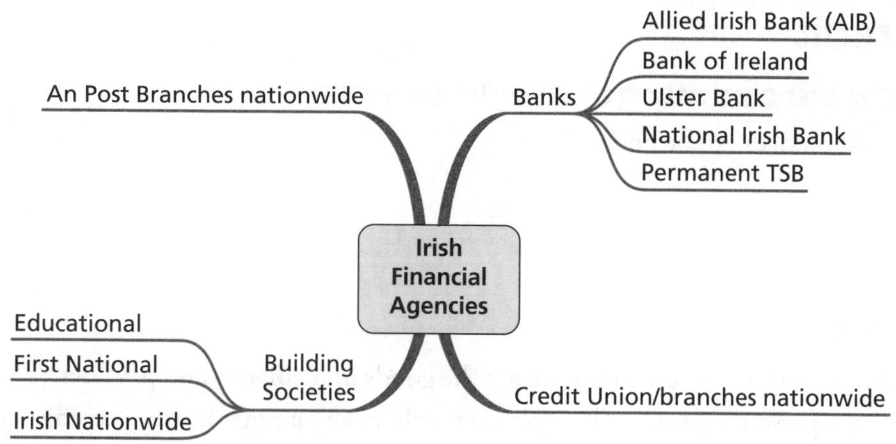

exam Q

See:

Ordinary Level	**Ordinary Level**	**Higher Level**	**Higher Level**
Section A	Section B	Paper I Section A	Paper I Section B
2007 Q15	2009 Q3	2008 Q8	2009 Q4
2006 Q8	2008 Q4	2007 Q12	2008 Q4
2006 Q17	2007 Q4	2006 Q1	2007 Q5a
2005 Q10	2006 Q4	2004 Q8	2006 Q6ab
2003 Q8	2005 Q4	2004 Q12	2005 Q4
2003 Q9	2004 Q4		2005 Q2a

9 Credit and Borrowing

From given data, to be able to:

- Compare cash with total credit cost
- Select an appropriate source of credit
- Present a written or oral application for credit
- Calculate and compare the cost of credit
- Compare the true vs flat rate of interest
- Compare rental, purchase and hire-purchase
- Identify the rights of the borrower
- Budget for the borrowing cost
- Match period of loan to the purpose

1. Credit

A. How we can buy goods and services

Goods and services can be bought by:

(1) Cash

(2) Credit

(3) Borrowing.

B. Credit

(1) When we buy goods on credit, we get the goods immediately and pay later.

(2) Before a person is given credit, a business will make sure that he/she is creditworthy, i.e. check to see if he/she will repay the money.

(3) Ways of checking creditworthiness/credit status:

- Bank can be asked for information on your financial position.
- Reference from other firms that you deal with.
- Credit Status Enquiry Agency.
- Get sales representatives to make enquiries.

Reasons for selling goods on credit

(1) To attract **new customers.**

(2) To **increase sales and profit.**

(3) To **help genuine customers** short of cash temporarily.

(4) To **compete** with other firms offering credit.

How a business can reduce its losses caused by bad debts

(1) Offer **discounts** for prompt payment.
(2) Have a **good credit control system** and good accounting system.
(3) **Retain ownership** of goods until payment is received.
(4) Sell for **cash only**.

C. Types of credit

1. Consumer credit

This is where consumers buy goods and use services and pay the seller/supplier at a later date, e.g. milk, electricity, telephone, local shop.

2. Credit card

When a consumer buys goods and services using a credit card, the bill is paid by the credit card company and the consumer then pays the credit card company within the agreed credit period. Examples include Visa and MasterCard.

3. Hire purchase

- Hire purchase is a system of buying goods on credit by paying an initial deposit and paying the balance owed by regular instalments over an agreed period of time.
- The buyer obtains **the immediate use of the goods** but does not become the legal owner until the **last instalment is paid**. It is expensive, as hire purchase companies charge a flat rate of interest.

Advantages to the consumer of buying on a hire purchase

(a) Immediate possession and use.
(b) Consumer has the use of item while paying for it.
(c) HP finance is easily available.
(d) Security is not required.

Disadvantages to the consumer of buying on hire purchase

(a) Expensive – a flat rate of interest is charged.
(b) Ownership acquired only after paying final instalment.
(c) Could encourage overspending.

4. Leasing/renting

(a) When you lease/rent something, you have the **use** of the item, e.g. television, car, video, but you will never **own** it.
(b) A regular payment is made for the use of the item.

5. Deferred payment/budget account

This is where an item is purchased, e.g. suite of furniture, with a deposit being paid and the balance paid in instalments. **Ownership of the goods passes to the buyer when the deposit is paid.** If the buyer defaults in payment, the goods cannot be repossessed but the seller can sue the buyer for the balance outstanding.

2. Borrowing

A. Borrowing

Borrow the money and repay the lending agency in the future with interest.

B. Factors to be considered before borrowing

Before borrowing, we must ask ourselves a number of questions:

(1) Do we need the goods or services?
(2) Can we meet the repayments? – Ability to repay.
(3) What security/collateral can we offer the lender?
(4) Rate of Interest – APR.
(5) Length of repayments.
(6) Amount required.
(7) Job security.
(8) Which financial institution best meets our requirements?

C. Collateral/security

Lender will require collateral or security. This means that you hand over/sign over some valuable asset. The lender will hold this asset until the loan is repaid. It may be liquidated by the lender if the borrower fails to repay.

Acceptable forms of security/collateral

- Deeds of premises or property.
- Life Assurance Policy.
- Share Certificates.
- Guarantor.

D. Advantages of borrowing

(1) Enables people to buy goods without saving for a long time.
(2) Increases standard of living.
(3) Helps people in difficult financial situations.

E. Disadvantages of borrowing

(1) Carries a high cost – rate of interest.
(2) Commits borrower to repayments in the future.
(3) High borrowings cause many social problems.

F. Applying for a loan

- Fill out loan application form.
- Meet lender.
- Agree terms of repayment.

G. Information required by lender on application form

- Name, address, age, occupation, employment, income.
- Amount of loan.
- Purpose of loan.
- Length of time required to repay.
- Security available.
- Track record.
- Other commitments.

H. Factors taken into consideration by bank before lending

(1) Current financial position of borrower. Are there outstanding debts.
(2) Creditworthiness of borrower. Previous record. Credit rating.
(3) Collateral/security available.
(4) Purpose of loan. Amount of loan.
(5) Duration of loan.
(6) Ability to repay. Job security. Occupation. Income.
(7) Savings record.
(8) Previous history with bank/other banks.

I. Cost of borrowing

The cost of borrowing is the rate of interest charged by the lender.

1. Flat rate of interest

Interest is charged on the **original loan amount over the full duration of the loan**. No credit is given for repayments made.

2. True rate of interest/APR

Interest is charged on the **reducing balance of the loan**, i.e. it is calculated on the amount outstanding after each instalment is paid. Another name for true rate is **Annual Percentage Rate** (APR), and it includes other costs in taking out a loan, e.g. administration fees, stamp duty and insurance. All lending institutions must by law show the annual percentage rate on any advertisement for a loan. This allows consumers to make comparisons between lending agencies.

J. Rights of borrower

- The right to change his/her mind and cancel the agreement within ten days.
- The right to pay off the loan earlier than when due.
- To be made aware of the Annual Percentage Rate (APR).
- To know the number of instalments.
- The amount of each instalment.
- To be informed of the Cash Price.
- To be told the Total Credit Price.
- To receive a copy of the agreement/contract.

K. Responsibilities of borrower

(1) To provide true and accurate information to the lender.
(2) To pay the monthly instalments on time.
(3) To repay the loan in full.

L. Bankruptcy

If a person borrows and is unwilling or unable to repay his debts, he can be declared bankrupt by the High Court.

M. Term of loans

Loans can be for the short term (up to one year), medium term (one to five years), or long term (five to twenty years). Here are some of the most **common reasons** for borrowing matched with the **sources available** and the **duration of the borrowing**.

Reasons	Sources Available	Duration
1. Christmas expenses	Bank overdraft, credit card, credit union	Short-term
2. Holidays	Bank overdraft, credit card, credit union	Short-term
3. College expenses	Credit union/Short-term loan	Short-term
4. Car/Computer	Bank term loan, credit union, hire purchase	Medium-term
5. House purchase	Building society mortgage, bank mortgage	Long-term

N. Lending agencies

1. Commercial banks

Commercial banks operate lending in a number of ways:

(a) **Term loan:** a loan given for a stated reason, for a specified period of time.

(b) **Bank overdraft:** where the bank manager gives permission to a current account holder to overdraw up to a certain limit.

(c) **Mortgage:** a home loan given by the bank for the purchase of a house.

(d) **Bridging loan:** short-term finance given to people who have a mortgage approved but are awaiting receipt of a building society loan.

2. Building societies

Building societies provide **home loans** and other **financial services**.

3. Credit union

You must be a member of a credit union with a savings record to qualify for a loan. The credit union will lend a multiple of the amount saved (two or three times). Loans are given for many purposes, including cars, furniture, holidays and electrical goods.

4. Hire purchase

This was dealt with earlier in the chapter (see p. 59).

5. Moneylenders

People will borrow from moneylenders if they have difficulty in borrowing from other financial institutions. Moneylenders charge extremely high rates of interest. Licensed moneylenders have a licence from the Revenue Commissioners to operate. APR must be quoted on all loans. An unlicensed moneylender lends without a licence.

Borrowing Question 1

Tom Morgan wishes to borrow in order to purchase some household appliances costing €6,000. He has the following options:

Option 1: Hire Purchase – €400 deposit and 36 instalments of €215 each.

Option 2: Loan – €6,000 at 7.5% APR over 3 years, with the loan amount to reduce by €2,000 each year.

(i) Calculate the total cost of **each** option. Show your workings.

(ii) Which option would you recommend? Give **one** reason for your answer. (16)

Solution

(i) Option 1: € 8,140 **(5 marks)**

Hire Purchase

Workings:

Deposit = € 400	(1)
Instalment € 215 @ 36	
= € 7,740	(1)
Total = € 8,140	(1)
	(5 marks)

(ii) Option 2: Loan € 6,900 **(8 marks)**

Workings:

€ 6,000 @ 7.5% (1)	= € 450	(1)
€ 4,000 @ 7.5% (1)	= € 300	(1)
€ 2,000 @ 7.5% (1)	= € 150	(1)
	= € 900	
Plus € 2,000 × 3	= € 6,000	(1)
Total	= € 6,900	(1)
		(8 marks)

(ii) Recommend Bank Loan – Option 2 (1) + (2) reason

- It's cheaper
- Acquire immediate ownership
- Interest can be treated as an expense in the profit & loss account
- Shopping is not confined to those offering hire purchase credit (3)

(16 marks)

Borrowing question 2

Answer (A), (B) and (C).

Rhona King, who is single, lives at 56 Banks Road, Cork, in a house which she purchased in 1990 with the help of a mortgage of €40,000 from the Startup Building Society and to whom she repays €200 per month. Her telephone number is 021–134567.

Rhona is employed as a legal secretary with Smart & Keane, Solicitors, Airport Road, Cork, where she started work in 1986. She earns a Gross Salary of €1,900 per month, out of which she pays income tax and PRSI totalling €650 per month.

Rhona wishes to buy a new car for her next birthday. She was 35 years old on 14 August 2000.

In order to buy the car, she needs to borrow €10,000, which she hopes to repay in monthly instalments of €230 over the next four years. She is already paying the Cork Credit Union €50 per month for a loan of €1,000, which she obtained in 1999.

She gets a Loan Application Form from her local branch of AIB Bank.

(A) Complete Rhona's Loan Application Form on today's date. (40)

(B) If the bank grants Rhona the loan for the car at €230 per month, how much interest will she have paid after four years? Show your workings. (8)

(C) Explain **three** of the following terms

Hire Purchase | Debtor
Collateral | Bankruptcy
Mortgage

(12)

(60 marks)

Source: Junior Certificate Ordinary Level.

Suggested solution

(A)

LOAN APPLICATION FORM			
PERSONAL DETAILS			
Name	Rhona King	Mr, Mrs, Ms.	Ms
Address	56 Banks Rd Cork		
Number of years at this address	10	Owner or Rented	Owner
Telephone	021–134567		**AIB Bank**
Date of birth	14/8/1965		
Mortgage amount (if any)	€10,000		
Annual repayments on mortgage	€2,400		
Mortgage borrowed from	Startup Building Society		
EMPLOYMENT DETAILS			
Occupation	Legal secretary		
Employer's Name & Address	Smart & Keane Solicitors, Airport Rd, Cork		
Net salary per month	€1,250		
No. of years in your present employment	14		

LOAN REQUIRED					
Amount	€10,000				
Purpose	To buy a car				
How long do you want the loan for?			4 years		
How much can you repay each month?			€230		
Details of other existing loans					
Lender	Cork Credit Union	Amount	€1,000	Annual repayments	€600
SIGNATURE	Rhona King		DATE	14/6/–	

(B) Total repaid €230 × 48 months = €11,040
Less amount borrowed = €10,000
Interest paid = €1,040

(C)
- Hire purchase: the customer buys a product from a retailer, the retailer is paid by the HP company, the customer repays the HP company plus interest. The customer does not own the goods until after the last repayment is made.
- Collateral: this is the security a borrower must give when taking out a loan.
- Mortgage: this is a long-term loan used to buy a house. The house is used as security, and the loan and interest are repaid usually over 20 years.
- Debtor: a person or a business who owes us money.
- Bankruptcy: this occurs when a person cannot pay his debts and his creditors go to court to have him declared bankrupt.

exam Q

See:

Ordinary Level	**Ordinary Level**	**Higher Level**	**Higher Level**
Section A	Section B	Paper I	Paper I
2008 Q18	2000 Q7	Section A	Section B
2007 Q16		2009 Q1	2007 Q5b
2004 Q4		2004 Q6	2006 Q6c
2002 Q14			2005 Q5ab
2001 Q18			2003 Q5d

10 Insurance

From data given, to be able to:

- Identify insurance requirements, personal and household
- Estimate cost
- Identify risk effects on premium
- Estimate compensation (including the average clause)
- Calculate a premium
- Explain terms used
- Complete a proposal or claim form
- Apply the Basic Principles of Insurance

A. What is insurance?

Insurance is protection against a possible loss that we hope will not happen, e.g. a house catching fire or a car accident. A fee called a premium is paid to the insurance company for this cover.

B. How insurance works

It is based on the idea of many people paying premiums into an insurance company fund and any person who suffers a loss being able to claim compensation.

C. Risks

Insurable risks and non-insurable risks

(1) Insurable risks are risks that can be insured against, e.g. house against fire and theft.

(2) Uninsurable risks are risks that cannot be insured against, e.g. damage caused by war or earthquakes, losses due to bad management.

D. Need for adequate insurance

Any insurance taken out by an individual or household should be adequate, that is, it should cover **all relevant risks** insured for the correct amount. Failure to insure risks for the correct amounts leads to underinsurance and reduction in compensation paid.

E. Basic principles of insurance

Insurance operates under a set of basic rules called the basic principles of insurance.

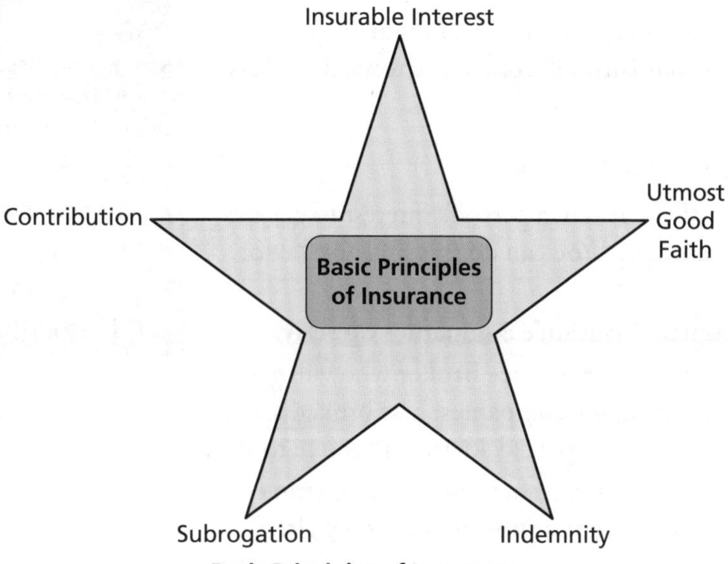

Basic Principles of Insurance

1. Insurable interest

In order to insure something one must have an **insurable interest** in the item. One must benefit financially by its existence and suffer financially by its loss, e.g. you can insure your own house but not your neighbour's house.

2. Utmost good faith

When completing a proposal form or claim form for insurance, one is obliged to answer all questions truthfully and disclose all material facts/relevant information which may affect the contract.

3. Indemnity

One cannot make a profit out of insurance. Compensation is limited to the value of the damage suffered irrespective of the level of cover. The aim of insurance is to place the insured in the same position financially as before the loss and not in a better position.

4. Subrogation

When an insurance company compensates the insured for the loss, it can proceed to claim compensation from the person who caused the loss. Once compensation has been paid, the damaged item becomes the property of the insurance company.

5. Contribution

This applies in the case where there are two or more insurers. If a person has the same risk insured with two companies, he cannot claim the full amount from each company. Each company will contribute toward the loss in proportion to the sum insured with it.

Know and be able to apply the five basic principles of insurance:

- Insurable interest
- Utmost good faith
- Indemnity
- Subrogation
- Contribution

F. Taking out insurance

Insurance is costly, so it is in a person's interest to get the best possible quotation. You can do this in a number of ways:

(1) You can contact **insurance companies directly**.

(2) You can contact an **insurance broker** who will get quotations from many companies. The broker is an insurance expert who arranges insurance, will give impartial advice and is free to sell any firm's policies.

(3) You can contact an **insurance agent** who is employed by a particular insurance company to sell insurance policies on its behalf.

1. Proposal form

This is an application form for insurance. All questions must be truthfully and **accurately answered giving all relevant details** – the principle of utmost good faith.

2. Actuary

An actuary will **assess the risk and calculate the premium**.

3. Premium

The **annual cost** of the insurance paid by the insured.

4. Policy

This is written **evidence** of the contract of insurance. It contains details of what risks are covered. Policy excess: means the insured has agreed to forego say the first €200 of any compensation.

5. Cover note

Sometimes there may be a delay in the preparation of the policy. In the meantime the insurance company will issue a cover note. This provides evidence that insurance cover exists.

6. Certificate of insurance

In motor insurance, a certificate of insurance is issued. **This is proof of the existence of insurance**. A portion of this document called the insurance disc is detached and displayed on the windscreen of the car to show that the car is insured.

7. Renewal notice

This is notice to remind you that the next premium is due.

8. Days of grace

These are additional days given by the insurance company to pay the renewal premium from the due date. There are no days of grace in motor insurance.

G. Making an insurance claim

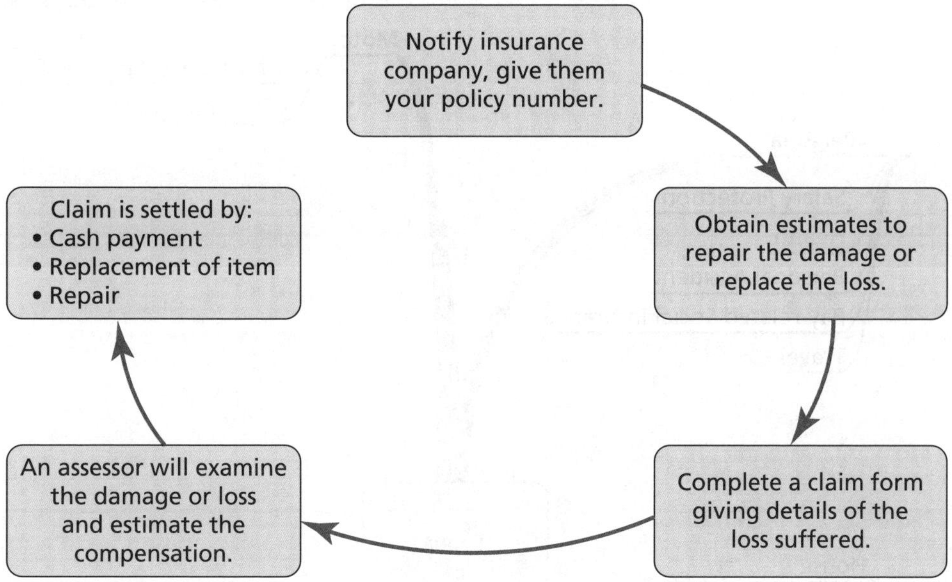

H. Overinsured/underinsured/average clause

1. Overinsured

If you have overinsured, you will receive only compensation amounting to **market value** of the item.

2. Underinsured

If you are underinsured and the item is completely destroyed, you will receive only compensation amounting to the value for which the item is insured.

3. Average clause – partial loss

Average clause applies in the case of a **partial** loss where the insurance cover is for less than the market value of the item lost, i.e. you are underinsured.

exam focus
Practise calculating insurance compensation using Average Clause.

Example – Average Clause

House valued at €200,000 insured for €160,000.

Fire causes €20,000 worth of damage.

Q. How much compensation will be paid?

A. House is only eight-tenths, i.e. four-fifths, insured so the amount of compensation will be four-fifths of €20,000, which is €16,000.

NB If you are only partly insured, you will receive only partial compensation.

I. Types of insurance

There are four main categories of insurance for the household and the individual. They are:

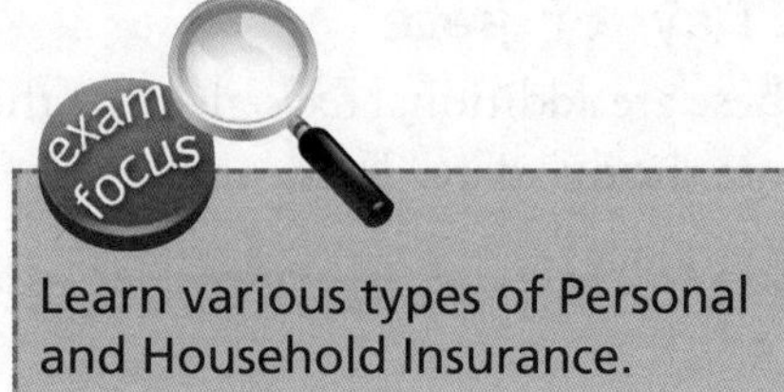

Learn various types of Personal and Household Insurance.

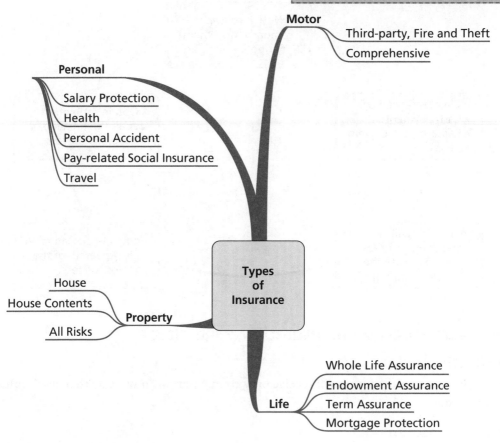

Personal insurance

(1) Salary Protection

Provides a payment of three-quarters of salary if you have to give up work because of accident or illness.

(2) Health Insurance (VHI, Hibernian Health, Quinn Insurance)

Protection against hospital and medical expenses incurred by the Insured.

(3) Personal Accident Insurance

Insures you against accidents.

(4) Pay-related Social Insurance (PRSI)

Covers loss of income due to illness or unemployment.

(5) Travel/Holiday Insurance

Covers goods and luggage stolen while travelling, plus medical bills.

Property insurance

(1) House Insurance

Covers building and contents against fire, or flooding or storm damage.

(2) House Contents Insurance

Covers theft or damage to contents.

(3) All Risks Policy

Householders can also take out an all risks policy which covers fire, burglary, public liability, as well as other risks such as storm damage, flooding, etc.

Motor insurance

Car insurance is compulsory under the Road Traffic Act 1933.

(1) Third Party, Fire and Theft Insurance

Compensation is provided to third parties for damage to them and their property by the insured while driving a car. It does not cover the insured person or his/her car for damage caused by the insured. Compensation is paid to the insured only when damage results from a fire or theft of the car.

(2) Comprehensive Insurance

Comprehensive insurance provides compensation to third parties for damage to them or their property by the insured while driving a car. It also covers the insured person's car against all risks.

FACTORS THAT WOULD INFLUENCE THE SIZE OF PREMIUM FOR CAR INSURANCE COVER

- Type of driving licence held.
- Age of insured.
- Driving history.
- Occupation of insured.
- Value of car/make.
- Purpose/use of car.
- Penalty points.

Life assurance

Life assurance is there to help families who lose the income earner through death. Life assurance covers risks that definitely happen – death.

(1) Whole life assurance

The assured pays premiums for the rest of his life. When the assured dies, a lump sum is paid to his dependants.

(2) Endowment policy

The assured pays premiums up to a certain age, e.g. sixty years. The lump sum is paid on the assured reaching this age or on death of assured, whichever comes first.

(3) Term assurance

This is where a policy is taken out for a specified period of time, e.g. ten years. If the assured dies within the ten years, his dependants will receive the lump sum. If the assured lives past the ten years, no payment is made. This type of policy is often used as security for a term loan.

(4) **Mortgage protection policy**
This policy is taken out by all mortgage holders. If the mortgage holder dies before the mortgage is paid, the policy will clear the mortgage and the house will become the property of the mortgage holder's dependants.

Surrender value

This arises **where a policy holder decides to stop paying** the premiums on a life assurance policy. The policy can be cancelled, usually after about two years, and a sum of money known as surrender value will be paid to the policy holder. However, it will be much less than the value of the premiums paid.

J. Calculating insurance premiums

The premium to be paid for insurance cover will be calculated by an actuary. The amount of the premium will depend on many things.

(1) Value of item.
(2) The risk involved.
(3) Age of insured.
(4) The loadings on the policy.
(5) The amount of no claims bonus (car insurance).

Loading: An amount added on to the premium because of an additional risk, e.g. previous claims, provisional licence, first insurance, being under twenty-five, penalty points, etc.

No Claims Bonus: A reduction/discount off the premium for not having sought compensation and for having accident-free driving.

HOW TO REDUCE COST OF HOUSEHOLD INSURANCE

(1) Fit a burglar alarm/fire alarm.
(2) Install a smoke detector.
(3) Become part of a community alert scheme.

K. Benefits of insurance

(1) Life assurance provides a lump sum payment to the assured's dependants on death of assured.
(2) Life assurance is a form of saving.
(3) A life assurance policy can be used as security for a loan.
(4) Insurance gives everyone protection against loss or damage.

L. Insurance companies operating in Ireland

(1) Irish Life Assurance
(2) New Ireland Assurance Company

(3) Hibernian Insurance Company
(4) Zurich
(5) AXA Insurance
(6) Quinn Insurance
(7) Eagle Star
(8) FBD Insurance
(9) Allianz
(10) One Direct

This is an Insurance question.

Answer all parts of this question:

(A) Elton and Orla Jones wish to insure the family home worth €300,000 and its contents worth €60,000.

They received a quotation of €17 per €10,000 for the house, and €25 for €5,000 for the contents from Fast Quotes Direct. They decided to insure the house to the value of €200,000 and the contents to their full value.

(i) Calculate the insurance premium that the Jones family will have to pay. Show your workings. (7)

(ii) What is the title of the person in an insurance company who calculates the premium? (2)

(iii) If a fire occurred causing €90,000 damage to the house and €20,000 damage to the contents, calculate the amount of compensation to which the Jones family will be entitled.

Show your workings and explain your answer. (8)

(B) Vicky Richards recently bought a car, she consulted a broker to advise her on insurance cover.

(i) Explain the term 'Insurance Broker'. (3)

(ii) Name the document to be completed by Vicky when seeking insurance. (2)

(iii) Vicky was confused by the terms **Third Party Insurance Cover** and **Comprehensive Insurance Cover**.

Explain the meaning of **each** of these terms. (6)

(iv) Vicky informed the broker that she had a 20% **No Claims Bonus**.

Explain what this means. (4)

(v) Vicky paid the **Premium** and the broker sent her the **Insurance Policy**.

Explain what this means. (6)

(vi) Name **two** factors which would influence the size of the premium paid by Vicky for car insurance cover. (2)

(40 marks)

Suggested solution and marking scheme

Insurance question

(A) (i) Calculation of Insurance Premium

Workings:

€17(1) × 20(1) = 340(1)

€25(1) × 12(1) = 300(1)

Total €640(1)

Answer: €640 (7 marks)

(ii) Title of person who calculates the premium:

ACTUARY (2 marks)

(iii) Calculation of Compensation

Workings:

House $\frac{€200,000 \times 90,000(1)}{(1)300,000}$

= 60,000(1)

Contents = 20,000(1)

80,000

Answer: €80,000 (5 marks)

Explanation of answer

They do not receive full compensation as **Average Clause** (1) applies in the case of the house as it was not **fully insured/underinsured** (1) and they **carried a third of the risk** (1). (3 marks)

(B) (i) Insurance Broker

An Insurance expert who **arranges insurance** and will give **impartial advice/independent** and is **free to sell any firm's policies**. The broker seeks the **best value/rate of premium** for the client.

One point @ 2 marks

One point @ 1 mark (3 marks)

(ii) Document to Be Completed with Seeking Insurance

Proposal Form (2 marks)

(iii) Third Party Insurance

Compensation is paid to third parties for damage to them or their property by the Insured while driving a car. (2)

It also covers the Insured Person's car against all risks. (1)

(2) + (1) = 3 marks

(iv) No Claims Bonus

A discount off the premium to the Insured(2)/for not having sought compensation(2) or for having an accident-free record. (4 marks)

(v) Premium

The Annual Cost(2) of the Insurance paid by the Insured(1). (3 marks)

Insurance Policy

This gives full details of what **exactly is covered**(1) and what is **excluded**(1). The policy will also give details of **any excess**(1) on the policy, e.g. excess €250. This means that the Insured must pay the first €250 of each claim. (3 marks)

(vi) Factors Which Would Influence the Size of The Premium

- Type of Licence held
- Age of Insured
- Driving history – previous accidents, etc.
- Occupation of Insured
- Value of car
- Make of car
- CC of engine
- Location/address
- Purpose/use of car
- Penalty points

Marking Scheme: any two factors @ 1 mark each **2 marks**

(40 marks)

exam Q

See:

Ordinary Level	**Ordinary Level**	**Higher Level**	**Higher Level**
Section A	Section B	Paper I	Paper I
2009 Q10	2007 Q3	Section A	Section B
2008 Q14	2003 Q7	2009 Q10	2009 Q5
2006 Q3	2001 Q3	2008 Q7	2006 Q5
2005 Q4		2007 Q5	2004 Q4
2004 Q6		2005 Q5	2003 Q5b
		2003 Q6	2001 Q2
		2000 Q18	

SECTION 2
Economic Awareness

National Business
Business Background
Services to Business
Work

National Business

Introduction to basic economic concepts and to the economic environment in which he/she lives.

11 Economic Framework

To understand the following:

- The nature of economics
- Choice, scarcity, limited resources
- Purposes of the economic system
- Rate of inflation
- Economic growth
- Factors of production

A. Needs and wants

An individual or family has three **basic needs** to survive: food, shelter and clothing. Once these needs are satisfied, people **want** other things, like cars and big houses – things people would like to have if they could afford them.

B. Scarcity and choice

To produce the goods that people need and want, four things are required: **land**, **money**, **workers** and someone with the **idea**. It is not possible to produce everything we need and want because resources are scarce. Thus choices must be made about which goods and services are to be produced.

C. Economics

Economics is the study of how scarce resources are used to produce the goods and services that people need and want.

D. Ireland's economic resources/factors of production

There are four main resources in the country used to produce goods and services. These resources are called factors of production and are **land**, **labour**, **capital** and **enterprise**.

Factors of production

Factors of Production	Explanation of Factors of Production	Payment for Use of Factor/Reward
1. Land	**All things supplied by nature for producing goods**, natural resources, i.e. land, sea, rivers, mines, gas fields, forests. From these we get raw materials which are made into finished goods.	Anyone with land is paid **rent** for the use of the land.
2. Labour	**People employed** to produce the goods or provide the service. Any productive human effort, e.g. block layer, hairdresser.	People are paid **wages** for the work they do.
3. Capital	Human created wealth, man-made items which help in further production, e.g. roads, factories, machinery.	People who provide money are paid **interest** for the use of their money.
4. Enterprise	Someone who has a **business idea** and is willing to take the risk of setting up a business for the purpose of making a profit. **Seeing an opportunity** to make a profit and investing in it. Combining other factors of production, e.g. self-employed people (entrepreneur), shop owner.	If the business is successful, the person gets a **profit** as payment for taking the risk of running a business.

E. Opportunity cost/making a choice

Because resources are scarce, choices have to be made when producing goods. When it is decided to produce one product, the opportunity cost is the other products that cannot be produced.

F. Economic systems

Each country wants to make best use of its scarce resources so choices must be made:

(i) What goods and services are to be produced?

(ii) Who will produce the goods and services?

The amount of choice that individuals or businesspeople have depends on the economic system that the country has.

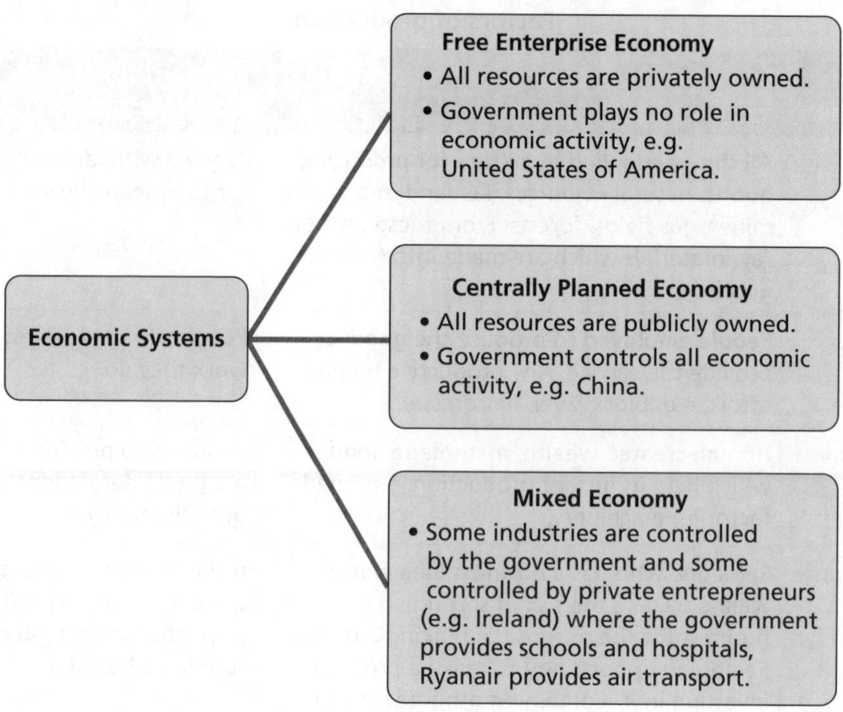

Economic Systems
Free Enterprise Economy
• All resources are privately owned.
• Government plays no role in economic activity, e.g. United States of America.
Centrally Planned Economy
• All resources are publicly owned.
• Government controls all economic activity, e.g. China.
Mixed Economy
• Some industries are controlled by the government and some controlled by private entrepreneurs (e.g. Ireland) where the government provides schools and hospitals, Ryanair provides air transport.

G. Economic growth

The total amount of goods and services produced in a country in a year is called Gross National Product (GNP).

If this total amount of goods and services produced (GNP) increases relative to the previous year, the country has economic growth.

exam focus

Formula for calculating economic growth

$$\text{Economic growth} = \frac{\text{Increase in production (GNP)}}{\text{Last year's production (GNP)}} \times 100\%$$

Example

Total production of goods and services 2014 = €600 million

Total production of goods and services 2015 = €660 million

$$\text{Economic growth} = \frac{€60\text{m}}{€600\text{m}} \times 100\% = 10\%$$

How can a country achieve economic growth?

(1) Keep inflation down.

(2) Keep interest rates down.

(3) Keep government borrowing down.
(4) Increase exports.

Advantages/consequences of economic growth

(1) Higher standard of living for people.
(2) More employment will be created and workers will earn more.
(3) More tax revenue for the government.
(4) More money available to government to provide services.

Recession

A Recession is a general slowdown in economic activity over a period of time:

- Productivity in economy decreases.
- Unemployment rate increases.
- Household incomes fall.
- Business profits and inflation fall.

H. Inflation

(1) Inflation is the increase in the general level of prices from one period of time to another.
(2) Rising prices mean that the cost of living is increasing, i.e. cost of food, clothes, fuel is increasing.
(3) An increase in the cost of living over a period of time is measured by the Consumer Price Index (CPI). This is a list of goods and their prices that is compared from one period to the next.

exam focus

Practise calculating economic growth and inflation rates.

Formula for calculating rate of inflation

$$\text{Rate of inflation} = \frac{\text{Increase in price}}{\text{Previous price}} \times 100\%$$

Example Cost of living 2014 €9,000
Cost of living 2015 €9,600

$$\text{Rate of inflation} = \frac{€600}{€9{,}000} \times 100\% = 6.6\%$$

Causes of inflation

(1) **Demand Pull Inflation** = Excessive demand in the market.
Demand > Supply → Prices rise.
(2) **Cost Push Inflation** = An increase in any of the following: taxes, wages, interest, oil, imports, material costs, service charges.

Advantages of low inflation to a country

(1) Economic growth is aided.

(2) Goods can be produced much more cheaply so it will be easier to sell them abroad.

Benefits of low inflation to the consumer

(a) Prices in shops are stable.

(b) Purchasing power of money is protected.

(c) Value of savings is protected.

(d) Wage demands are lower.

(e) Value of money is maintained.

Deflation

- Deflation occurs when prices are declining over time. This is the opposite of inflation.
- When the inflation rate is negative the economy is in a deflationary period.
- Deflation occurs in an economy when the annual inflation rate falls below zero per cent.

I. Interest rates

An interest rate is the price borrowers pay for the use of money they borrow from a lender. Interest rates of Euro countries are set at the same level and are controlled by the European Central Bank.

Benefits of low interest rates to the economy/general public

(1) Mortgages and loans will be cheaper.

(2) Encourages new investment and enterprise.

(3) Increased consumer spending.

(4) Boosts economic activity and employment.

(5) Reduces the cost of servicing the national debt.

(6) Reduces business costs.

(7) Gives people more disposable income.

Disadvantages of high interest rates to the economy/general public

(1) Discourages new investment.

(2) Reduces consumer demand.

(3) Increases business costs.

(4) Increase cost of living – leading to wage demands.

This is a Factors of Production, Economic Growth and Inflation Question.

Answer all parts of this question:

(A) In any economy, factors of production are required to produce goods and services. Name the **four** factors of production and the reward/payment associated with each. (8).

(B) Many countries have achieved high levels of economic growth in recent years.

(i) Explain the term 'economic growth'.

(ii) Outline **one** advantage of economic growth to a country.

(iii) From the following data, calculate the percentage of economic growth for a country from 2010 to 2011. Show your workings.

	€
2009	800 million
2010	850 million

(10)

(C) (i) Explain the term **'Inflation'**.

(ii) State **two** causes of inflation.

(iii) State **two** benefits to the consumer of low inflation.

(iv) The cost of living in a country in 2010 was €5,000. In 2011 it was €5,100. Calculate the rate of inflation (show your workings).

(v) In Ireland what is the official measure of inflation called? (13)

Suggested solution and marking scheme (31 marks)

Factors of Production, Economic Growth and Inflation Question.

(A) Land(1) – rent(1)
Labour(1) – wages(1)
Capital(1) – interest(1)
Enterprise(1) – profit/loss(1) (8 marks)

(B) (i) Economic Growth: An increase in the quantity of goods and services(2) produced in a country in a given period(2). (4 marks)

(ii) Advantages:

- Increase in the number employed.
- Higher standard of living/people are materially better off.
- Increase in government income.
- More money available to government to provide services.
- May give rise to lower tax rates.

(One advantage @ 3 marks)

(iii) 6.25%

Workings:

$\frac{50}{800} \times 100 = 6.25\%$ (3 marks)

(C) **(i)** Inflation is the **increase in the price of goods** (5) and services in general **over a period of time**. An increase in the cost of living as measured by the Consumer Price Index (CPI). (5 marks)

(ii) Demand Pull: Excessive demand in the market due to cheap money. (1)

Cost Push: An increase in any of the following: taxes, wages, interest, oil, mark-up, imports, material costs, refuse charges, service charges, exchange rates. (1) (2 marks)

(iii) Benefits:

- Stable price in the shops.
- Purchasing power of money is maintained.
- Value of saving is protected.
- Less pressure for increases in incomes/wages.
- Value of money is maintained.
- Easier to budget.

Two benefits of low inflation @ 1 mark each (2 marks)

(iv) The cost of living in a country in 2010 was €5,000. In 2011 it was €5,100. Calculate the rate of inflation (show your workings).

Workings:

$$\frac{€100}{€5{,}000(1/2)} \times 100\%(1/2) = 2\%(2)$$

Correct answer 2 marks

(v) Official measure of inflation in Ireland:

Consumer Price Index/CPI(2) (4 marks)

See:

Ordinary Level	**Ordinary Level**	**Higher Level**	**Higher Level**
Section A	Section B	Paper I	Paper I
2009 Q2	2009 Q8b	Section A	Section B
2007 Q3	2008 Q8b	2009 Q8	2008 Q3a
2006 Q13	2006 Q8de	2009 Q20	2007 Q3c
2005 Q8		2008 Q4	2006 Q3ab
2005 Q9		2007 Q8	2005 Q6ab
2005 Q11		2006 Q17	2004 Q3d

12 National Budgeting

From given data, to be able to:
- Draft a simple budget
- Identify a surplus or deficit

A. National budget

(1) A national budget is a **plan** of the government's expected future **income** and **expenditure** for a period of time, usually a year.

(2) The government plans where the income will come from and how the money will be spent (expenditure).

(3) Each government department **estimates** how much money it will need to run the department for the year.

(4) The **Department of Finance** decides how much each department can spend for the year ahead.

(5) The Department of Finance also decides how it is going to find this money.

(6) The **Minister for Finance** makes the budget speech in the Dáil in December each year telling the nation about the budget.

B. Government budgets

exam focus

Know how to prepare a National Budget and identify a surplus/deficit.

The government must prepare two budgets:

(1) **Current Budget:** This outlines the expenditure needed to run the country on a day-to-day basis and where income to finance this will come from.

(2) **Capital Budget:** This outlines the expenditure on capital projects (long-term projects) and where the income to finance these projects will come from.

C. Current budget

1. Current expenditure

This is ongoing, recurring expenditure on the day-to-day running of the country.

(a) **Wages and salaries** of civil servants, teachers, gardaí, army, prison officers.

(b) **Social welfare benefits**, e.g. unemployment benefit, old age pensions, children's allowances, etc.

(c) **Running costs of government departments**, e.g. telephone, stationery, heating and lighting.

(d) **Interest on borrowings**, i.e. national debt. Interest must be paid on money borrowed by the government over the years.

2. Current income

This is income received by the government on a regular basis (monthly/annually) and it is used to cover current expenditure. The main sources of current income are set out below, the principal one being taxation.

Taxation revenue

(a) **Income Tax:** Tax paid by all workers through the PAYE system.
(b) **Value Added Tax (VAT):** Tax on goods and services.
(c) **Customs Duties:** Tax on goods entering a country. It acts as a deterrent to imports.
(d) **Excise Duties:** Tax on certain goods produced in the country, e.g. whiskey, petrol, cigarettes, beer.
(e) **Corporation Tax:** Tax on the profits of companies paid to the government.
(f) **Deposit Interest Retention Tax (DIRT):** Tax on interest earned in a deposit account.

Non-tax revenue

(a) Profits earned by State companies.
(b) Sale of lottery tickets/profits from the National Lottery.

D. Balancing current budget

1. Balanced budget

Current expenditure = Current income

2. Budget surplus

Current income is greater than Current expenditure

What can the government do with a budget surplus?

(a) Reduce taxation.
(b) Increase social welfare.
(c) Pay off some of the national debt.
(d) Put some of the surplus toward capital expenditure, thus reducing borrowing.
(e) Increase spending in some departments to give a better service, e.g. health and education.

3. Budget deficit

Current expenditure is greater than Current income.

How can the government reduce a budget deficit?

(a) Increase taxation.
(b) Reduce expenditure by cutting back on some services.
(c) Cut public sector pay.
(d) Borrow the amount of the shortfall.

E. Capital budget

1. Capital expenditure

This is non-recurring, one-off expenditure on buying fixed assets, e.g. new roads, new schools, new hospitals, airports, railway stations, government jet. These items are called the **infrastructure** of the state.

Public utilities

Much of the government spending is on services that are essential for the efficient running of the state, e.g. roads, railways, airports, harbours, ports, telephone, electricity, gas, water, sewerage, postal service, schools, hospitals.

2. Capital income

This is income received 'once only' and is used for capital expenditure. **Borrowing** is the main source of capital income. Capital income has also been received by the government from the **sale of state companies** to private shareholders, called **privatisation**, e.g. Eircom, and from **EU Grants** and sale of state property.

F. Balancing capital budget

The capital budget will always balance because the amount of capital expenditure will be matched by capital income and borrowing.

G. National debt

National debt is the **total amount of money that has been borrowed** by the government over the years. Interest has to be paid on this debt.

H. Local authorities

County councils and corporations provide many services in the local area, e.g. water supply, sewerage schemes, refuse collection. They get most of their income from central government, but they also charge for their services. These charges are known as service charges, e.g. service charges for water supply and refuse collection.

This is a National Budget Question.

(A) The following figures were presented on Budget Day as projections for 2011.

Main items of Revenue and Expenditure	Estimated figures in millions €
PAYE	7,590
Corporation Tax	2,560
Agriculture	690

Health Services	7,420
VAT	8,360
Education	5,390
Debt Servicing	1,320
Social Welfare	9,680
Excise Duties	1,640

(i) Draft the National Budget for 2011 from the above information. State whether it is a Surplus or Deficit budget. (12)

(ii) State **two** effects of an increase in unemployment on the above National Budget. (2)

(iii) Distinguish between Capital Income and Current Income for the government. Use **one** example of **each** type of income to explain your answer. (6)

(iv) Distinguish between Capital Expenditure and Current Expenditure for the government. Use **one** example of **each** type of expenditure to explain your answer. (6)

(26 marks)

Suggested solution and marking scheme

National Budget

(A) (i)

National Budget for 2011 (1)

INCOME	€	EXPENDITURE	€
PAYE	7,690(1)	Agriculture	690(1)
Corporation Tax	2,560(1)	Health Services	7,420(1)
VAT	8,360(1)	Education	5,390(1)
Excise Duties	1,640(1)	Debt Servicing	1,230(1)
		Social Welfare	9,680(1)
	20,250		24,410

DEFICIT(1)
4,160(1)

Words and figures must be linked for marks. (12 marks)

(ii) Effect of an increase in unemployment on the National Budget:

- Decrease in Revenue from PAYE/Decrease in PAYE
- Decrease in Revenue from VAT/Decrease in VAT
- Decrease in Revenue from Excise Duties/Decrease in Excise Duties
- Increase in Social Welfare payments/Dole

2 effects @ 1 mark **2 marks**

(iii)

CAPITAL INCOME	CURRENT INCOME

This is income which the **government receives** (1) on a **one-off** basis or **borrows** (1).
Examples: sale of a state company, e.g. Eircom
Borrowing
EU Grants
One example @ 1 mark
	Income which the **government receives on a regular basis each year**(1). The principal **source of Current Income is taxation**(1).
	Examples:
	• Taxation – PAYE
	• VAT
	• Customs duty
	• Excise duties
	• Corporation Tax
	• Deposit Interest Retention Tax
	  • Profits from state firms
	  • Lottery receipts
	One example @ 1 mark **(6 marks)**

(iv)

CAPITAL EXPENDITURE	CURRENT EXPENDITURE
Non-recurring, one-off expenditure(1) in **buying fixed assets**(1). Example: new schools, hospitals, roads, government jet **One example: 1 mark**	**On-going, recurring, day-to-day expenditure**(1) in the **running of the country**(1) Example: wages of Gardaí, civil servants and TDs, cleaning, repairs and medicine for hospitals. **One example @ 1 mark** **(6 marks)**

See:

Ordinary Level
Section A
2007 Q19
2003 Q10
2000 Q20

Ordinary Level
Section B
2009 Q8a
2008 Q8c
2006 Q8f

Higher Level
Paper I
Section B
2009 Q3a
2008 Q3bc
2007 Q3ab
2005 Q6c
2004 Q3abce

13 Foreign Trade

From given data, be able to:

- Identify sources/destinations of Ireland's main exports/imports
- Identify the member states of the EU, their language and currency
- Identify the currencies of other main markets
- Convert one currency into another currency
- Prepare Balance of Trade and Balance of Payments Account
- Identify surpluses and deficits

A. Foreign trade

Foreign trade occurs when Ireland buys goods and services from other countries or sells goods and services to other countries.

B. Importing

1. Visible imports

These are physical **goods** that Ireland buys from other countries, e.g. cars, oil, fruit, coffee, wine, clothes, coal.

2. Invisible imports

These are **services** that Ireland buys from other countries. Examples include:

- Irish students going abroad on a school tour – **Irish money goes to a foreign country**.
- Irish people going on holiday abroad.
- Foreign bands playing in Ireland.
- Giving foreign firms a contract to build our roads.

Be able to distinguish between imports and exports, visible and invisible trade.

3. Why does Ireland import goods and services?

(a) **Unsuitable climate**, e.g. oranges, bananas, tea.

(b) **Raw materials** required for production, e.g. oil, coal, steel, timber.

(c) Irish consumers want **variety**.

(d) Certain countries have **natural skills**, e.g. French wines.

(e) Availability of products we cannot produce.

4. Sources and types of imports

Principal sources of imports	Visible imports (goods)	Invisible imports (services)
UK US Japan Germany France	Food, fruit, coffee, wine Oil, petrol, coal Clothes and footwear Electrical goods Timber Computers/Transport equipment Machinery, communication equipment Motor vehicles	Foreign entertainers on tour in Ireland Irish students on foreign school tours Irish people holidaying abroad Irish football supporters travelling to an away match Irish people getting insurance from a foreign insurance company

C. Exporting

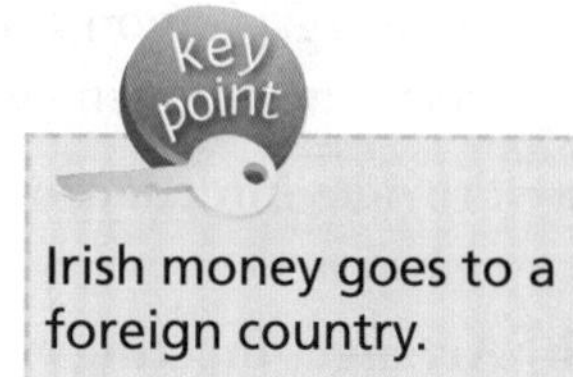

Irish money goes to a foreign country.

1. Visible exports

These are **goods** that Ireland sells to other countries, e.g. meat, dairy products, live animals, chemicals.

2. Invisible exports

These are **services** that Ireland sells to other countries, e.g. Spanish students coming to Ireland to learn English during the summer. **Foreign money comes into Ireland.**

3. Why does Ireland export goods and services?

(a) To **earn essential foreign money** to pay for imports.
(b) The Irish market is too small.
(c) Surplus production, e.g. beef.
(d) Demand for Irish products by consumers abroad, e.g. Kerrygold butter.
(e) Maintains jobs in Ireland.
(f) Ireland's ability to export encourages foreign firms to establish in Ireland.
(g) Helps balance of payments.

4. Difficulties that an Irish firm would experience when exporting goods

(a) Different languages.
(b) Different currency.
(c) Transport costs.
(d) Insurance costs.
(e) Cultural differences.
(f) Regulations to be adhered to.
(g) Standards to be met.

5. Destinations and types of exports

Principal destinations of exports	Visible exports (goods)	Invisible exports (services)
UK Germany US France Netherlands	Live animals Meat Dairy products Chemical and pharmaceuticals Engineering products Computer equipment Scientific equipment	Irish entertainers giving concerts abroad A foreigner taking out insurance with an Irish company Irish people working abroad and sending money to Ireland Foreign tourists visiting Ireland

6. State involvement in exporting

The state organisation **Enterprise Ireland** assists Irish exports in the following ways:

Foreign money comes into Ireland.

(a) Provides **information on foreign markets**, shipping and transport.

(b) **Arranges meetings with foreign buyers.**

(c) Provides **information** on **trade regulations**, packaging and language.

(d) Organises **trade fairs and exhibitions** abroad.

(e) Arranges **training courses for salespeople.**

D. European Union

The EU was established in 1957 with the aim of eliminating **trade barriers between member states.** This means there is **free trade** between the members. Ireland joined in 1973. The EU is now a group of twenty-seven member countries.

E. Aims of EU

(1) **Free trade** between member countries.

(2) **Free movement of people** between member countries.

(3) **Free movement of money** between member states.

(4) **Common currency.**

(5) To provide **financial assistance** to the less prosperous regions of the EU.

F. Benefits of EU membership to Ireland

(1) Access to a European market – 500 million people.

(2) EU finance for farmers and industry.

(3) EU finance for infrastructure, i.e. roads, communications, etc.

(4) Increased consumer choice – goods imported from EU.

(5) Irish people can work in any EU member state (freedom of movement within EU).

G. European union, countries, currency, language

Country	Currency	Language
Lithuania	Liras	Lithuanian
France	Euro	French
Germany	Euro	German
Italy	Euro	Italian
Belgium	Euro	French/Flemish
Netherlands	Euro	Dutch
Luxembourg	Euro	French/German
United Kingdom	Pound Sterling (£)	English
Ireland	Euro	English/Irish
Denmark	Krone	Danish
Greece	Euro	Greek
Spain	Euro	Spanish
Portugal	Euro	Portuguese
Austria	Euro	German
Finland	Euro	Finnish/Swedish
Sweden	Krona	Swedish
Cyprus	Euro	Greek/Turkish
Czech Republic	Czech Crown	Czech
Estonia	Euro	Estonian
Hungary	Florint	Hungarian
Latvia	Lats	Latvian
Malta	Euro	Maltese/English
Poland	Zloty	Polish
Slovakia	Euro	Slovak
Slovenia	Euro	Slovene
Romania	Leu	Romanian/German/Hungarian
Bulgaria	Lev	Bulgarian/Turkish

H. Rate of exchange

Every country has its own currency. If you want to buy goods or services from another country or travel to another country, you must convert your € (Euro) into that currency. Foreign currency can be bought at banks, building societies and Bureaux de Change. The cost of this currency is the rate of exchange.

Example

John is touring the US and wishes to convert €200 into US Dollars.

'Sell at' rate: 2.60, 'Buy at' rate: 2.74.

This means that for every €1 John will get US$2.60.

1. Buying foreign currency
Use 'Sell at' rate.

Formula: Converting € to foreign currency
Multiply € by bank sell rate

Answer: €200 × US $2.60 = US$520.

Example

John has US$25 left on returning from the US. He wishes to convert it back to Euro.
'Sell at' rate: 2.60, 'Buy at' rate: 2.74.
This means that for US$2.74 John will get €1.

2. Selling foreign currency
Use 'Buy at' rate.

Formula: Converting currency into €
Divide foreign currency by bank buy rate

Answer: US$25 ÷ US$2.74 = €9.12.

Practise questions on Balance of Trade and Balance of Payments.
Be able to identify surplus/deficit.

I. Balance of trade

Balance of Trade = Visible Exports − Visible Imports.
If visible exports are greater than visible imports, it is a trade surplus.
If visible exports are less than visible imports, it is a trade deficit.

J. Balance of payments

Balance of payments is the difference between all money coming into a country (total **exports**) and all money going out of a country (total **imports**).

Balance of Payments = Total Exports − Total Imports.
If total exports are greater than total imports = surplus on balance of payments.
If total exports are less than total imports = deficit on balance of payments.

Example – Higher Level

Visible exports €16.6 billion. Invisible exports €17.1 billion.
Visible imports €13.1 billion. Invisible imports €19.2 billion.

Answer

Balance of payments:			€
Balance of Trade	Visible exports		16.6 billion
	Visible imports		13.1 billion
	Balance of trade surplus		3.5 billion
Invisible Trade	Invisible exports	17.1 billion	
	Invisible imports	19.2 billion	
	Deficit on invisible trade		2.1 billion
	Balance of payments surplus		**1.4 billion**

Balance of payments includes visible and invisible trade.

This is a question on International Trade and Balance of Payments.

'International Trade is very important to the success of the Irish Economy'.

(i) (a) State **two** reasons why exporting is very important for the success of the Irish economy. (4)

(b) Give **two** benefits of imports for the Irish Consumer. (4)

(ii) The following data relates to the International Trade of a country.

	€
Invisible Imports	16.4 billion
Visible Exports	14.6 billion
Invisible Exports	24.8 billion
Visible Imports	19.2 billion

(a) From the above data, calculate the Balance of Trade and the Balance of Payments. Show your workings.

(b) Indicate in **each** case whether it is a surplus or a deficit balance. (10)

(iii) Explain the difference between visible and invisible imports and give one example in each case. (8)

(24 marks)

Suggested solution and marking scheme

International Trade, Balance of Payments

(i) (a) Reasons why exporting is important to the success of the Irish Economy

- To obtain foreign currency to pay for imports.
- The Irish market is too small, Irish manufacturers need to export to boost sales and profits.
- Exporting helps maintain employment in Ireland.
- Ireland's climate is very suitable for agricultural production, surplus production can be exported to other countries, e.g. beef, butter, pork.
- Exporting helps Balance of Payments.
- Demand for Irish products abroad, e.g. Kerrygold.
- Ireland's ability to export encourages foreign firms to establish in Ireland.

2 reasons @ 2 marks each **4 marks**

(b) Benefits of imports to the Irish consumer

- Availability of products we cannot produce.
- Greater variety and choice of products.
- Cheaper prices due to more competition.
- Better standard of living.

2 benefits @ 2 marks each **4 marks**

(ii) (a) and (b) BALANCE OF TRADE AND BALANCE OF PAYMENTS

	Billion	Billion	
Visible Exports(1)	14.6		
Visible Imports(1)	19.2		
(A) Balance of Trade(1)		4.6(1)	Deficit(1)
Invisible Exports	24.8		
Invisible Imports(1)	16.4		
Invisible Earnings		8.4	
(B) Balance of Payments(1)		3.8(1)	Surplus(1)

Words and figures must match **(10 marks)**

OR BALANCE OF PAYMENTS

	Billion	Billion	
Total Exports(1)	39.4		
Total Imports(1)	35.6		
(B) Balance of Payments(1)		3.8(1)	Surplus(1)

(iii) **Visible Imports:** refers to the purchase of physical items from another country.

Examples: Cars/oil/fruit.

One example @ 2 marks

Invisible Imports: refers to the purchase of services from another country.

Examples: Holidays abroad/going to the World Cup/foreign bands playing in Ireland.

One example @ 2 marks

See:

Ordinary Level	**Ordinary Level**	**Higher Level**	**Higher Level**
Section A	Section B	Paper I	Paper I
2009 Q13	2006 Q8abc	Section A	Section B
2009 Q17	2004 Q8cde	2008 Q17	2009 Q3b
2008 Q4	2001 Q8	2007 Q13	2006 Q3c
2008 Q6		2006 Q6	2003 Q4
2008 Q11		2005 Q10	
2007 Q5		2004 Q5	
2006 Q6			

Business Background

Introduction to the general background and structure of business nationally, and to commercial services available to business.

14 Forms of Business

From given data, be able to:

- Identify forms of ownership
- Recommend forms of ownership

In Ireland businesses are owned by one person, two or more people, or by the state.

Main forms of business unit

- Sole Trader – owned by one person.
- Co-operatives – owned by eight or more people, called members.
- State Companies – owned by state.
- Private Limited Company – owned by people, called shareholders.

A. Sole trader

A sole trader is a person who owns and manages his own business.

Characteristics	Types	Advantages	Disadvantages
(1) Owned by **one person**. (2) Owner makes **all decisions**. (3) Owner keeps all **profit** – suffers all losses. (4) Owner has **unlimited liability**.	(1) Retailers. (2) Services. (3) Professional Services.	(1) Easy to **set up**. (2) **Personal attention** to customers. (3) **Owner makes all decisions**. (4) Owner can keep all **profit**. (5) May give credit. (6) May offer a delivery service.	(1) **Unlimited liability** – if the business fails, the sole trader can also lose his/her own private assets. (2) **Lack of capital** hinders expansion. (3) Extra work outside trading hours. (4) Owner bears all **losses**. (5) **No continuity of business** – on death, the business ceases to exist.

B. Co-operatives

A co-operative is a business owned and managed by its members for the members' benefit. Each member has one vote and an equal say in the running of the business, regardless of how much they invest in the business.

Characteristics	Formation	Advantages	Disadvantages
(1) To become a member a person must buy **one share**. (2) Each member has **one vote**. (3) Profit is **distributed** among members. (4) Members have **limited liability**. (5) Managed by a committee.	(1) Eight people are required. (2) Apply to Registrar of Friendly Societies. (3) Certificate of Incorporation is issued. (4) Report annually to Registrar of Friendly Societies.	(1) Shareholders have **limited liability**. (2) **One vote per member**. (3) Members own co-operative – a big incentive to do their business with co-operative. (4) Profits are returned to members.	(1) Lack of finance. (2) No incentive to buy more shares. (3) Management committee may not have the business expertise to run a modern business.

Types of co-operative

(1) Producer co-operatives

Producer co-operatives are mainly agricultural co-operatives. They collect the raw material from the farmers, e.g. milk, process it and sell the finished product, e.g. cheese.

(2) Consumer co-operatives

These co-operatives buy directly from the manufacturer and sell to members and non-members.

(3) Worker co-operatives

These are set up where businesses close down and the workers decide to put in money and set up a worker co-operative.

(4) Financial co-operatives, a credit union is an example of a co-operative in the financial sector.

These are set up by people sharing a common interest, e.g. same town, same job (ASTI Credit Union for teachers). They encourage savings and provide loans at a reasonable rate of interest.

Co-operatives becoming public limited companies – PLCs

One of the major problems co-operatives have had in the past is the **lack of capital for expansion**. To overcome this problem, some of the major co-operatives have converted their status from co-operatives to PLCs (Public Limited Companies). For example, Kerry Group PLC, Glanbia PLC.

Advantages of converting to PLCs

(a) Finance is available by selling shares to the public.

(b) Shareholders can sell their shares at the Stock Exchange.

C. State ownership

State companies are owned and controlled by the state.

Reasons For State Involvement	Formation	Characteristics	Advantages	Disadvantages
(1) To provide **essential services.** (2) To develop the country's **natural resources.** (3) To rescue firms in **danger of closing down.** (4) To promote **Irish businesses at home and abroad.** (5) To provide **training for unemployed,** e.g. FÁS.	Most state companies were set up by passing an Act of the Oireachtas.	(1) **Owned, financed** and **controlled** by the **government**. (2) Each state company is responsible to a government minister. (3) The minister appoints a **board of directors** to run the company. (4) Profit is **reinvested** in the company or given to the government.	(1) **Provide essential services.** (2) Provide a lot of **employment.**	(1) Some are in a **monopoly** situation with no competition, which may lead to inefficiency. (2) **No profit motive**, which also leads to inefficiency. (3) Some state firms suffer **large losses** borne by taxpayer.

Names, initials and main activity of state companies

Name	Main Activity
(1) Production	
Electricity Supply Board (ESB)	Provision of electricity throughout Ireland.
Bord na Móna	Development of peat resources.
Bord Gáis Éireann (BGE)	Distribution of natural gas.
Coillte	Planting of forests and sale of timber.
(2) Transport	
Coras Iompair Éireann	Provision of transport by roads and rail throughout Ireland.
Three Companies:	
(a) Dublin Bus	Dublin city bus service.
(b) Bus Éireann (CIE)	Bus service for rest of Ireland.
(c) Iarnród Éireann (Irish Rail)	Rail service for passengers and goods throughout the country.

(3) Marketing/Export	
Enterprise Ireland	Encourages development of indigenous industry (Irish-owned).
Fáilte Ireland	Promotion of Irish tourist industry.
An Bord Bia	Responsible for promotion of Irish food and drinks products.
Bord Iascaigh Mhara (BIM)	Promotion of Irish Sea fishing industry.
(4) Training	
Foras Aiseanna Saothair (FÁS)	Training workers and the unemployed.
(5) Research	
Teagasc	Research in agriculture and horticulture.
(6) Communications	
Radio Telefís Éireann (RTE)	Radio and television services.
An Post	National postal service.
(7) Promotion and development	
IDA Ireland	Encourages transnational companies to set up in Ireland.
(8) Health Insurance Services	
Voluntary Health Insurance (VHI)	Provision of hospital insurance cover.

Nationalisation

State takes over a firm previously owned by shareholders.

Privatisation

State sells off a state company to the public. A number of state companies have been privatised, including Irish Life, Irish Sugar Company, now called Greencore, Telecom Éireann, now called Eircom.

Reasons for privatisation

(1) Raises finance for government.

(2) State no longer responsible for these state companies.

How state companies are financed

(1) Borrowing.

(2) Grants.

(3) Issuing government stock to public.

(4) Charging for services.

D. Private limited company (Ltd)

A private limited company is where a group of people numbering between one and ninety-nine come together and form a business. The owners are called shareholders. They invest money in the company. The profit is divided up among the shareholders and distributed in the form of **dividends**.

Characteristics	Advantages	Disadvantages
(1) Between one and ninety-nine shareholders. (2) Shareholders have limited liability. (3) 'Ltd' written after the name. (4) The annual accounts are sent to the Registrar of Companies. They are not published. (5) Control is shared. **Those with most shares make the decisions.** (6) Profits are shared between shareholders (called dividends).	(1) Shareholders have **limited liability**. (2) **Extra capital** available. (3) **Continuity of existence**.	(1) **Costly** to set up. (2) A lot of **legal requirements** when forming a company. (3) Shares **cannot be transferred** to the general public.

Formation of a private limited company

(1) The following legal documents must be completed:
- Memorandum of association
- Articles of association
- Declaration of compliance of companies acts
- Statement of nominal share capital
- Declaration of consent to become a director.

(2) Documents are sent to the registrar of companies.

(3) The registrar issues a certificate of incorporation. This is the birth certificate of the company.

(4) The company can begin trading.

Learn the procedure of the formation of a private limited company.

Documents involved in the formation of a company

(1) Memorandum of Association

This sets out the relationship of the company to the general public, i.e. external rules and regulations governing the company's dealings with the public.

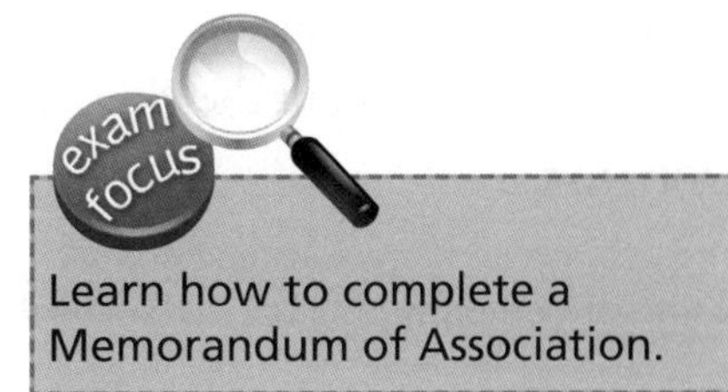

Learn how to complete a Memorandum of Association.

CONTENTS		SAMPLE MEMORANDUM OF ASSOCIATION	
(a) Name of company with 'Ltd' after last word.	→	(a) Name of company is Lakeside Fruit Farm Ltd.	
(b) Objectives of company (i.e. type of business).	→	(b) Objects for which company is established are fruit-growing.	
(c) Statement of limited liability.	→	(c) The liability of the company is limited.	
(d) Share capital of company. How much money can be raised from selling shares.	→	(d) The share capital of the company is €50,000 divided into 50,000 shares @ €1 each.	
		We the several persons whose names, addresses and descriptions are subscribed wish to be formed into a company in pursuance of the Memorandum of Association and we agree to take the number of shares in the capital of the Company set opposite our respective names.	
(e) Names of those forming the company and number of shares taken.	→	(e) Name, address and description of each subscriber.	Number of shares taken by each subscriber.
	→	John O'Mahony Director Cork	15,000
	→	Claire O'Mahony Director Cork	15,000
(f) Date and signatures.	→	(f) Date 01. 1. 15	Signatures: John O'Mahony Claire O'Mahony

(2) Articles of Association

This document sets out the internal rules and regulations of the company.

CONTENTS		SAMPLE ARTICLES OF ASSOCIATION	
Name of Company	→	Articles of Association of Lakeside Fruit Farm Ltd.	
(a) Details of share capital.	→	(a) Share capital of company is €50,000 divided into 50,000 shares @ €1 each.	
(b) Shareholders' voting rights.	→	(b) Shareholders' voting rights. One vote per share.	
(c) Regulation regarding General Meetings.	→	(c) General Meetings AGM will be held on first Tuesday in January.	
(d) How directors are to be elected.	→	(d) Election of directors at AGM and will hold office for one year.	
(e) Powers and duties of directors.	→	(e) Powers and duties of directors. Responsible for day-to-day running of company.	
(f) Borrowing powers of company.	→	(f) Borrowing powers of company. Up to €1,000,000.	
(g) Procedure for winding up company.	→	(g) How company can be wound up. Company can be wound up if it becomes insolvent.	
(h) Directors' names and addresses.	→	(h) DIRECTORS' NAMES	AND ADDRESSES
		John O'Mahony	Cork
		Claire O'Mahony	Cork
(i) Date and signature	→	(i) Date 01.1.15	Signatures John O'Mahony Claire O'Mahony

(3) Declaration of Compliance with Companies Acts 1963–2003

This document states that the directors will comply with the rules of Companies Law.

(4) Statement of Nominal Share Capital

This document states the **Authorised Share Capital** of the company, i.e. the maximum amount of capital that the company can raise.

Registrar of Companies

The documents are sent to the Registrar of Companies. The Registrar will check all the documents carefully to see if they are in order. If everything is in order a **Certificate of Incorporation** is issued.

Certificate of incorporation

(1) This is the birth certificate of a company. It is written proof that a company has been registered as a limited company.
(2) It has a separate legal existence from its owners.
(3) The shareholders have limited liability.
(4) Company can sue and be sued in its own name.

Board of directors

When the company is incorporated it will hold a meeting of shareholders, who elect a board of directors to run the company on a day-to-day basis. They report to the shareholders annually on the performance of the company at the Annual General Meeting (AGM).

Recording share capital in the books of a private limited company

From the memorandum and articles we see that on 1 January 2015 John and Claire O'Mahony formed a private limited company called Lakeside Fruit Farm Ltd. They each purchased 15,000 shares @ €1 each in the company. The money received by the company was lodged in a company bank account. On 10 January they purchased equipment for €20,000.

(1) Record the issue of the shares in the ordinary Share Capital A/C and Bank A/C.
(2) Record the purchase of the equipment in the appropriate accounts.
(3) Make out the trial balance of Lakeside Fruit Farm Ltd on 11 January 2015.

Answer

(1) Lakeside Fruit Farm Ltd has received €30,000, which was lodged in the bank. **Debit bank account** (receiving account). Company now owes €30,000 to its shareholders, John and Claire O'Mahony, who purchased the shares. **Credit share capital account** (giving account).

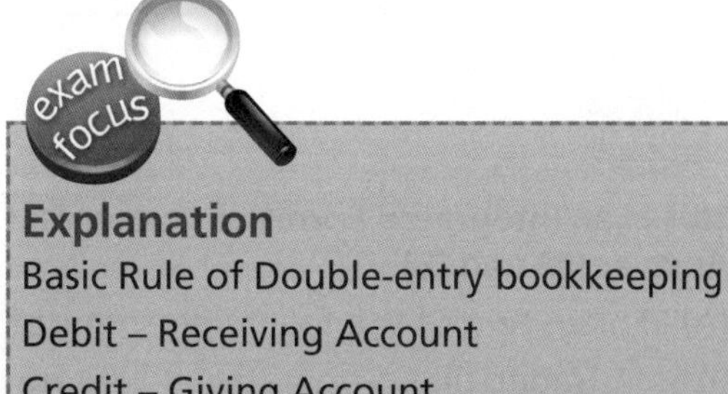

Bank Account					
		€			€
01.1.15	Ordinary Share Capital A/C	30,000	10.1.15	Equipment A/C	20,000
			11.1.15	Balance C/d	10,000
		30,000			30,000
11.1.15	Balance C/d	10,000			

Ordinary Share Capital Account					
					€
			01.1.15	Bank	30,000

(**2**) On 10 January 2015 Lakeside Fruit Farm Ltd purchased equipment for €20,000. **Debit equipment account** (receiving account). **Credit bank account** (giving account).

Equipment Account			
		€	
10.1.15	Bank	20,000	

(**3**) Trial Balance of Lakeside Fruit Farm Ltd on 11.1.15

The trial balance brings together the balance from the accounts and lists them in two separate columns, **Debit** and **Credit**.

Bank €10,000 Debit.

Ordinary Share Capital €30,000 Credit.

Equipment €20,000 Debit.

The trial balance must balance.

Trial Balance of Lakeside Fruit Farm Ltd on 11.1.15		Debit	Credit
		€	€
	Bank	10,000	
	Ordinary Share Capital		30,000
	Equipment	20,000	
		30,000	30,000

This is an Integrated Forms of Ownership and Company Formation Question. Answer (A) and (B).

(A) Explain **two** of the following forms of ownership.

(i) Sole Trader, (ii) Co-operative, (iii) State Ownership. (12)

(B) On 1 May 2012 Nora Martin, 5 Marino Close, Bray, Co. Wicklow and Joseph O'Connor, 14 Strand Road, Bray, Co. Wicklow formed a Private Limited Company called EDUCU BOOKS Ltd. They prepared a Memorandum of Association and sent it with all the necessary documents to the Registrar of Companies.

The objectives of the company are to publish and sell educational books.

The Authorised Share Capital of EDUCU BOOKS Ltd is 100,000 €1 ordinary shares.

On 12 May 2012 Nora Martin and Joseph O'Connor purchased 25,000 €1 ordinary shares each. The money received from the issue of the shares was lodged to the company bank account.

You are required to:

(i) Complete the Memorandum of Association. (16)

(ii) Record the issue of shares on 12 May 2012 in the Ordinary Share Capital and Bank Accounts.

Prepare the Opening Balance Sheet of the company as on 12 May 2012. (12)

(40 marks)

Source: Junior Cert Higher Level

Suggested solution and marking scheme

(A) Two forms of ownership explained.

Sole Trader

- This is a business owned and run by one person.
- This person puts up all the capital, keeps all the profits made.
- Has unlimited liability, i.e. if the business fails the sole trader can also lose his/her own private assets.
- Takes all the risks and bears all the losses made.
- On death this business ceases to exist (there is no continuity of existence).

Co-operative

- This is a business started by a number of people for their own benefit.
- Each person has one vote regardless of the amount they invested.
- The liability of each member is limited to the amount each invested.
- Even if one person dies or leaves the co-operative the co-operative will continue to exist (a co-operative has continuity of existence).

State Ownership

- These are businesses formed, financed and run by the government.
- The government appoints top management.
- Profits earned are reinvested or taken by the government.

Any two points on two forms of ownership @ 3 marks each. (12 marks)

(B)(i)

MEMORANDUM OF ASSOCIATION

1. The Name of the Company is EDUCU BOOKS Ltd (2)
2. The Objects for which the Company is established are:

   To publish and sell educational books (2)
3. The Liability of the members is limited.
4. The Share Capital of the Company is €100,000 (1) divided

   into 100,000 €1 ordinary shares (1)

   We the several persons whose names, addresses and descriptions are subscribed wish to be formed into a Company in pursuance of the Memorandum of Association and we agree to take the number of shares in the Capital of the Company set opposite our respective names.

Name, Address of each Subscriber	Number of Shares taken by each Subscriber
Nora Martin (1) 5 Marino Close Bray Co. Wicklow	25,000 (2)
Joseph O'Connor (1) 14 Strand Road Bray, Co. Wicklow	25,000 (2)
Date 1 May 2012 (2)	

For use with Question (B)(ii)

Date	Details	F	Amount €	Date	Details	F	Amount €
			Ord. Share Capital A/C (p. 1)				
				12/5/12	Bank (1)	CB	50,000 (1)
				(1)			
			Bank A/C (p. 2)				
12/5/12	Ordinary Share						
(1)	Capital (1)	GL	50,000 (1)				

Balance Sheet as on 12/5/2012

Current Assets			
Bank			50,000 (1)
Financed By	Authorised	Issued	
10,000 €1 Ordinary Shares	100,000 (2)	50,000 (2)	50,000

See:

Ordinary Level	**Ordinary Level**	**Higher Level**	**Higher Level**
Section A	Section B	Paper I	Paper II
2008 Q20	2009 Q4	Section A	2009 Q6
2003 Q18	2006 Q7	2009 Q14	2005 Q6abc
2001 Q14	2005 Q8	2007 Q6	2004 Q5a
2000 Q8	2002 Q7	2006 Q12	2002 Q3
		2005 Q11	
		2004 Q4	

Services to Business

Introduction to services available to business
Note: Chapters 15–19 are for Higher Level Students only.

15 Finance for Business

Note: Chapter 15 is for Higher Level students only.

To be able to:

- Identify suitable sources of finance
- Prepare and present a loan application
- Calculate the cost of a loan
- Compare costs of finance

Sources of finance

Why companies need finance	Length of time money is needed	Match use with source	Collateral required on loans
(1) Purchase assets (2) Pay expenses	Short-term (0–1 yr) Medium-term (1–5 yrs) Long-term (over 5 yrs)	Purchase premises → Long-term source Purchase stock → Short-term source	(1) Title deeds (2) Personal guarantor (3) Life policies (4) Stocks and shares

Short-term Sources (0–1 year)		
Purpose	**Sources**	**Explanation**
Purchase of stock Payment of wages Insurance Telephone, rent	Taxation	VAT, PAYE, PRSI, paid every two months, used as a free loan until collection.
	Trade credit	Buy goods on credit, usually thirty days = free loan.
	Bank overdraft	Overdraw current account up to a certain limit.
	Expenses accrued	Delayed payment of bills – use of free money.
	Factoring	Selling debtors for cash.

Medium-term Sources (1–5 yrs)		
Purpose	**Sources**	**Explanation**
Vehicles Furniture and fittings Computers	Hire purchase	Pay by instalments. The firm will not own goods purchased until last instalment is paid.
	Term loan	Loan for a period up to five years, given for specific reason and repaid by instalments.
	Leasing	Similar to renting, pay rentals but the firm will never own asset.

Long-term Sources (5 yrs upwards)		
Purpose	**Sources**	**Explanation**
Land Premises Extensions Equipment Machinery	Capital	Invested by owner – sole trader/partnership. Companies sell shares to public – shareholders.
	Retained earnings	Profit made retained in business.
	Sale and leaseback	Sell an asset for cash and arrange to lease it back.
	Mortgage	Long-term loan – repayable with interest within an agreed time. Title deeds of premises are given as collateral.
	Government grants and EU grants	Government agencies provide grants to business, e.g. Fáilte Ireland, BIM, FÁS, IDA Ireland. Non-repayable/interest free source of finance, but the receiver must comply with the grant conditions.

Question 1.

Tick the most suitable source of finance for each of the following items required by Ideal Motors Ltd:

Items	Sources		
	Short-term	Medium-term	Long-term
Buildings			✓
Computer		✓	
Cars for resale	✓		
Advertising	✓		

(4 marks)

Answer ALL Sections. This is a Business Finance and Loan Application Question.

(A) Study the following advertisement for loans and answer the question below.

> ***Let M & M Finance Ltd Lend You A Financial Hand***
>
> Loans available on the following conditions:
>
> Capital Repayments are distributed evenly over the period of the loan.
>
> Interest 9% APR.

MURPHY Ltd obtained a **three year** loan of €12,000 from M & M Finance Ltd. Calculate the total interest payable (show workings). (12)

(B) S&R CONCRETE Ltd is a manufacturer of concrete products operating from Quarry Lane, Sligo. It has two directors, Maura Stone and Paddy Rock. S&R CONCRETE Ltd owns quarries worth €2,000,000 and machinery and trucks valued at €250,000. It has a monthly income of €60,000 and it forecasts that this will increase by 20% if it obtains new buildings costing €85,000, machinery costing €120,000 and purchases five new trucks costing €50,000 each.

S& R CONCRETE Ltd has reserves of €35,000. The directors will invest €40,000 each and it will receive a grant of €75,000.

On 1 June 2015 it applied for a ten-year loan from the M & M Finance Ltd. The loan was granted on 15 June 2015.

You are required to:

(i) Calculate the amount of the loan required (show workings).

(ii) Complete the Loan Application Form.

(iii) Record the receipt of the loan in the *M & M Finance Ltd Loan and Bank Accounts.* (28)

(40 marks)

Suggested solution and marking scheme

Business Finance and Loan Application Question

(A)

Year	Principal €	Interest €
1	12,000	1,080(8)
2	8,000	720(1)
3	4,000	360(1)
	Total Interest Paid:	**2,160**(2)

(12 marks)

(B) (i) Amount of loan required

Building		€85,000
Machinery		€120,000
New Trucks		€250,000
Total cost of project		**€455,000(1)**
Less finance available		
Directors' investment	€80,000	
Reserves	€35,000	
Grant	€75,000	€190,000(1)
Amount of loan required		**€265,000(5)**

(7 marks)

Note on Calculation of Annual Income

Present monthly income + 1% increase multiplied by 12

€60,000 + €12,000 (20% of €60,000) × 12 = €864,000

Business Finance and Loan Application Question.

(ii) Loan Application Form

M & M Finance Ltd LOAN APPLICATION FORM		
NAME OF BORROWER:	S&R CONCRETE Ltd.	(1)
ADDRESS OF BORROWER:	Quarry Lane,	
	Sligo.	(1)
NAMES OF COMPANY DIRECTORS:	Maura Stone	(1)
	Paddy Rock	(1)
NATURE OF BUSINESS:	Manufacturer of concrete products	(1)
FORECASTED ANNUAL INCOME:	€864,000	(3)
AMOUNT OF LOAN REQUIRED:	€265,000	(1)
PURPOSE OF LOAN:	Purchase of new buildings, machinery and	
	five new trucks	(1)
TERM OF LOAN:	10 years	(1)
SECURITY AVAILABLE:	Quarries	(1)
SIGNATURES OF DIRECTORS:	Maura Stone	(1)
	Paddy Rock	(1)
DATE:	1 June 2015	(1)

(15 marks)

(iii) LEDGER OF S&R CONCRETE Ltd

Date	Details	F	Amount	Date	Details	F	Amount
M&M Finance Ltd LOAN A/C (page 1)							
				15/6/15 (½)	Bank(1)	ACB (½)	265,000 (1)
BANK A/C (page 2)							
15/6/15 (½)	M&M Loan (1)	GL (½)	265,000 (1)				

(6 marks)

exam Q

See:

Higher Level
Paper I
Section A
2008 Q9
2005 Q9
2000 Q3

Higher Level
Paper II
2005 Q5
2002 Q4bcd
2000 Q5

16 Financial Planning for Business

Note: Chapter 16 is for Higher Level students only.

From given data, to be able to:

- Prepare a Business Plan
- Prepare a Cash Flow Forecast

A. Applying for a loan

Financial institution will need information on the following:

(1) Purpose of loan.
(2) Size of loan.
(3) Repayment period.
(4) Security available.
(5) Ability to pay.

B. What documents must be presented to the bank when seeking a loan?

(1) Loan application form.
(2) Business plan.
(3) Cash flow forecast.
(4) Final accounts.
(5) Details of collateral.
(6) Proof of ability to repay.

C. Business plan

When applying for a loan, it will be necessary to prepare a Business Plan which will show how the owners see their business developing in the future. A business that fails to plan, plans to fail. A good business plan should cover the following areas: company details, product, market research, sales promotion, finance.

Contents of a business plan

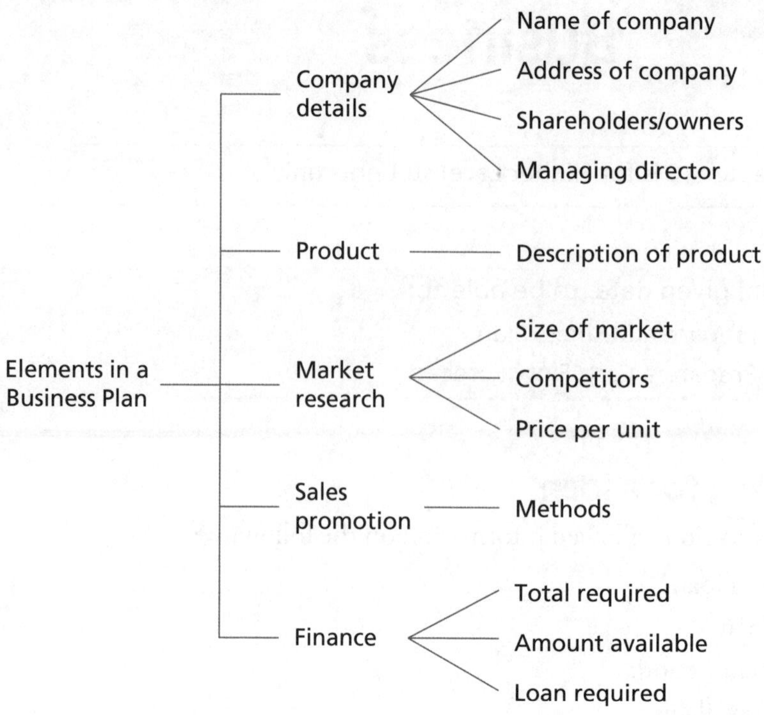

Costings

There are two costs involved in producing a product:

(1) Fixed costs – Must be paid irrespective of how much is produced, e.g. rent, insurance.

(2) Variable Costs – Increase as production increases, e.g. materials, labour.

Fixed costs + variable costs = Total costs.

$$\textbf{Cost per unit} = \frac{\textbf{Total Cost}}{\textbf{Unit Produced}}$$

Reasons why a company would prepare a business plan

- To establish the firm's objectives/goals.
- To establish targets against which achievement can be measured.
- To support an application for finance from agencies.
- To set out a framework within which to run the business.

D. Cash flow forecast

A Cash Flow Forecast shows **expected receipts** and **expected payments**: Net Cash, Opening Cash and Closing Cash (similar to a household budget).

Receipts of a business	Payments of a business
Sales, owners' capital, sale of assets, receipts from debtors, bank interest received, loans received, government grants.	Purchases of stock, purchase of premises, machinery, equipment, computers, wages, rent, rates, insurance, heat and light, repayment of loans, telephone, advertising.

Reasons for preparing a cash flow forecast

A business prepares a cash flow forecast for the following reasons:

(1) To project future inflows/receipts of cash.

(2) To project outflows/payments of cash.

(3) To identify monthly net cash/calculate monthly surplus or deficit.

(4) To identify monthly closing cash/shortfalls – need for borrowing or surplus for investing.

E. Details of collateral/security

This is the security that a business offers to a bank when it looks for a loan. If the business cannot pay back the loan the bank can take over the item the loan was secured against. Acceptable security would be land and buildings.

F. Recording the loan in the books of the company

When the business receives the loan, it must be recorded in the books as follows:

- Debit bank account of business.
- Credit loan account.

This is a Question on Cash Flow Forecast.

Answer all parts of this question:

(A) State **two** reasons why a business would prepare a Cash Flow Forecast. (4)

(B) On the sheet supplied with this question there is a partially completed cash flow forecast for RETLOW Ltd. You are required to complete the forecast for the months September, October, November and December together with the Total Column.

The following information should be taken into account.

- Monthly Cash Sales are expected to increase by 25% beginning in December.
- RETLOW Ltd is expected to receive a loan of €50,000 in October.
- Shareholders are expected to invest €100,000 in September.
- Buildings are expected to be sold in December for €120,000.
- Monthly Cash Purchases are expected to increase by 15% in December.
- Rent is expected to remain the same every month.
- New equipment will be purchased in November for €279,000.
- Shareholders will be paid a dividend of €27,000 in December.
- Light and Heat is expected to increase by 25% in the months of October and December.
- Wages are expected to remain the same, except in December when a Christmas bonus of €14,000 will be paid. (28)

(C) RETLOW Ltd forgot to allow for overtime payments of €8,000 for this period. Show the new Closing Cash figure for December after taking this overtime into account. (4)

(D) List **two** possible ways a business could deal with a Net Cash Deficit in a particular month. (4)

(40 marks)

Suggested solution and marking scheme

(A) Two reasons why a business would prepare a Cash Flow Forecast.

- To find out if the business can live within its means, i.e. Receipts > Payments.
- To identify future liquidity problems.
- Cash flow forecasts are needed for obtaining bank loans/grants.
- Cash flow forecasts need to be prepared as part of a business plan.
- For future expenditure, i.e. to see if they can afford to buy a fixed asset.
- To show whether repayments can be met.

2 reasons @ 2 marks **(4 marks)**

(B) Cash Flow Forecast for RETLOW Ltd for the period September to December.

	Jul €	Aug €	Sep €	Oct €	Nov €	Dec €	Total Jul–Dec €
Receipts							
Cash Sales	153,000	153,000	153,000	153,000	153,000	191,250	956,250(2)
Loan				50,000			50,000(1)
Share Capital			100,000				100,000(1)
Buildings						120,000	120,000(1)
A. Total Receipts	153,000	153,000	253,000	203,000	153,000	311,250	1,226,250
Payments							
Cash Purchases	72,000	72,000	72,000	72,000	72,000	82,800	442,800(2)
Rent	7,200	7,200	7,200	7,200	7,200	7,200	43,200(1)
Equipment					279,000		279,000(1)
Dividend						27,000	27,000(1)
Light and heat		14,400		18,000		18,000	50,400(2)
Wages	54,000	54,000	54,000	54,000	54,000	68,400	338,400(2)
B. Total Payments	133,200	147,600	133,200	151,200	412,200	203,400	1,180,800
Net Cash (A–B)	19,800	5,400	119,800(1)	51,800(1)	(259,200)(1)	107,850(1)	45,450(1)
Opening Cash	1,800	21,600	27,000	146,800(1)	198,600(1)	(60,600)(1)	1,800(1)
Closing Cash	21,600	27,000	146,800(1)	198,600(1)	(60,600)(1)	47,250(1)	47,250(1)

(28 marks)

(C) €39,250 **(4 marks)**

(D) Two ways a business could deal with a Net Cash Deficit in a particular month:

- Spread payments over a number of months.
- Obtain a bank overdraft for the month (not loan).
- Move a payment to a different month.
- Reduce or defer planned payments for that month.
- Move a receipt into the month in question.

2 possible ways @ 2 marks **(4 marks)**

Answer must be short-term ways as it is for a particular month. **(40 marks)**

Self-Employment and Business Plan Question. Answer (A) and (B).

(A) State **two rewards** and **two risks** of being self-employed. (8)

(B) Mary Burke and John Smyth decide to set up a sandwich making and delivery business. The name of their company is SAMBOS Ltd, located at 25 Low Street, Kells, Co. Meath.

Mary Burke is managing director.

Their market research has provided the following information:

– there are two thousand potential customers;

– there are four businesses in the area supplying sandwiches but none of them offers a delivery service;

– they estimate that they can sell five hundred sandwiches per day at €1.85 each.

They estimate their costs as follows: Equipment €5,500; Delivery van €12,000; Lease of premises €14,000; Working capital €7,500.

They have savings of €5,500 to invest in the business and can obtain a grant of €10,000 if they produce a Business Plan. They seek your help in preparing this plan.

(i) Calculate the amount of money they would need to borrow in order to set up this business.

(ii) Outline **two** suitable methods of advertising and promoting their sandwiches.

(iii) Complete the blank Business Plan document using today's date.

(32)

(40 marks)

Source: Junior Certificate Higher Level.

Suggested solution

(A) Rewards of being self-employed:

(i) Keep all the profit.

(ii) Make all the decisions.

(iii) Be one's own boss.

2 rewards @ 2 marks each (40 marks)

Risks of being self-employed:

(i) Lose one's investment if the business fails.

(ii) Has unlimited liability, could lose one's personal wealth (house, etc.) if the business fails.

(iii) Final decisions up to the owner, may not make the correct decision.

(iv) Stress – Family problems.

2 risks @ 2 marks each (4 marks)

(B) (i) Amount of money required:

	€	€
Equipment	*5,500*(1)	
Delivery Van	*12,000*(1)	
Lease of premises	*14,000*(1)	
Working Capital	*7,500*(1)	*39,000*(1)
Less amount of money available	€	€
Own savings	*5,500*(1)	
Grant	*10,000*(1)	*15,500*(1)
Amount of money required		***23,500***(1)

(9 marks)

(ii) Two suitable methods of advertising and promoting sandwiches.

Leaflets drop, Local paper, Local radio, Personal callers, Free samples, Street signs, Billboards, Local TV, Cinema.

2 methods @ 3 marks each (6 marks)

(iii) Business Plan

COMPANY DETAILS	
Name of Company	Sambos Ltd (1)
Address of Company	25 Low Street
	Kells
	Co. Meath (1)
Shareholders/Owners	Mary Burke, John Smyth (2)
Managing Director	Mary Burke (1)
PRODUCT	
Description of product	Sandwich making and delivery (1)
MARKET RESEARCH	
Size of market	Two thousand customers (1)
Competitors	Four businesses but no delivery services (1)
Price per unit sandwich	€1.85 (1)
SALES PROMOTION	
Methods	Leaflets (1), free samples (1)
FINANCE	
Total required	€39,000 (1)
amount available	€15,500 (1)
loan required	€23,500 (1)
Signed	Mary Burke (1)
	John Smyth (1)
Date	16/6/15 (1)

(17 marks)

See:

Higher Level
Paper I
Section A
2008 Q15
2008 Q19
2006 Q18

Higher Level
Paper II
2007 Q3
2007 Q5
2004 Q5b
2003 Q6

17 Commercial Banks and Business

Note: Chapter 17 is for Higher Level students only.

To understand the following:

- Financial services
- Money transfer facilities
- Procedure for opening accounts
- Operating accounts

A. Summary of services provided by commercial banks for business

exam focus

Begin by rereading chapter 8 – Money and Banking.

1. Deposit accounts

2. Money transfer facilities

(a) **Cheque payments.**

(b) **Bank draft** – a cheque drawn by a bank on its own bank account.

(c) **Standing order** – to make certain fixed payments, e.g. rent, insurance, interest payments.

(d) **Direct debit** – to make variable payments from an account at regular intervals, e.g. ESB, telephone.

(e) **Credit transfer** (bank giro) – to pay ESB or telephone bills, make VAT returns.

(f) **PayPath** – wages transferred directly into employee's bank account.

3. Card payments

(a) **ATM (Automated Teller Machines)** – a business can lodge, withdraw, request a statement, order a cheque book or pay a bill.

(b) **Company credit cards** – used in business to pay for lunches, hotel accommodation, petrol/diesel.

4. Transferring money abroad

(a) **Foreign draft** – to pay a creditor abroad.

(b) **Traveller's cheques** – used by salespeople travelling abroad.

5. Lending

(a) **Bank overdraft.**

(b) **Term loan** – given for a **stated reason** for a **specified period of time**, it has an **agreed repayment schedule.**

(c) **Commercial mortgage** – for purchasing property.

6. Safe keeping

(a) **Strongroom facilities** – a business can store important documents and other valuables in the bank's strongroom.

(b) **Night safe facilities** – money can be lodged in the bank late at night through a chute located in the bank wall. A leather wallet and key are provided.

7. Foreign exchange

8. Financial services

(a) **Financial advice.**

(b) **Income tax advice.**

(c) Facility for **purchase and sale of shares.**

(d) Advice on **insurance** or **assurance**.

(e) Help with **financial planning,** e.g. cash flow statements.

9. Help with exporting

(a) Foreign currency **exchange**.

(b) Checking **creditworthiness** of foreign customers.

(c) **Information** on foreign markets.

(d) Arranging **collection of payment** from abroad.

(e) **Export credit insurance** covers risk of non-payment.

(f) **Loans**, while firms are waiting for payment from foreign customers.

10. Bank statements and bank reconciliation statements

These are dealt with fully in chapter 8.

B. Operating a business bank account

(1) Usually two signatures required on all cheques and withdrawal forms.

(2) Record all lodgments and payments in the business bank account.

(3) Request a weekly bank statement.

(4) Prepare bank reconciliation statement regularly.

Some information that a private limited company can provide when opening a current account in a bank

(1) Memorandum of association/articles of association.

(2) Signatures of people who can write company cheques.

(3) Name and address of company, names of directors.

(4) Certificate of incorporation.

(5) Objectives of the company.

(6) Details of company accounts.

Factors that banks consider when granting a loan

(1) Amount of money required.

(2) Purpose of the loan.

(3) Period of time the loan is required for.

(4) Ability to repay loan.

(5) Security available.

(6) Business history.

(7) Market research details.

(8) Creditworthiness of business seeking the loan.

18 Insurance for Business

Note: Chapter 18 is for Higher Level students only.

From given data, be able to:

- Identify insurance requirements for a business.

A. Reasons for business insurance

(1) **Protection of assets** against fire, theft, etc.

(2) Protection against **legal action** as a result of accidents to the public or staff.

(3) **Legal reasons** – motor insurance.

There are many risks in business and every business should be adequately insured.

B. Main types of business insurance

(1) **Motor insurance** – compulsory on all company vehicles.

(2) **Employer's liability** – covers claims by employees arising out of accidents at work.

(3) **Building insurance** – covers damage to property and contents.

(4) **Burglary/Theft insurance** – covers damage arising from a break-in and theft of contents or property.

(5) **Cash in transit insurance** – covers theft of cash while in transit between the business and the bank.

(6) **Goods in transit insurance** – covers theft or damage to goods while being transported.

(7) **Fidelity guarantee insurance** – compensates an employer for loss of cash arising from the dishonesty of employees.

(8) **Plate glass insurance** – covers the breakages or damage to expensive shop window glass.

(9) **Sprinkler leakage insurance** – covers loss or damage caused to stock by water as a result of accidental switching on of the sprinkler system used for fire-fighting.

(10) **Consequential loss insurance** – covers the firm for loss of profits while a business is closed as a result of a fire or flood.

(11) **Public liability insurance** – covers claims made by members of the public who are injured while on the firm's property.

(12) **Bad debts insurance** – covers a loss arising because a debtor does not pay what he/she owes.

(13) **Product liability insurance** – provides cover against a claim made by a person that he/she was harmed or suffered a loss or damage through using the firm's products.

(14) **PRSI (Pay-related Social Insurance)** – PRSI is a payment to the government. The employee pays a percentage of gross wages, but the employer must also make a contribution for each employee on the payroll.

(15) **Key person insurance** – provides compensation for the loss of valuable employees through death, for example, the managing director or a highly talented employee.

C. Non-insurable risks

(1) Bankruptcy.

(2) Stock becoming obsolete (out of date).

(3) Bad management decisions.

D. Recording the payment of insurance in the books of the business

When insurance is paid, money goes out of the business.
- Debit insurance account (expense).
- Credit bank account (asset).

Example

A payment of €600 was made by cheque for insurance on 1 September 2016.

Bank Account (Asset)

			1/9/16	Insurance	600

Insurance Account (Expense)

1/9/16	Bank	600	1/9/16	Profit & Loss A/C	600

The figure of €600 insurance will appear under expenses in the profit and loss account.

Profit and Loss Account

	Expenses		
	Insurance		600

This is a Report Writing and Insurance Question. Answer ALL Sections.

NPD ELECTRIC Ltd, 34 Live Wire Drive, Galway, manufactures and distributes electrical appliances for the home. It sells its products in Ireland.

NPD ELECTRIC Ltd wishes to review its insurance policies and requires advice on its insurance requirements. It supplies the following information:

Its assets include: Premises, Equipment, Motor Vehicles, Stock of electrical appliances. It has eighty employees.

NPD ELECTRIC Ltd lodges its cash twice weekly in a bank ten kilometres away.

(A) Assume you are Martina Toban, Insurance Consultant, 10 Castle View, Roscommon. Prepare a report, on today's date, for the directors of NPD ELECTRIC Ltd, setting out the following:

(i) **Two** types of insurance that NPD ELECTRIC Ltd is required to have by law.

(ii) **Four other** relevant types of insurance you would advise it to have and the reasons for having these.

(iii) The importance of having adequate insurance for NPD ELECTRIC Ltd. (32)

(B) Martina advised the directors of NPD ELECTRIC Ltd that when calculating their insurance premium they must take into account, the basic premium, loadings and deductions. The basic premium was €25,000, loadings were 30% of basic and deductions were 12% of basic plus loadings.

(i) List **one** example of a loading and **one** example of a deduction that NPD ELECTRIC Ltd might have to take into account when calculating its premium.

(ii) Calculate the total premium for NPD ELECTRIC Ltd (show workings). (8)

(40 marks)

Suggested solution and marking scheme

(A) Report

From: 10 Castle View
Roscommon (2)

15 June 2011 (2)

Title: Report on the Insurance requirements of NPD ELECTRIC Ltd (2)

To: The Directors
NPD ELECTRIC Ltd, (1)
34 Live Wire Drive,
Galway (1)

Introduction:
I was asked on behalf of the Directors of NPD ELECTRIC Ltd to prepare a report on the insurance requirements of the Company. I have studied all the details supplied to me by the directors and I set out my report below. (2)

The Company is required by law to:
(i) have third party motor insurance on all its vehicles. (2)
(ii) pay its portion of PRSI. (2)

It is advisable to have:

Type

1. Product Liability (1)
2. Employer's Liability (1)
3. Cash in Transit Insurance (1)
4. Fire and Theft Insurance (1)

Reason

1. This is in case customers, who are injured by a faulty product, make a claim. (1)
2. This is in case any of its employees are injured at work. (1)
3. This is in case cash is stolen while being transported to the bank, ten kilometres away. (1)
4. This is in case of loss through fire damage or goods being stolen. (1)

Importance of Adequate Insurance (2)

Adequate insurance is having **all relevant risks insured** for the **correct amounts**. Failure to insure risks for the correct amounts leads to **underinsurance** and reduction in compensation paid. (2)
[Reason (2) and Consequence (2)]

I am available to discuss this report if required.(2)

Martina Toban,(2)
Insurance Consultant.(2)

(32 marks)

Other types of insurance, with appropriate reasons, that would be acceptable to include are: Fidelity Guarantee, Consequential Loss, Goods in Transit, Public Liability, Bad Debts.

(B) (i) One **example of a loading** includes a charge for:
previous claims, nature of industry, location, age, type of work. (1)
One example of a deduction includes a reduction for:
having fire/ burglar alarms, no claims bonus, having security. (1)

(ii) Calculation of Insurance Premium

Basic Premium	€25,000
Add Loadings 30% of basic	€7,500
	€32,500
Less Deductions 12% of basic plus loadings	€3,900
Total Premium	**€28,600**

(8 marks)

(Must show workings for full marks)

See:
Higher Level
Paper II
2005 Q3
2004 Q4

19 Communications

Note: Chapter 19 is for Higher Level students only.

From given data, be able to:

- Recommend a form of communication
- Prepare a suitable graph/chart

A. Factors to be considered when choosing a form of communication

(1) **Cost** – How expensive is the method of communication: telephone call or letter?

(2) **Speed** – How fast can the information be transferred?

(3) **Safety** – Will the item reach its destination safely?

(4) **Written record** – It is important to keep a written record for future reference.

(5) **Secrecy** – If information is confidential, choose a secret form of communication.

(6) **Destination** – Over what distance is the communication, national or international?

(7) **Accuracy** – Will method chosen transfer the information exactly?

key point

Communication is the exchanging of information. The message should be **brief**, **clear** and **simple**.

B. Who does a business communicate with?

(1) Directors, managers, employees, supervisors – **internal communication**.

(2) Customers, public, shareholders, insurance companies, bank, suppliers, tax office – **external communication**.

C. Communication

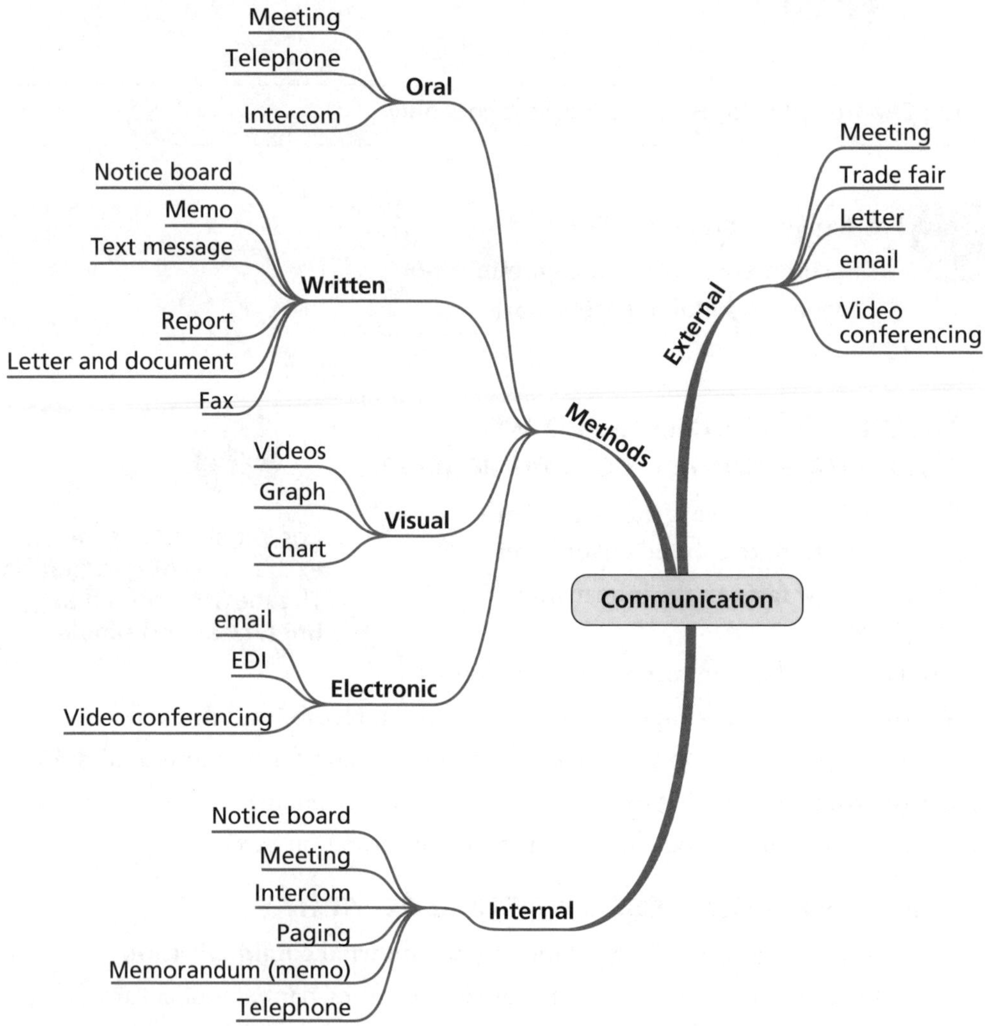

Communication

- **Methods**
  - **Oral**
    - Meeting
    - Telephone
    - Intercom
  - **Written**
    - Notice board
    - Memo
    - Text message
    - Report
    - Letter and document
    - Fax
  - **Visual**
    - Videos
    - Graph
    - Chart
  - **Electronic**
    - email
    - EDI
    - Video conferencing
- **External**
  - Meeting
  - Trade fair
  - Letter
  - email
  - Video conferencing
- **Internal**
  - Notice board
  - Meeting
  - Intercom
  - Paging
  - Memorandum (memo)
  - Telephone

D. Agencies involved in communication

Eircom

EIRCOM provides a national and international broadband and phone service.

(1) **Telephone** – Popular form of communication for local, national and international calls.

(2) **Teleconferencing** – A meeting or conference can be held over the telephone.

(3) **Videoconferencing** – A way of conducting meetings without travelling to the meeting. Video cameras are used to transmit the picture and sound of the meeting over the telephone.

(4) **Fax (facsimile)** – Exact copy of a document can be transmitted over the telephone to another fax machine

(5) **Internet** – This gives access to the World Wide Web and email.

An Post

An Post provides a national and international telecommunications service.

(1) **Postal services**

All services have been designed according to what is important to the customer.

- **Standard post**: If cost is the main concern, standard post should be used. It offers a cost-effective worldwide delivery.
- **Registered post**: If security is the main concern, registered post should be used. It offers the securest delivery method available.
- **Express post**: If speed and next-day delivery are required, express post should be chosen. It offers a guaranteed next-working-day delivery within the Republic of Ireland, with optional signature and insurance available for a small fee.
- **Courier post**: If the item is especially urgent, courier post is the service to use. It provides a next-day delivery before 12.00 p.m. in major urban areas within the Republic of Ireland. International delivery times vary according to destination.

(2) **Freepost** – Allows customers to write to a business free of charge. Customers must write 'FREEPOST' on the envelope

(3) **Business Reply Service** – Business provides special business reply envelopes.

E. Visual communication – charts and graphs

There are three main ways of showing information visually.

Line graph, bar chart, pie chart.

1. Line graph

A line graph shows a trend, i.e. how things change over time.

2. Bar chart

A bar chart is very useful when making comparisons. Information is displayed in a series of bars.

3. Pie chart

A pie chart is a circle divided into sections, each section showing figures as a percentage of the total.

F. Modern communication technology

Electronic data interchange (EDI)

EDI is an automated method of processing transactions between suppliers and customers, e.g. ordering stock, invoicing, payment, etc. EDI is dependent on the supplier and customer having compatible EDI software.

The Internet

- The Internet is a global network of computers facilitating the transfer of data and communication between users.
- All computer users who are networked to the Internet through an Internet service provider can access information via the **World Wide Web** – using a website address or through a search engine, e.g. Google.
- Users may also communicate with each other via **email**. Broadband is the fastest Internet access.

Internet services

Electronic mail (Email)

The sending and receiving of documents, messages, images, and video clips electronically by means of a computer.

World Wide Web (WWW)

A vast network of linked documents stored on computers throughout the world that can provide a computer user with information on a huge variety of subjects.

E-commerce/E-business

This consists of the buying and selling of products or services over the Internet.

Videoconferencing

- A meeting between people in different locations. A computer, a video camera and a network such as the Internet are used. People can see and hear each other using electronic communication.
- Videoconferencing is an extremely useful method of communication because it saves people the time and expense of travel and can often accomplish many of the things a physical meeting can.

This is a Question on Graphs and Charts

A country called Skyland trades with other countries each year. In 2010 it had the following exports to other countries (m = million).

Exports	€
Germany	300 m
Britain	700 m
Netherlands	200 m
France	400 m
US	600 m
Spain	500 m

Show the above figures in the form of a pie chart **or** a bar chart. **(20 marks)**

Solution

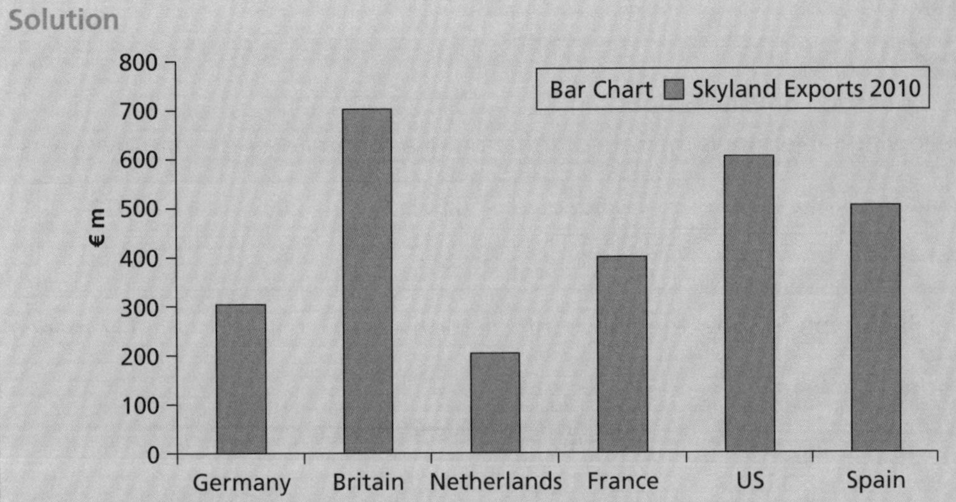

Marking Scheme

Title = 2 marks

6 bars drawn to scale @ 2 marks each = 12 marks

Bars correctly labelled 1 mark each = 6 marks

OR

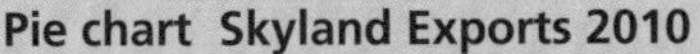

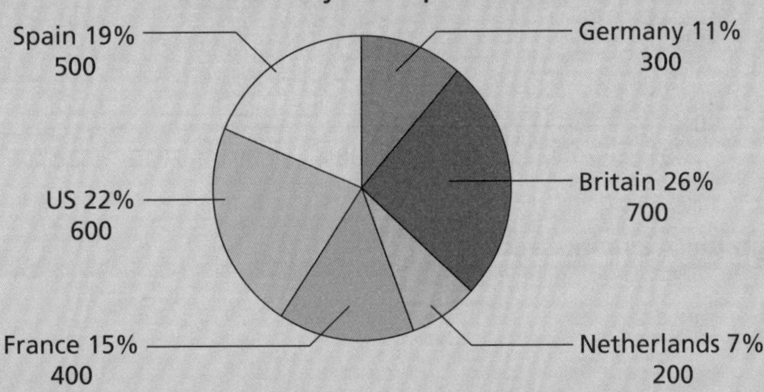

Marking Scheme

Title = 2 marks

6 segments drawn to scale @ 2 marks each = 12 marks

Segments clearly labelled 1 mark each = 6 marks

This is a question on Line Graphs.

The following table shows the rate of inflation in a country over the past five years.

Year	2006	2007	2008	2009	2010
Rate	8%	4%	6%	5%	2%

Draw a line graph to show the above information. **(12 marks)**

Solution

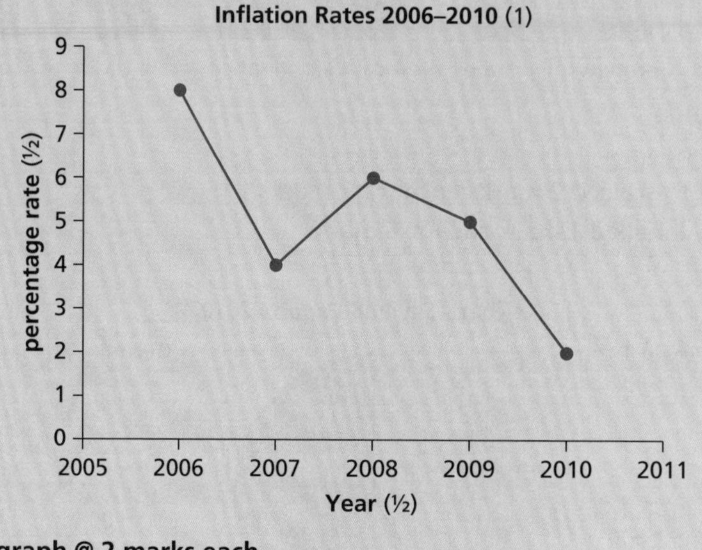

5 points on graph @ 2 marks each **(10 marks)**

See:

Ordinary Level
Section A
2005 Q18

Higher Level
Paper I
Section A
2007 Q1
2006 Q2
2003 Q16
2001 Q14

Work

Introduction to the chain of production and to the people who work in the chain including industrial relations.

20 Chain of Production and Channels of Distribution

From given data, be able to:

- Identify different units in the chain of distribution
- Distinguish between different types of retailing
- Distinguish between different types of wholesalers
- Identify types of industry

A. Types of production

Primary Production – the **extracting of materials** from the sea and land for use by consumers or for further processing.

Examples: fishing, forestry, mining, quarrying, oil extraction, turf cutting.

Secondary Production – **converting raw materials** from the primary production stage into finished products.

Examples: manufacturing industries such as car manufacturing, brewing, food processing, and construction: roads, hospitals, schools.

Tertiary Production – service industries are businesses who **do not manufacture anything** but who provide assistance, goods or materials for consumers and other businesses.

Examples: banking, advertising, insurance, retailing, hairdressing, transport, communications, medical/dental, etc.

B. Public sector and private sector

Public sector – working for government, e.g. teachers.

Private sector – all other workers not employed by government, e.g. bank officials.

C. Channels of distribution

Channels of distribution are the ways that goods go from the manufacturer to the consumer.

The most common channels of distribution are:

1. Manufacturer/Producer → Consumer

- Goods are made to customers' specifications.
- Suitable for fitted furniture, buying a computer direct from the manufacturer, a farmers' market.

2. Manufacturer/Producer → Retailer → Consumer

- Used where large retailer buys direct from manufacturer, e.g. Tesco, Dunnes Stores.
- Newspapers and magazines are distributed in this way as product can't be stored.
- Product may be perishable and has to be delivered to the market quickly, e.g. bread, milk.

3. Manufacturer/Producer → Wholesaler → Retailer → Consumer

- Suitable for goods where retailer is too small to deal directly with the manufacturer, e.g. household food items.

D. Manufacturer

The manufacturer turns raw materials into finished goods.

E. Wholesaler

The wholesaler buys in bulk from manufacturer and sells in smaller quantities to the retailer.

Services to manufacturer	Services to retailer
(1) Buys in bulk.	(1) Gives credit to retailer.
(2) Blends, grades, packs goods.	(2) Delivers goods to retailer.
(3) Advertises manufacturer's goods.	(3) Provides wide choice of goods.
(4) Gives information.	(4) Informs retailers about new products.

Types of wholesaler

(1) Traditional wholesaler

Retailer sends in order. Goods are delivered to retailer's premises. Credit is given.

(2) Cash and carry wholesaler

Sells a wide variety of goods. Retailer goes to the wholesaler's premises, selects and pays for goods and transports them to his premises.

Why would the wholesaler be omitted from a channel of distribution?

(1) Storage may not be required.

(2) If it is important to get product to consumer quickly.

(3) If product has short shelf life.

(4) Retailer wishes to buy in bulk from manufacturer.

F. Retailer

The retailer buys goods from the wholesaler and sells to the consumer.

Functions of retailer

(1) Sells goods or services at a convenient location.
(2) Offers a wide range of goods to the consumer.
(3) May give **credit**.
(4) May **deliver** goods.
(5) May offer personal service and advice.
(6) Brings new products to the attention of the consumer.

Types of retailer

(1) **Independent shops/Sole traders**
- Small shops owned and managed by one person.
- **Examples:** butcher, newsagent.

(2) **Multiple shops/Chain stores**
- A number of shops/branches owned by same firm.
- Multiple shops **specialise** in a particular type of product, e.g. Eason's.
- Chain stores **sell a wide range** of goods, e.g. Tesco, Dunnes.

(3) **Department stores**
- Large retail shop selling a wide range of goods in many different departments, e.g. furniture, clothing, electrical.
- **Examples:** Marks & Spencer, Brown Thomas.

(4) **Supermarkets**
- Large self-service stores selling a variety of goods, e.g. Dunnes Stores, Superquinn.

(5) **Shopping centres**
- A number of shops under one roof usually located on the outskirts of large towns or cities.

(6) **Franchising**
- Purchasing from the parent firm a licence to set up a branch of their firm in accordance with their policy.
- An annual fee is paid for the use of their trade name.
- There is ongoing support and advertising from the parent company.
- **Examples:** McDonald's, Burgerland, Subway.

(7) **Voluntary groups**
- A number of small retailers link with a wholesaler to form a group.
- **Examples:** Super Valu, Spar, Gala.

(8) Mail order

- Customer chooses goods from catalogue.
- **Example:** Family Album, Argos.

Developments in retailing

(1) In-store banking – Customers can pay directly from their bank accounts e.g. Laser.

(2) Bar codes/Bar code scanner – stores prices, acts as cash register, produces receipt and updates stock levels.

(3) Increase in the use of environmentally friendly products, e.g. reusable bags.

(4) More foreign competition e.g. ALDI, LIDL.

(5) E-commerce – Sale of goods and services over the Internet.

exam Q

See:

Ordinary Level	**Ordinary Level**	**Higher Level**	**Higher Level**
Section A	Section B	Paper I	Paper II
2009 Q1	2008 Q8a	Section A	2006 Q5ab
2008 Q9	2004 Q8ab	2009 Q12	
2007 Q7		2007 Q7	
2007 Q14		2006 Q5	
2006 Q19		2006 Q19	
2004 Q5		2005 Q2	
		2005 Q15	

21 People at Work

From given data, be able to:

- Draft an organisational structure for a business
- Match names to jobs
- Outline rights and responsibilities of employees
- Identify risks and rewards of self-employment

A. Work

Human effort **without payment**, such as club members doing voluntary work, e.g. GAA.

B. Employment

- Working **for payment**, i.e. employees of firms.

C. Nature and extent of employment

- People who are employed work in three main areas: agriculture, industry, services.
- People who cannot find employment are said to be unemployed.
- The labour force = those who are employed and those available for work.

D. Unemployment

People are unemployed when they are willing to work for payment but cannot find a job.

Reasons for unemployment	How to reduce unemployment
(1) Fall in the number employed in agriculture. **(2)** New technology replacing workers. **(3)** Firms have reduced staff numbers because of competition. **(4)** Business closing down and relocating to other countries to avail of lower wage rates. **(5)** Economic recession.	**(1)** Put more money into job creation. **(2)** Encourage more enterprise and self-employment. **(3)** Become more competitive abroad and increase sales, thus creating more jobs. **(4)** Introduce early retirement and job-sharing schemes. **(5)** Buy more Irish-produced goods and create more jobs.

E. Emigration

Leaving the country in search of employment.

F. Self-employment

Why people become self-employed

(1) Cannot find employment.

(2) Made redundant.

(3) See an opportunity to start own business.

Rewards of Self-employment	Risks of Self-employment
• Own boss and working for oneself. • Make all the decisions and answerable to no one. • Keep all the profit after paying the taxes. • Increased motivation to work harder. • More job satisfaction when it's for oneself. • Potential to be wealthy as the business grows.	• Risk of financial failure/lose one's original investment. • Must bear the losses incurred and pay from one's own resources, may go bankrupt. • Can be overworked doing all the tasks if one can't afford to employ others. • Can be stressful having full responsibility for all aspects, particularly borrowings. • Unstable income as profits may fluctuate or be non-existent.

G. Organisation of the workplace

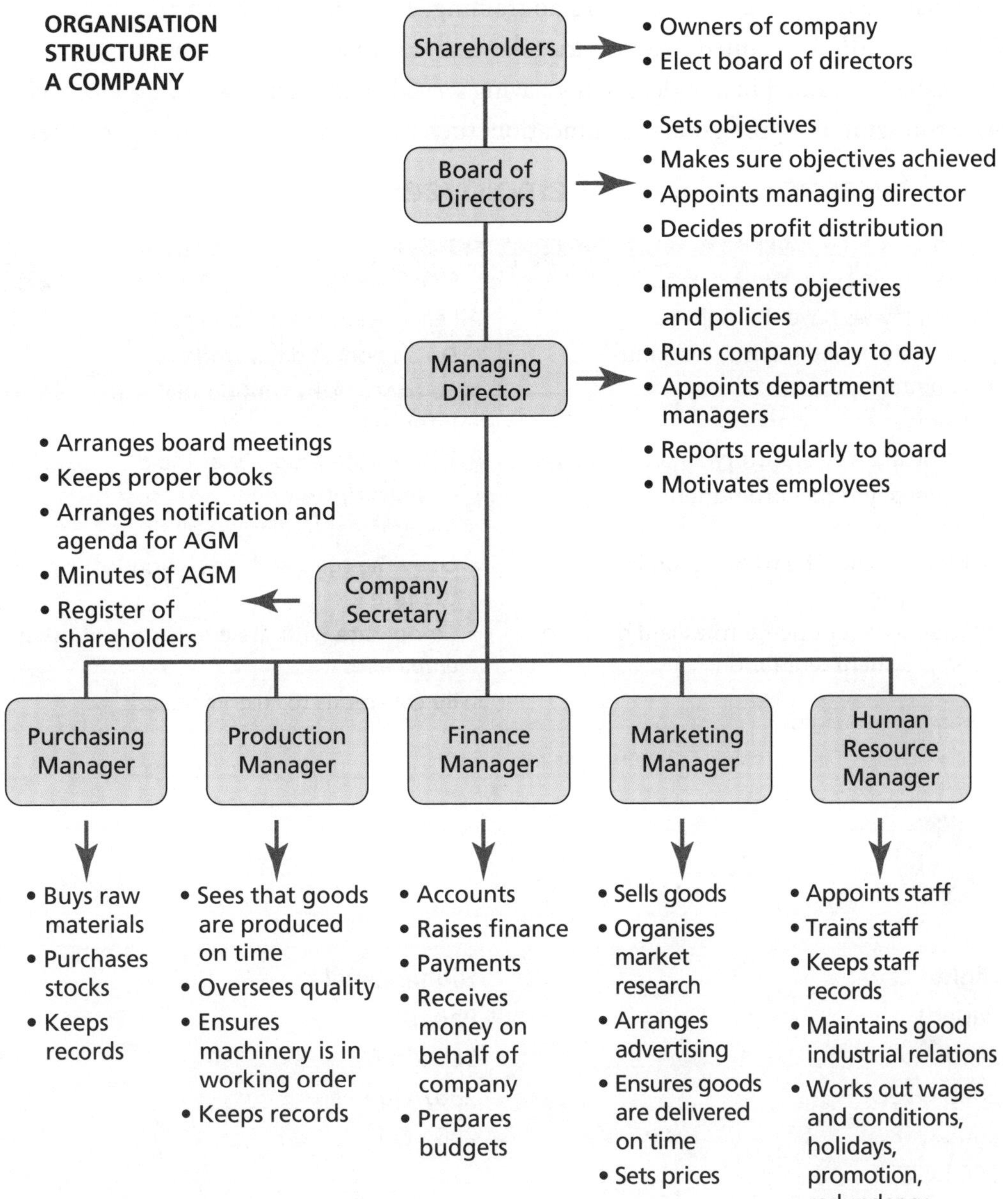
ORGANISATION STRUCTURE OF A COMPANY
Shareholders
• Owners of company
• Elect board of directors
Board of Directors
• Sets objectives
• Makes sure objectives achieved
• Appoints managing director
• Decides profit distribution
Managing Director
• Implements objectives and policies
• Runs company day to day
• Appoints department managers
• Reports regularly to board
• Motivates employees
Company Secretary
• Arranges board meetings
• Keeps proper books
• Arranges notification and agenda for AGM
• Minutes of AGM
• Register of shareholders
Purchasing Manager
• Buys raw materials
• Purchases stocks
• Keeps records
Production Manager
• Sees that goods are produced on time
• Oversees quality
• Ensures machinery is in working order
• Keeps records
Finance Manager
• Accounts
• Raises finance
• Payments
• Receives money on behalf of company
• Prepares budgets
Marketing Manager
• Sells goods
• Organises market research
• Arranges advertising
• Ensures goods are delivered on time
• Sets prices
Human Resource Manager
• Appoints staff
• Trains staff
• Keeps staff records
• Maintains good industrial relations
• Works out wages and conditions, holidays, promotion, redundancy

H. Types of job

(1) **Services** – providing a service to individuals or to business, e.g. teacher.
(2) **Administration** – in either a management or a supervisory role.
(3) **Artistic/Creative** – using one's imagination or creative abilities, e.g. artist.
(4) **Technical** – understanding how things work, e.g. computer programmer.
(5) **Manual** – physical work, e.g. builder.
(6) **Clerical** – office work.

Types of skill

(1) **Unskilled** – no qualifications and no training, e.g. builder's labourer.
(2) **Semi-skilled** – trained to do a particular task, e.g. machine operator.
(3) **Skilled** – trained in a trade, usually having served an apprenticeship, e.g. electrician.
(4) **Professional** – professional qualification, such as a university degree, e.g. teacher.

I. Rights/responsibilities of employees

Rights of employees	Responsibilities of employees
All employees have the right to: • Safe, clean and healthy working conditions. • Fair wages for work done. • To be allowed statutory annual holidays. • Equal pay, equal promotion opportunities. • Membership of a trade union if they wish. • Their legal entitlements as laid down in employment legislation.	All employees are obliged to: • Do an honest day's work. • Be trustworthy/confidential with information. • Respect the property of the employer/firm. • Be punctual to work at all times. • Obey the rules and regulations of the firm. • Co-operate with the employer and other employees. • Be courteous to customers.

exam Q

See:

Higher Level
Paper I
Section A
2008 Q12
2005 Q18
2004 Q2
2002 Q12

Higher Level
Paper I
Section B
2007 Q6a
2004 Q6

22 Being an Employer

From given data, be able to:

- Draft a job advertisement
- Calculate the wages book for a small business
- Complete a wages slip
- Prepare cash analysis statement

A. Rights/responsibilities of employer

Rights of employer	Responsibilities of employer
(1) To decide on the **objectives** and **policies** of the business. **(2)** To select suitable employees. **(3)** To dismiss dishonest or unsuitable staff. **(4)** To expect loyalty from staff.	**(1)** To make sure workplace is safe and healthy. **(2)** To give employees a contract of employment in writing. **(3)** To give statutory holiday entitlements. **(4)** To pay agreed wages. **(5)** To obey all employment laws. **(6)** Keep all necessary employee records.

B. Procedure for employing staff

1. Draw up job description describing the duties and responsibilities of the job and the skills and qualifications required.
2. Advertise the job.
3. Short-list candidates. Interview candidates.
4. Select most suitable candidate. Prepare contract of employment.
5. Introduce new employee to firm, organise training, register them for tax and PRSI.

C. Calculating wages

Employees are paid by time rate, piece rate or on a commission basis.

1. Time rate

Employees are paid a certain rate per hour or per day.

2. Piece rate

Employees' gross pay would depend on output/the number of units produced, e.g. €1 per block laid, €5 per item made.

3. Commission

Income calculated as a percentage of the value of sales. This is usually used for paying sales personnel, e.g. 10% of gross sales in Euros.

Gross Pay = Basic Pay + Overtime + Commission
Net Pay = Gross Pay − Deductions

D. Income tax forms

1. P60

At the end of the tax year each employee receives a P60, which shows gross pay, tax and PRSI deducted during the tax year.

2. P45

Given to an employee leaving the firm. This shows gross pay, tax and PRSI paid to the date of ceasing employment.

3. P12

This is the taxpayer's income tax return for the year. It also acts as an application form for a tax credit.

E. Wages slip

When employees are paid they receive their pay plus a payslip. This shows gross pay, deductions and net pay.

F. Wages book

The employer will keep a record of all wages/salaries paid in a wages book. From the wages book the employer can calculate the total cost of wages and employer's PRSI.

G. Payment of wages and salaries

Wages and salaries may be paid in any one of the following ways:

(1) **By cash**.
(2) **By cheque** – safe method of payment.
(3) **By credit transfer** directly into the bank account of employee (PayPath).

By cash

If wages are paid by cash the employer will have to do a cash analysis to show the breakdown of the wages into the various denominations of money required for paying each employee.

H. Recording the total cost of wages in the books of Premier Ltd

- Debit wages account.
- Credit bank account.

I. Employee records

Employers keep records on all employees.

(1) Personal details.
(2) Job application form.
(3) Curriculum vitae.
(4) Job performance.
(5) Behaviour – absence, lateness, personal days taken.
(6) Copy of contract of employment.
(7) PAYE and PRSI records.

Why are employee records kept?

(1) A reference if an employee leaves.
(2) Employee records such as CVs and contracts are required for promotion/dismissal purposes.
(3) PAYE and PRSI records are compulsory.
(4) Employee records are required by law, e.g. evidence of age.

Information given on a CV

(1) Personal details.
(2) Educational achievements.
(3) Work experience details.
(4) Interests/Hobbies/Achievements.
(5) Referees.

This is a question on Employment and Wages.

(A) CRISPY FAST FOOD has two employees who are paid on a monthly basis. Each employee pays PRSI at the rate of 8%. The employer's rate of PRSI is 12%.

(i) Complete the Wages Book for the month of May 2011 *using the partially completed Wages Book.*

(ii) Calculate the **total cost of wages** for the month of May 2011. (16)

(B) Record the **total cost of wages** for the month of May 2011 in the Wages and Bank accounts of CRISPY FAST FOOD, provided. (6)

(C) CRISPY FAST FOOD paid their wages in cash. Fill in the note/coin analysis. (18)

(40 marks)

Solution and marking scheme

(A) (i)

WAGES BOOK

Date	Name	Gross Wages	Deductions			Net Wages	Employer's PRSI
			PAYE	PRSI	Total		
		€	€	€	€	€	€
31.5.2011	Mary Fish	1,800	600	144 (1)	744 (1)	1,056 (1)	216 (1)
31.5.2011	Luke Curry	1,400	460	112 (1)	572 (1)	828 (1)	168 (1)
	Total	3,200 (1)	1,060 (1)	256 (1)	1,316 (1)	1,884 (1)	384 (1)

(ii)

TOTAL COST OF WAGES	(3,200 + 384) €3,584 (2)

(B)

Date	Details	F	Amount €	Date	Details	F	Amount €
			Wages A/C (p. 1)				
31.5.2011 (1)	Bank (1)	CB	3,584 (1)				
			Bank A/C (p. 2)				
				31.5.2011 (1)	Wages (1)	CB	3,584 (1)

(C)

Note/Coin Analysis Sheet for CRISPY FAST FOOD															
Name	Total	€500	€200	€100	€50	€20	€10	€5	€2	€1	50c	20c	10c	5c	2c	1c
Mary Fish	€1,056	2			1			1		1						
Luke Curry	€828	1	1	1		1		1	1	1						
Total	€1,884	3	1	1	1	1		2	1	2						
	(2)	(2)	(2)	(2)	(2)	(2)		(2)	(2)	(2)						

This is a question on People at Work and Wages.

Cormac Fallon is employed as an electrician with McMahon Electric Ltd. His basic wage rate is €925 for a 37-hour week. Overtime is paid at time and a half for the first six hours and double time for hours in excess of that. In week No. 30 he worked 48 hours. Cormac pays income tax at the rate of 41% and PRSI at 8%. His annual tax credit is €7,488. Each week he pays €6 Trade Union membership and invests €40 in a pension fund. Both of these are deducted at source by his employer.

(i) Complete Cormac's wage slip for Week No. 30 using the blank document. Show your workings. (22)

(ii) State **two** benefits that Cormac may receive from his PRSI contributions. (4)

(iii) Outline **three** responsibilities that Cormac has to his employer. (6)

Suggested solution and marking scheme **(32 marks)**

Gross Pay		€	PAYE		
Basic Pay		925	Gross Pay		
Overtime 6 hrs × €37.50 = 225(1)			1,400 × 41% =	574 (1)	
5 hrs × €50.00 = 250(1)		475	Less Tax Credit	144 (1)	
Gross Pay:		€1,400	PAYE	€430	
Tax credit			Other		
$\frac{€7,488\ (1)}{52\ \ (1)}$ = €144 per week			PRSI €1,400 × 8% = €112		

(i)

Wage Slip		
Name: Cormac Fallon (1)		
Week No.: 30 (1)		
Basic Pay	€925 (2)	
Overtime	€475 (3)	
GROSS PAY	→	€1,400
Tax Credit	€144 (3)	
Deductions:		
PAYE	€430 (3)	
PRSI	€112 (3)	
Trade Union	€6 (2)	
Pension	€40 (2)	
Total Deductions	→	€588
NET PAY	→	€812 (2)

(22 marks)

(ii) Benefits from PRSI Contributions

- Contributory pension
- Unemployment benefit (dole)
- Dental benefit
- Optical benefit
- Widow's pension
- Disability benefit
- Sickness benefit

2 benefits @ 2 marks (4 marks)

(iii) Responsibilities that Cormac has to his employer

- To do an honest day's work.
- To be punctual.
- To protect employer's property, stock and good name.
- To attend every working day.
- To follow employer's instructions.
- To co-operate with other employees.
- To work in the best interest of the firm.
- To maintain confidentiality regarding business matters.

3 responsibilities @ 2 marks (6 marks)

exam Q

See:

Ordinary Level	**Ordinary Level**	**Higher Level**	**Higher Level**	**Higher Level**
Section A	Section B	Paper I	Paper I	Paper II
2009 Q12	2007 Q7	Section A	Section B	2008 Q3a
2009 Q18	2006 Q4	2002 Q18	2009 Q6	2006 Q3
2008 Q19	2004 Q3		2008 Q6	2001 Q5
2007 Q17	2002 Q4		2007 Q6b	
2004 Q9	2001 Q7		2006 Q4b	
2004 Q12			2005 Q3	

23 Industrial Relations

From given data, be able to:

- Identify types and causes of industrial disputes
- Outline types and functions of trade unions
- Explain Arbitration, Conciliation, Shop Steward, Human Resource Manager
- Identify steps in the resolution of an industrial dispute

A. Introduction

Industrial relations is the term used to describe the relationship between management and employees. If relationships are good, workers will be well **motivated**, **morale** and **productivity** will be high. There will be industrial peace, no strikes and good co-operation between employers and employees. If industrial relations are poor, employees are discontented resulting in **poor motivation**, **absenteeism**, **high labour turnover** and **low productivity**.

B. What is a trade union?

A trade union is an organisation that represents workers and speaks on their behalf with employers on issues such as pay and working conditions.

C. Functions of a trade union

(1) To protect the **rights** of its members.
(2) To **negotiate wages and salaries** for members.
(3) To **negotiate conditions of work**.
(4) To negotiate with employers if a dispute occurs.
(5) To **protect** members from unfair dismissal.
(6) To negotiate in a redundancy situation.

Benefits of joining a trade union

(1) Higher standard of living for members – improved wage rates, improved conditions.
(2) Greater job security if union is powerful.
(3) Increased bargaining power, one voice for all workers.
(4) The benefit of having skilled negotiators on behalf of employees.
(5) Protection against discrimination or unfair treatment.
(6) Support members if in dispute with employer.

D. Types of trade union

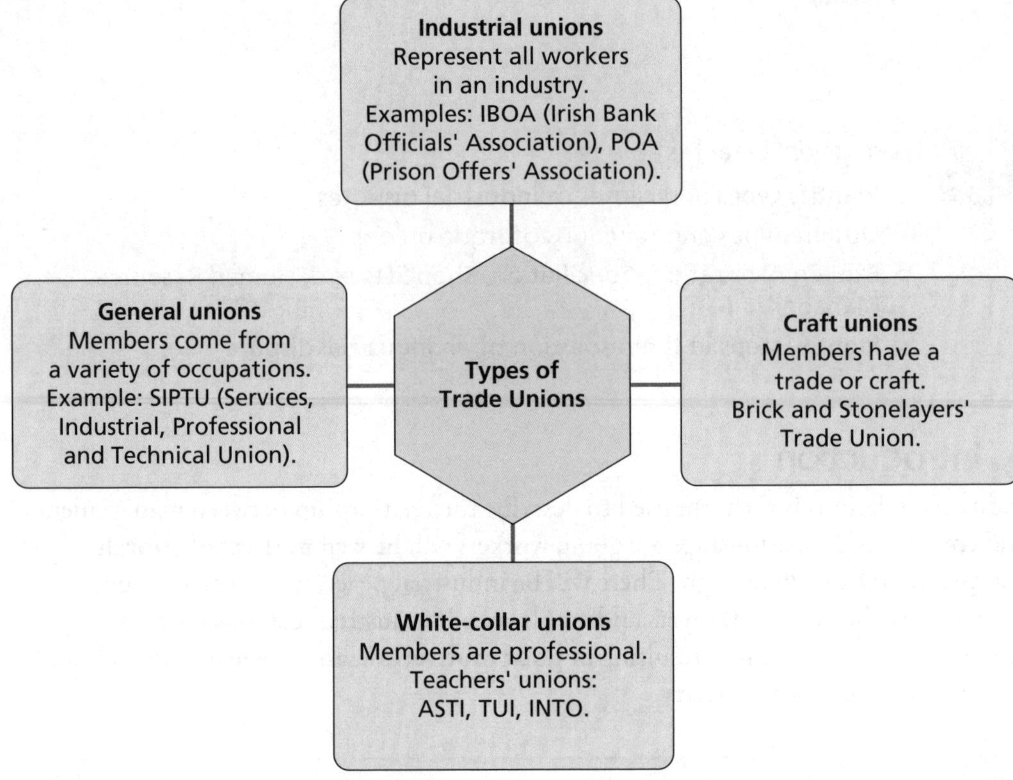

Industrial unions
Represent all workers in an industry.
Examples: IBOA (Irish Bank Officials' Association), POA (Prison Offers' Association).
General unions
Members come from a variety of occupations.
Example: SIPTU (Services, Industrial, Professional and Technical Union).
Types of Trade Unions
Craft unions
Members have a trade or craft.
Brick and Stonelayers' Trade Union.
White-collar unions
Members are professional.
Teachers' unions:
ASTI, TUI, INTO.

E. How to join a trade union

(1) Contact shop steward (union representative).

(2) Fill in application form.

(3) Pay annual subscription.

Shop steward

Shop Steward is the local union representative, elected by union members, who negotiates with management and ensures that agreements are kept. S/he organises meetings of union members to keep them up to date with developments. S/he also recruits new members for the union.

F. Duties of a shop steward

(1) Acts as intermediary between union members and union head office.

(2) Represents members in their dealings with management.

(3) Recruits new members.

(4) Attends union meetings.

(5) Collects subscriptions.

(6) Communicates information to (or from) union head office.

(7) Gives advice to members on industrial relations issues.

G. Irish Congress Of Trade Unions (ICTU)

ICTU represents all trade unions. It is the governing body of trade unions. It represents trade unions in negotiations with employers and the government with regard to pay and working conditions.

STRONGER TOGETHER
CONGRESS
Irish Congress of Trade Unions

H. Irish Business Employers' Confederation (IBEC)

IBEC represents all employers in negotiations with trade unions and the government. It gives a voice to members on all aspects of industrial relations.

I. Management role

The Human Resource Manager, also known as the personnel manager, is employed by the employer to recruit new employees, organise their training and deal with their problems. S/he tries to sort out problems with unions before industrial action takes place.

J. What is a dispute?

A dispute is a disagreement between employees and management.

K. Main causes of disputes/strikes

(1) **Pay** – employees looking for pay for extra work done, e.g. teachers implementing syllabus changes.

(2) **Working Conditions** – employees look for better and safer places to work.

(3) **Dismissal of Workers** – Employees feel that some workers are unfairly dismissed.

(4) **Unequal Treatment** – Employees feel that the employer favours one employee over another.

(5) **Redundancy** – When employees are being let go because there is no work, disputes can arise as to who should be let go first. The normal way is **Last In First Out**.

(6) **Demarcation Disputes** – These are disputes arising when an employer asks some employees to do the work of other employees, thus endangering the other employees' jobs.

(7) **Union Recognition** – These are disputes over the employer refusing to accept that employees are in a trade union.

L. Types of industrial action (strikes)

1. Strike

Workers withdraw labour, i.e. refuse to work. There are two types of strike:

(a) **Unofficial strike** – not approved by trade union.

(b) **Official strike** – approved by trade union.

2. All-out strike

All unions in the firm stop work in support of the union on strike.

3. Work to rule (i.e. go slow)

Workers go to work but do only the bare essentials.

4. A 'sit-in'

Employees sit in, in the premises where they work.

5. Picketing

Workers on strike usually **picket** the employer's premises.

M. How to resolve an industrial dispute

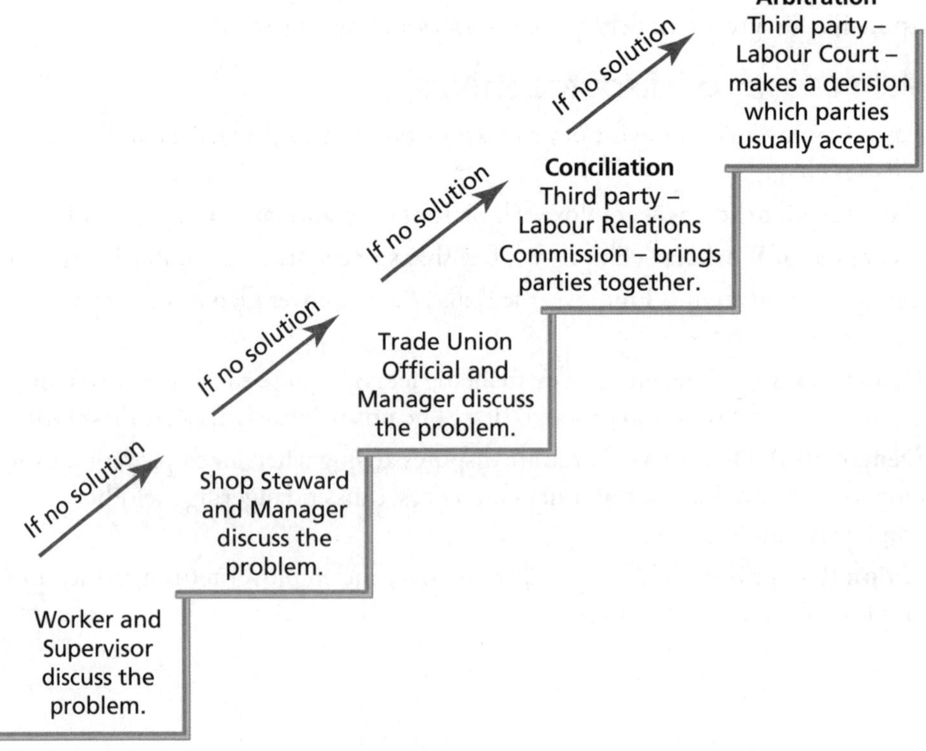
Worker and Supervisor discuss the problem.
If no solution
Shop Steward and Manager discuss the problem.
If no solution
Trade Union Official and Manager discuss the problem.
If no solution
Conciliation
Third party – Labour Relations Commission – brings parties together.
If no solution
Arbitration
Third party – Labour Court – makes a decision which parties usually accept.

N. Functions of Labour Relations Commission (LRC)

(1) **Conciliation service.** Parties are brought together, and are encouraged to come up with a settlement themselves.

(2) **Advisory service.** LRC offers advice to employers and employees on industrial relations matters.

(3) It appoints **Rights Commissioners.** Investigates disputes concerning individual workers or small groups of workers.

(4) It appoints **Equality Officers.** Investigates disputes on issues of equality and discrimination in the workplace.

O. Labour Court

The Labour Court is a court of last resort to help to settle industrial disputes.

Function of labour court:

- Investigates disputes.
- Court of Appeal.
- Investigates breaches of codes of practice.
- Registers employment agreements.

P. Difference between conciliation and arbitration

Conciliation

- A third party, the Labour Relations Commission or a mediator brings both sides of a dispute together and helps them find a resolution.
- The proposal of the conciliator is not binding in industrial relations.

Arbitration

- Both parties in a dispute present their case to an independent body or Labour Court, which then recommends a resolution.
- The parties may agree to the recommendation of the arbitrator.
- It is normal for the disputing parties to accept the finding of the arbitrator.

Q. Equality in employment

(1) It is illegal to discriminate on the grounds of marital status, gender, family status, religious belief, age, disability, race, membership of traveller community, sexual orientation.

(2) There must be equal pay for men and women.

R. National wage agreement

This is a pay agreement between the social partners, i.e. ICTU (workers), IBEC (employers) and the government. It is binding on all employers and employees nationally.

This is a question on Employment and Industrial Relations.

Answer all parts of this question.

(A) State **three** rights and **three** responsibilities of employers. (6)

(B) Study the newspaper extract below and answer the questions that follow.

Unions at Eircom are expected to serve strike notice on the company today after discussions to resolve a pay dispute collapsed. The unions must provide a week's notice of industrial action to management. The biggest union at the firm, the CWU, believes that the issue will go to the Labour Relations Commission when the notice is served. The CWU voted overwhelmingly in favour of industrial action after Eircom refused to pay workers a 2% increase due to them under the National Wage Agreement until they agreed to change their work practices.

(i) Name the **two** parties involved in the dispute.

(ii) What form of industrial action is being proposed?

(iii) Identify the third party who might help solve the dispute. (10)

(C) (i) Other than pay, explain **three** possible reasons for industrial disputes.

(ii) Explain **three** of the following terms:

Arbitration

Conciliation

Shop Steward

Human Resource Manager.

(24)

(40 marks)

Solution and marking scheme

(A) Rights of employers include:

- To set up in business.
- Select suitable employees.
- Dismiss dishonest employees.

(3 rights @ 1 mark each)

Responsibilities of employers include:

- Pay agreed wage/minimum wage.
- Provide safe and healthy working conditions.
- Obey all employment laws.
- Keep all necessary employee records.

(3 responsibilities @ 1 mark each)

(B) (i) Eircom and the Eircom employees/unions/CWU.

(two parties in the dispute @ 2 marks each)

(ii) Strike – withdrawal from work. **(3 marks)**

(iii) The Labour Relations Commission **(3 marks)**

(C) (i) Examples of disputes that can arise for reasons **other than pay:**

Working Conditions – Employees look for better and safer places to work and eat in.

Dismissal of Workers – Employees feel that some workers are unfairly sacked.

Unequal treatment – Employees feel that the employer favours one employee over another.

Redundancy – When employees are being let go because there is no work, disputes can arise as to who should be let go first. The normal way is **L**ast **I**n **F**irst **O**ut.

Demarcation Disputes – These are disputes arising when an employer asks some employees to do the work of other employees, thus endangering the other employees' jobs.

Union Recognition – These are disputes over the employer refusing to accept that employees are in a trade union.

(Three reasons for industrial disputes @ 4 marks each

2 marks naming point

2 marks explaining point)

(ii) Explanation of Terms – Examples.

Arbitration is where an acceptable third party is asked, by both parties in dispute, to examine why a dispute has taken place and to make a recommendation as to how the dispute can be settled.

Conciliation is the use of an acceptable third party to help the parties in a dispute reach an agreement. For example, in section (B) above the Labour Relations Commission can help Eircom and the employees reach a settlement.

A **Shop Steward** is the local union representative, elected by union members, who negotiates with management and ensures that agreements are kept. S/he organises meetings of union members to keep them up to date with developments. S/he also recruits new members for the union.

The **Human Resource Manager,** also known as the personnel manager, is employed by the employer to recruit new employees, organise their training and deal with their problems. S/he tries to sort out problems with unions before industrial action takes place.

3 explanations @ 4 marks each (2 points of information required on each point)

See:

Ordinary Level	**Higher Level**	**Higher Level**	**Higher Level**
Section A	Paper I	Paper I	Paper II
2009 Q19	Section A	Section B	2008 Q3bc
2008 Q10	2009 Q16	2006 Q4a	2003 Q3
2007 Q20	2007 Q10	2002 Q4bc	
2005 Q6	2005 Q14		
2003 Q12	2003 Q5(i)		
2003 Q15			

SECTION 3
Enterprise

Marketing and Distribution

Business Transactions and Business Documents

Double-entry Bookkeeping

Final Accounts of a Private Limited Company

Reporting on Accounts

Applied Accounts

Marketing and Distribution

Introduction to simple market research, identification of a market, to the purchase and sale of goods, and, to working out the level of gross profit (or loss!).

24 Marketing

To be able to:

- Identify target markets from given data.
- Suggest suitable sources of information on the market.
- Carry out simple research projects on markets and marketing.
- Select an appropriate method for promoting a product or service from given data.

A. Market

A market is a place where goods are bought and sold.

B. Types of market

(1) Retail Market – where goods and services are sold to the public.

(2) Wholesale Market – where goods and services are sold to retailers.

(3) Street Market – fruit, vegetables, clothes.

(4) Stock Exchange – where stocks and shares are bought and sold.

(5) Export Market – exporting to other countries.

C. Target market

The target market is the total number of potential customers for a product or a service, e.g. the target market for Junior Certificate Business Studies Revision Notes is Junior Certificate students studying Business Studies.

D. Market segmentation

Producing many different models of the same product to satisfy customers.

E. Marketing

Marketing is concerned with all the stages involved in getting the product or service to the final customer.

F. Four 'P's of marketing/marketing mix

(1) Product – Product/service that a company offers to the target market. It includes quality and packaging.

(2) Place – This is where the product is available to the target consumers.

(3) Price – Amount of money customer has to pay to obtain the product.

(4) Promotion – This consists of the activities that communicate the merits of the product and persuade the target customer to buy.

To be successful a business must have the **right product** on sale in the **right place** at the **right price** using the **right promotion.**

G. Market research

Market research involves collecting, recording and detailed examination of all information relating to the transfer of goods and services from the producer to the consumer. The main objective is to find out information.

H. Reasons for market research

(1) To identify consumers' needs and wants.

(2) To identify size of the market.

(3) To identify the main competitors.

(4) To find out the best methods of advertising.

(5) To find out best means of distribution.

(6) To discover a suitable selling price.

I. Methods of collecting information for market research

1. Desk research/secondary research

This involves researching existing information, e.g. examining business records, looking up suitable Internet sites, examining census of population, Central Statistics Office.

2. Field research/primary research

This involves obtaining new information directly from the customer.

(a) **Observation** – Researcher watches and records behaviour rather than asking questions.

(b) **Questionnaire** – Document containing a series of structured questions designed to generate information.

(c) **Telephone interview** – Researcher telephones the people being surveyed.

(d) **Personal interview** – Researcher asks questions and records responses.

J. Test marketing

A new product is tested on a small number of people to find their reaction.

K. Product development

It is important to **improve existing products** and **develop new products**. If a new product is to be successful, it must be:

- better quality
- better value
- better presented.

Factors that a business should consider before deciding to produce a new product

(1) Is there a **demand** for the product?
(2) Will it be **profitable**?
(3) What kind of product should it be?
(4) What **price** should be charged?
(5) How should it be **promoted**?
(6) In what place should it be sold?
(7) What type of **packaging** should be used?
(8) What is the **target market**?
(9) How is it different from/better than competitors' products?

L. Advertising

Advertising is informing consumers about products or services.

M. Reasons for advertising

(1) To inform the public of a new product or service the firm is offering for sale.
(2) To increase sales and profit.
(3) To persuade the consumers to buy their products.
(4) In response to advertising by competitors.
(5) To maintain/increase a firm's share of the market.
(6) To promote a particular industry and its production.

N. Types of advertising

(1) **Informative advertising** – giving information to the consumer.
(2) **Persuasive advertising** – trying to convince the consumer.
(3) **Competitive advertising** – comparing with competitors.
(4) **Generic advertising** – industry promotes the product.

O. Advertising media (i.e. where to advertise)

(1) Newspapers (Press)
(2) Television
(3) Radio
(4) Posters and Hoardings
(5) Magazines
(6) Cinemas
(7) Trade Fairs and Exhibitions
(8) Leaflets
(9) Window Displays
(10) Vehicle Displays
(11) Shopping Bags
(12) Journals
(13) Internet

P. Sales promotion

This is used to back up advertising and the aim is the same – to increase sales. Techniques include:

(1) Free samples
(2) Special offers
(3) Coupons/Tokens
(4) 'Money-off Vouchers'
(5) In-store promotions
(6) Competitions and draws

Q. Selling techniques

1. Branding

A brand is a name/sign/symbol/design used by a firm to identify its products and distinguish them from other similar products. Examples include Levi's, Reebok, Primark, Cadbury, Tayto and St Bernard.

2. Loss leaders

Selling products below cost price.

3. Trade marks and logos

A trade mark is the name given to the product or firm, while a logo is the symbol, which is usually designed in a very distinctive style.

4. Merchandising

Arranging products on shelves or in display cabinets for maximum impact on the consumer.

R. Public relations (PR)

Presenting a good image of the company to the public.

Duties of public relations officer

(1) Issuing press releases.
(2) Arranging trade fairs and exhibitions.
(3) Arranging sponsorship.
(4) Arranging radio and TV coverage of events.
(5) Organising company literature for employees and the public.

S. Sponsorship

Business supporting teams and events and in return having their names and logos displayed.

T. Export markets

Exports are essential if Irish firms are to survive and expand.

Difficulties in Exporting

(1) Language.
(2) Currency.
(3) Documentation.
(4) Transport costs.
(5) Risk of non-payment is very great.

Recording the payment of advertising in the books of the Business

Example: A payment of €10,000 was made by cheque for advertising on 31/12/16

Bank A/C

					€
			31/12/16	Advertising	10,000

Advertising A/C

		€			€
31/12/16	Bank	10,000	31/12/16	Profit & loss A/C	10,000

The figure for €10,000 advertising will appear under Expenses in the Profit and Loss Account.

Profit and Loss Account for year ending 31/12/16

	Expenses		€
	Advertising		10,000

This is a Marketing Question. Answer ALL sections.

(A) State **four** factors that a business should consider before deciding to produce a new product. (8)

(B) Explain **two** methods of obtaining information about a market. (6)

(C) Knockair is a low-cost airline flying from Knock Airport to ten European capitals. The company is launching a new route from Knock to Paris. Flights, available seven days a week, will depart at 6.30 a.m. This new route will commence on 1 June 2004 and will cost €15, one way, plus government taxes. Booking is online at www.knockair.com.

(i) Draft a suitable advertisement, for this new route, that could be inserted in a national newspaper.

(ii) State **three** methods, other than newspapers and the Internet, of advertising a low-cost airline. (24)

(40 marks)

Suggested solution and marking scheme

(A) The factors that should be considered include:

(i) Is there a demand for the product?
(ii) Will it be profitable?
(iii) What kind of **product** should it be?
(iv) What **price** should be charged?
(v) How should it be **promoted**?
(vi) In what **place** should it be sold?
(vii) Packaging?
(viii) Target market?

Four factors @ 2 marks each

(B) Methods of obtaining information about a market include:

(i) **Desk Research** – using **existing information** – examining business records, looking up suitable Internet sites, examining the census of population, Central Statistics Office.
(ii) **Field Research** – obtaining **new information** – carrying out surveys, using questionnaires, interviewing people.
(iii) **Market research** – find out about competitors, customers, laws, etc.

Two methods @ 4 marks each – 2 marks stating point
2 marks explaining

(C) **(i)**

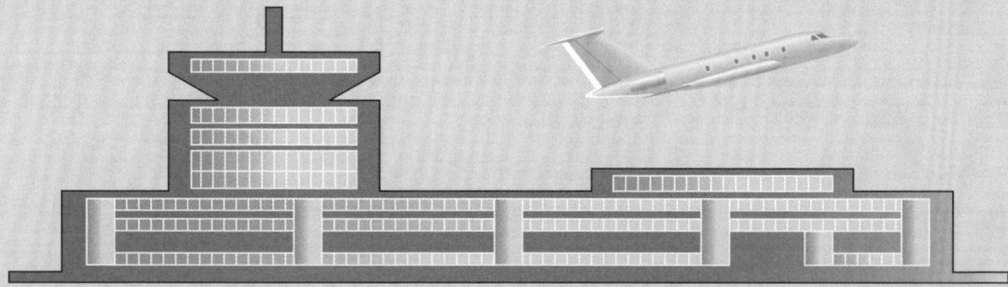

Another first for **Knockair, the low-cost airline, serving ten European capitals**. A new route from **Knock to Paris**, operating **seven days per week**, will **commence on 1 June 2004.**

Departs at 6.30 a.m. each morning.

Flights cost €15 one way, plus government taxes.

Flights can only be booked online – **www.knockair.com**

Any five points @ 3 marks each.
Plus 3 marks for presentation/creativity.

(ii)

Three methods of advertising a low-cost airline, other than in newspapers and the Internet, include:

television, radio, cinema, magazines, billboards, holiday brochures.

3 methods @ 2 marks each.

See:

Ordinary Level	**Ordinary Level**	**Higher Level**	**Higher Level**
Section A	Section B	Paper I Section A	Paper II
2009 Q11	2008 Q7c	2009 Q3	2009 Q3
2008 Q3	2004 Q7	2007 Q3	2006 Q6ab
2007 Q11		2006 Q4	2004 Q3
2005 Q17		2006 Q10	2001 Q3
2003 Q2		2005 Q8	

25 Delivery Systems

To be able to:

- Select an appropriate delivery system, giving reasons
- Calculate delivery times
- Calculate cost of delivery

A. Importance of delivery in the chain of distribution

A good efficient delivery system is important to business.

(1) To deliver raw materials to the manufacturer.

(2) To deliver finished goods.

(3) To transport workers to their jobs.

(4) To transport goods abroad.

B. Factors to be considered when choosing a delivery system

(1) **Cost** – Business wants to keep costs low. It is important to keep business going.

(2) **Reliability** – System chosen must be reliable and punctual – a late delivery can mean a lost sale.

(3) **Speed** – Speed of delivery is an important factor especially for perishables or something urgently required.

(4) **Safety** – Important for valuable goods and people.

(5) **Distance** – Distance between buyer and seller will be an important factor in choosing a delivery system.

(6) **Type of goods** – will influence the delivery system chosen. Is the product perishable, bulky or fragile?

C. Types of delivery system

The following are the main types of delivery system used in Ireland.

Types	Advantages	Disadvantages
Road	1. Fast over short distances 2. Door-to-door deliveries 3. Minimum handling 4. Flexible, convenient and cheap	1. Congestion/Poor roads – delays 2. Bad weather – delays 3. Not suitable for bulky goods 4. Slow over long distances
Rail	1. Fast over long distances 2. Suitable for bulky goods 3. Reliable 4. Cheap for bulky goods	1. Not flexible – fixed timetable 2. Lot of handling 3. Not all parts of country have a rail link 4. Expensive over short distances
Sea	1. Suitable for bulky goods 2. Cheaper than air 3. Suitable for containers 4. Good facilities at ports 5. Modern ships – large loads	1. Slow over long distances 2. Weather conditions – delays 3. Not flexible – fixed timetable 4. Must link with other forms of transport 5. High insurance costs
Air	1. Fastest method over long distances 2. Suitable for expensive goods 3. Good safety record 4. Less packing – reduced cost 5. Modern aircraft – large loads	1. Expensive 2. Bad weather – delays 3. Must link with other forms of transport 4. Not flexible – fixed timetable 5. Not suitable for bulky goods
Pipeline	1. Safe 2. Cheap to maintain	1. Expensive to install 2. Suitable only for liquids or gases

D. Modern developments in transport in Ireland

Some of the modern developments in transport in Ireland include new **motorways, tunnels, regional airports, toll roads** and the **Luas system**.

(1) **Motorways** – Large roads often three or more lanes wide that go directly from one major city to another bypassing towns and villages.

Improve transport by speeding up delivery times.

(2) **Regional Airports** – Smaller airports (usually not international) that serve a particular region or area.

They improve transport by allowing delivery of goods and passengers near to the final destination.

(3) **Tunnels** – Used to reduce the amount of traffic on a route or to enable the distance to be shortened.

They improve transport by removing heavy traffic from roads, speeding up the journey.

(4) **Toll roads** – As roads are upgraded and improved the money to pay for them is sometimes collected by a charge called a **toll**. Modern technology enables the toll to be collected without holding up traffic.

This improves transport by shortening journey times and bypassing towns.

(5) **Luas** – a light rail system used in Dublin City to help commuters travel quickly to the city.

It improves transport by helping people move quickly in and out of the city.

E. Calculating delivery time

When calculating delivery time we must:

(1) Work out distance involved (use a distance table).

(2) Calculate average speed of vehicle (km per hour).

(3) Allow for stopovers, traffic delays and time for loading and unloading.

Formula for Calculating Time

$$\frac{\text{Distance}}{\text{Average Speed per Hour (km)}}$$

Question 1.

Look at the distance table and answer the following questions:

(A) How many kilometres from Tralee to Limerick?

Distance Table (km)

Dundalk									
256	Ennis								
238	70	Galway							
240	37	105	Limerick						
92	16	144	148	Mullingar					
246	246	274	210	204	Rosslare				
168	195	138	232	135	326	Sligo			
346	94	162	105	254	290	288	Tralee		
242	164	220	130	170	82	292	210	Waterford	
118	228	254	190	185	19	306	275	62	Wexford

(B) How long would it take for a lorry to travel from Galway to Waterford at an average speed of 44 kilometres per hour? (5)

Source: Junior Certificate Ordinary Level.

Solution

(A) 105 km.

(B) Time $= \frac{\text{Distance}}{\text{Av. speed}} = \frac{220 \text{ km}}{44} = 5$ hrs

F. Calculating delivery costs

As delivery expenses increase the cost of the goods, it is important to choose the cheapest method of transport. It is also important to be able to calculate the cost of delivery accurately.

Firm using own vehicles

When using own vehicles there are two costs involved.

Fixed costs must be paid no matter how much the vehicle is used and must be divided out over each day the vehicle is used in the year, e.g. maintenance, road tax, vehicle insurance.

Variable costs vary with the usage of the vehicle and are associated with a particular delivery, e.g. petrol/diesel, wages.

Reasons why a business might use its own fleet of delivery vans

(1) Transport is available when required – flexibility.
(2) Vehicles can be used for advertising.
(3) Business not affected by a strike of transport hauliers or of Iarnrod Éireann.
(4) Return load can be collected.
(5) It is not confined to a fixed timetable.
(6) It can be cheaper in the long term than hiring outside transport.
(7) It is more secure and requires less handling of the goods.

This is a question on Cost of Delivery.

Calculate the total cost of a journey from Cork to Dublin and back to Cork from the following data:

- Distance from Cork to Dublin 260 km.
- Diesel van will do 10 km per litre of diesel.
- Cost of diesel is €1 per litre.
- Van driver's wages are €100 a day.
- Annual van tax is €250.

- Annual van insurance is €750.
- Annual repairs €500.
- The company operates 250 days in the year.

Solution

	Total distance	260 km × 2 (return journey)	= 520 km
	Number of litres used	$\frac{520}{10}$	= 52 litres
Variable Costs	Cost of diesel	= 52 litres × €1	= €52
	Driver's wages		= €100
Fixed Costs	Motor tax per day	= $\frac{€250}{250 \text{ days}}$	= €1
	Insurance per day	= $\frac{€750}{250 \text{ days}}$	= €3
	Repairs per day	= $\frac{€500}{250 \text{ days}}$	= €2
	Total cost of delivery		= €158

Recording the total cost of delivery in the books of the business.

Assume cost is €158 × 250 days = €39,500

Bank Account

					€
			31/12/16	Delivery/carriage out	39,500

Delivery/carriage out A/C

		€			€
31/12/16	Bank	39,500	31/12/16	Profit & Loss account	39,500

The figure of €39,500 delivery expenses will appear under Expenses in the Profit and Loss A/C.

Profit and Loss account for year ending 31/12/16

			€
	Expenses		
	Delivery Expenses		39,500

exam Q

This is a question on Integrated Delivery Systems.

Answer all parts of this question.

(A) Transport is very important in the Distribution of Goods.

(i) Give **three** reasons why transport is important in the distribution of goods. (3)

(ii) State **three** sources of finance that could be used to obtain delivery vans. (3)

(iii) State and explain **two** factors that should be taken into account when deciding on the type of delivery system to be used in business. (4)

(B) Calculate the cost of transport for **one day** from the following details provided by DUGGAN DELIVERIES Ltd, a licensed carrier (show your workings).

DUGGAN Ltd operates 320 working days per year:

The diesel van used can do 35 kilometres per litre.

The distance travelled per day is 875 kilometres.

The cost of diesel is €1.20 per litre.

Gross wage of driver is €360 per day.

Employer's PRSI is 12.5%.

Annual motor insurance is €3,840.

Annual motor tax is €1,920.

Annual motor repairs is €2,240.

Toll charges are €20 per day. (16)

(C) On 10 March 2009 DUGGAN Ltd purchased a new delivery van on credit from PLUNKETT MOTORS Ltd for €85,000.

Record the purchase of the delivery van in the General Journal and appropriate ledger accounts of DUGGAN Ltd. (14)

(40 marks)

Suggested solution and marking scheme

(A) (i) Reasons why transport is important in the distribution of goods.

- To transport raw materials to the manufacturer.
- To transport finished goods from the manufacturer to the wholesaler/retailer/customer.
- To bring employees to their workplace.
- To transport customers to the retailers or to transport goods from the retailer to the customer.

3 reasons @ 1 mark each (3 marks)

(ii) Sources of finance that could be used to obtain delivery vans.

Medium-term Sources

- Bank Term Loan
- Leasing
- Hire Purchase

Long-term Sources

- Share Capital
- Reserves
- Grants
- Sale and Leaseback
- Long-term Loan

3 sources @ 1 mark each (3 marks)

(iii) Factors that should be taken into account when deciding on the type of delivery system to be used in Business.

- Speed – very important for perishable and urgently required goods.
- Cost – the cost of delivery adds to the price of the goods.
- Reliability – delivery must be on time and agreed.
- Convenience – available when and as required.
- Destination/location – the location of the supplier and the customer may require a number of forms of transport.

2 factors @ 2 marks → 1 name → 1 explain (4 marks)

Name and relevant statement

(B) COST OF TRANSPORT FOR ONE DAY FOR DUGGAN LTD

Cost of Transport = Cost of diesel + wages + annual costs + toll charges

- **Cost of diesel**

$$\frac{\text{Distance travelled in km}}{\text{Kilometres per litre}}$$

$$= \frac{875 \text{ km (1)}}{35} = 25 \text{ litres (1) @ €1.20 per litre (1)} \quad = €30 \text{ (1)}$$

- **Cost of Wages**

Driver's wages + employer's PRSI

€360 (2) + €45 (2) = €405

- **Annual Costs**

320 working days per year

Motor Insurance	$\frac{€3,840}{320}$	= €12 (1)	
Motor Tax	$\frac{€1,920}{320}$	= €6 (1)	
Motor Repairs	$\frac{€2,240}{320}$	= €7 (1)	€25 (1)

- **Toll Charges** €20 (1)

Total Cost of Transport (1) → **€480** (2) **(16 marks)**

(C) General Journal of Duggan Ltd

Date	Details	F	DR €	CR €
10/3/09 (1)	Delivery Van (1)	GL	85,000 (1)	
	Plunkett Motors Ltd (1)	CL (1)		85,000 (1)
	Purchase of Delivery Van on credit from Plunkett Motors Ltd (1)			

Seven pieces of information @ 1 mark each **(7 marks)**

Ledger of Duggan Ltd

Date	Details	F	Total €	Date	Details	F	Total €
	Delivery Van (1) A/C						
10/3/09 (½)	Plunkett Motors Ltd (1)	GJ (½)	85,000 (½)				
	Plunkett Motors (1) A/C						
				10/3/09 (½)	Delivery Van (1)	GJ (½)	85,000 (½)

Marking scheme

2 account names @ 1 mark each 2 marks

2 correct details @ 1 mark each 2 marks

6 other pieces of information @ ½ marks each 3 marks 7 marks

(40 marks)

exam Q

See:

Ordinary Level	**Ordinary Level**	**Higher Level**	**Higher Level**
Section A	Section B	Paper I	Paper II
2006 Q16	2009 Q7	Section A	2008 Q5
2004 Q11	2008 Q7ab	2007 Q14	2006 Q5cd
2003 Q17	2007 Q8	2003 Q4	2003 Q5
2001 Q20	2005 Q7	2002 Q9	2001 Q6
2000 Q17	2002 Q8	2001 Q4	

Business Transactions and Business Documents

26 Purchases and Sales

To understand the following:

- Effective purchasing
- Source of supply
- VAT
- Simple terms of trade
-  Stock control
- Finance for purchase
- Method of payment
-  Mark-up and margin
- Computerised stock control

1. Purchases

A. Effective purchasing

Purchasing the **right goods** in the **right quantity** at the **right price** at the **correct time**.

B. Enquiring about goods and services

When suitable suppliers are identified, contact can be made by letter, telephone, fax or personal call. A number of suppliers may be contacted with **an enquiry** about prices, quality, delivery terms, discount terms and payment terms. Most suppliers will reply by means of **a quotation** and on comparing these a decision can be made from which company to **order** the goods.

C. Prices

(1) **Price list** – a list of all goods and their price.

(2) **Catalogue** – a book containing details and descriptions of all goods for sale.

(3) **Quotation** – contains details about the price at which the seller is prepared to supply his goods.

D. Delivery terms

(1) **Carriage paid** – price quoted includes all transport costs (paid by seller).

(2) **Ex-works/Ex-factory** – buyer pays for delivery.

E. Discount terms

1. Trade Discount

Discount given by the seller to the buyer off the list price of the goods to enable the buyer to make a profit when he resells the goods. Trade discount is deducted on the invoice.

2. Cash Discount

Discount given to the buyer to encourage him to pay promptly.

F. Payment terms

(1) **CWO (Cash With Order)** – customer must pay when ordering.

(2) **COD (Cash On Delivery)** – customer must pay on delivery.

G. VAT – Value added tax

VAT is a tax on goods and services sold. Businesses with a certain turnover must register for VAT. They will pay VAT on their purchases and must charge VAT on their sales.

2. Sales

A. Selling on credit

A credit sale is where goods are sold and the customer pays for them at a later date.

Reasons why businesses sell goods on credit

- To increase sales and profit.
- To compete with businesses who only sell for cash.
- To facilitate customers who require some time to pay for goods purchased.

Methods of checking the credit rating of customers before selling goods on credit

- **Trade Reference**
  This is where a business, who previously gave the customer credit, recommends that credit can be given to customers.
- **Bank Reference**
  This is where the customers' banks recommend that credit can be given to the customers (the customers are creditworthy).
- **Status Enquiry Service**
  This is where a special agency checks out the creditworthiness of the customers, to provide proof of income and ability to repay.
- **Business Records**
  This is where the records of the business are examined to see if the customers were given credit in the past and if they paid up on time and in full.

B. Stock control

It is very important for a business to have the correct level of stock at all times. This is the optimum stock level.

Overstocking costs	Understocking costs
1. Cash tied up. 2. More storage space required. 3. Higher insurance costs. 4. More security staff required. 5. Risk of pilferage. 6. Risk of stock becoming obsolete.	1. Loss of orders. 2. Loss of sales. 3. Loss of customers. 4. Loss of profit.

To ensure that a firm has always the correct amount of stock, it is important to have a proper stock control system.

Setting up a stock control system

(1) Code every item in stock.

(2) Decide the correct level of stock for each item.

(3) Develop a method of recording stock.

(4) Carry out regular stocktaking.

C. Computerised stock control

When a business is computerised, the computer will give an automatic update on stock position. Each time a product is sold the bar code on the product is passed over a scanner and the stock count of the product is reduced by one.

D. Mark-up and margin

HL

The aim of being in business is to make a profit. A business will buy goods at cost and add on its profit to give the selling price.

COST + PROFIT = SELLING PRICE

Mark-up and margin are expressed as percentages.

Example Cost price €100 Selling price €120 ∴ Profit = €20

Mark-up – Profit expressed as a percentage of cost.

$$\text{Mark-up} = \frac{\text{Profit} \times 100\%}{\text{Cost Price}} = \frac{€20 \times 100\%}{€100} = 20\%$$

Margin – Profit expressed as a percentage of selling price.

$$\text{Margin} = \frac{\text{Profit} \times 100\%}{\text{Selling Price}} = \frac{€20 \times 100\%}{€120} = 16.66\%$$

E. Filing

Filing is the storing of documents so that they can be easily and quickly found when required. There are many methods of filing. The most common are alphabetical and numerical.

1. Alphabetical

This is where the customer files are arranged in the filing cabinet in **alphabetical order.** Steel cabinets are used. A folder is used for each customer and the name of the customer is written on a tab.

2. Numerical

Each customer file is given a **number** rather than the customer name. Files are arranged in the filing cabinet in numerical sequence. A card index system showing each customer's name and address and file number is used in conjunction with numerical filing.

It is very important to file all business documents carefully, so that they can be found when needed.

Question 1.

(A) Given a cost price of €40 and a selling price of €45.60, calculate the percentage mark-up. (4)

(B) Given a buying price of €50 and a selling price of €60, calculate the percentage profit 'margin'. (4)

Solutions

(A)

ANSWER

14%

Workings

$$\text{Mark-up} = \frac{\text{profit} \times 100}{\text{Cost Price}}$$

$$= \frac{€5.60 \times 100}{€40.00} = 14\%$$

Source: Junior Certificate Higher Level.

(B)

ANSWER

16.66%

Workings

$$\text{Profit Margin} = \frac{\text{Profit} \times 100}{\text{Selling Price}}$$

$$= \frac{€10 \times 100}{€60.00} = 16.66\%$$

Source: Junior Certificate Higher Level.

See:

Ordinary Level	**Higher Level**
Section A	Paper I
2009 Q8	Section A
2008 Q2	2004 Q3a
2007 Q6	2004 Q9
2006 Q4	2004 Q10
2006 Q20	2003 Q3
2004 Q18	2000 Q5
	2000 Q15

27 Business Letters/Report Writing

To be able to:

- Write a business letter
- Prepare a business report

Business letters are an important form of communication. A letter will reveal what a business is like. A good business letter should be accurate, brief and clear.

Question 1.

This question is about writing a Letter.

Sarah McKenna is Treasurer of Fairways Golf Club, Links Road, Cork. The annual subscription for members is €1,000. On 20 April 2014 she received a cheque for €300 from Jack Palmer, one of the members, who lives at 29 Salt Road, Mallow. Mr Palmer stated that he would pay the rest of the annual subscription in September.

Sarah immediately wrote a letter to Mr Palmer, thanking him for the €300 and enclosing a Receipt. In the letter, she pointed out that the Golf Club was not in a position to wait until September for the rest of his annual subscription, as this would not be fair to all the other members who had already paid in full. She also stated that, according to the rules, anyone whose full annual subscription was not paid by 1 May would no longer be a member of the club. She hoped that Mr Palmer would forward the balance due before that date.

Assume you are Sarah McKenna. Write the letter that Sarah sent to Mr Jack Palmer.

Source: Junior Certificate Ordinary Level. **(45 marks)**

Solution

LETTER

[1] Fairways Golf Club
Links Road
Cork

Tel (021) 926311

[2] 20 April 2014

[3] Mr Jack Palmer
29 Salt Road
Mallow

[4] Re: Annual Subscription

[5] **D**ear Mr Palmer

[7] **[6]** I wish to **thank you for your cheque** of €300, for which a receipt is enclosed. Unfortunately, the Golf Club **is not in a position to wait until September for the rest of your annual subscription**, as this would not be fair to all the other members who have paid in full.

According to the rules, **anyone whose full subscription is not paid before the first of May will cease to be a member** of this club.

[8] I hope you can **forward the balance due of €700** before that date.

[9] Yours sincerely

[10] Sarah McKenna
Treasurer.

[11] ENC 1

A. Layout of a business letter

[1] **Address of sender** – This is printed information on the top of company or club notepaper as follows:

Full name and address of company or club, telephone number, fax number and VAT number.

[2] **Date** – The most acceptable order for the date in a business letter is day, month, year.

[3] **Inside address** – This is the person to whom the letter is addressed.

[4] **Re-Regarding** – This outlines what the letter is about.

[5] **Salutation** – This is the greeting with which every letter begins, i.e. Dear Sir, Dear Madam.

[6] **Introduction** – If the letter is a reply to a letter received thank the writer and briefly mention the subject-matter (state what the letter is about).

[7] **Body of the Letter** – The body of the letter should be written in clear concise English. It should be divided into paragraphs.

[8] **Follow-up** – Stating what should happen next.

[9] **Complimentary Close** – This is the ending of a business letter and must match the salutation. The most used are Yours faithfully/Yours truly, Yours sincerely.

[10] **Signature and position/Title** of letter writer

[11] **Enc – Enclosures 1** – This shows that something else has been enclosed with the letter, e.g. receipt, and the number of items.

B. What marks are awarded for in business letters

(1) **Format/Layout** – Address of sender, date, inside address, salutation, Yours sincerely, signature, regarding, enclosures.

(2) **Content/Body of Letter** – Generally four points of information are required as bold underlined in the solution.

(3) **English** – Marks are awarded for paragraphs, punctuation, grammar, spelling.

(4) **Presentation/Neatness** – Marks will be awarded for a well-presented and neat letter.

C. Report writing

LAYOUT OF A REPORT

1. Title of report.
2. Address of report writer.
3. Date.
4. Who the report is for.
5. Introduction – reasons for report and how the information was collected.
6. Main body of report – conclusions and recommendations.
7. Follow-up – report writer available to discuss report.
8. Signature of report writer.
9. Position/Title of report writer.

(see reports on pages 127, 181, 286 and 298)

This is a Consumer and Report Writing Question

Aoife Slattery, Gortrue, Tullamore, had a new heating system installed in her home by Rads Ltd, Heating Contractors, Portlaoise, at a cost of €3,000. She was dissatisfied with it as it was very noisy and not very effective for heating. Aoife complained to Rads Ltd but they stated that everything was in order.

Aoife was unhappy with the response and contacted H and C Engineers Ltd, Tuam, Co. Galway, for their opinion. Niall O'Riordan, a consultant engineer with H and C Engineers Ltd, examined the heating system and wrote a report to Aoife outlining the following:

- The boiler used was a very old, second-hand model which consumed a lot of oil.
- Pipes of the wrong size were used in the plumbing installation thereby causing noise.

Niall recommended that a new, modern boiler be installed and that the system be replumbed using pipes of the correct size.

Assume that you are Niall O'Riordan, consultant engineer, and write the report sent to Aoife Slattery dated 25 April 2011 outlining your findings and recommendations. **(16 marks)**

Suggested solution and marking scheme

H and C Engineers Ltd,
Tuam,
Co. Galway. (1) Layout

25 April 2011 (1) Layout

Report on Domestic Heating System (1) Layout

To: Aoife Slattery
Gortrue
Tullamore. (1) Layout

I was asked to examine a central heating system recently installed by a firm of heating contractors at your home. After spending some time examining and observing it, the following are my findings:

(i) *The boiler was an old second-hand model which consumed a lot of oil.* (1) (Content)
(ii) *The piping used in the plumbing was the incorrect size, thereby creating noise.* (1) (Content)

To make the system work effectively, I recommend a new modern boiler be installed (1) (Content) and the system be re-plumbed using pipes of the correct size. (1) (Content)

I am available to discuss this report if required. (1) (Layout)

Niall O'Riordan (1) (Layout) (English 2 marks)
Consultant Engineer (1) (Layout) (Paragraphs 1 mark)

C = Content 4 marks (Grammar/punctuation 1 mark)
L = Layout 7 marks (Layout/Neatness 1 mark)

See:
Ordinary Level
Section B
2000 Q3

28 Business Transactions and Business Documents

To be able to:

- Complete or interpret the following documents (including VAT):
  - letter of enquiry
  - quotation
  - order form
  - invoice
  - credit note
  - delivery docket
  - statement of account
  - cheque
  - receipt
  - file documents
  - record data in accounts from source documents
- Compose a reply to queries – tracing a transaction to its origin through documents and accounts.

A. Cash transaction

A cash transaction is where goods are purchased and payment is made at the time of purchase either by cash or by cheque.

B. Credit transaction

A credit transaction is where goods are purchased and payment is made at a later date.

C. Business documents

Business documents are a very efficient way of putting business transactions on paper. They give both the buyer and the seller a written record of the transaction.

Stages in a Business Transaction

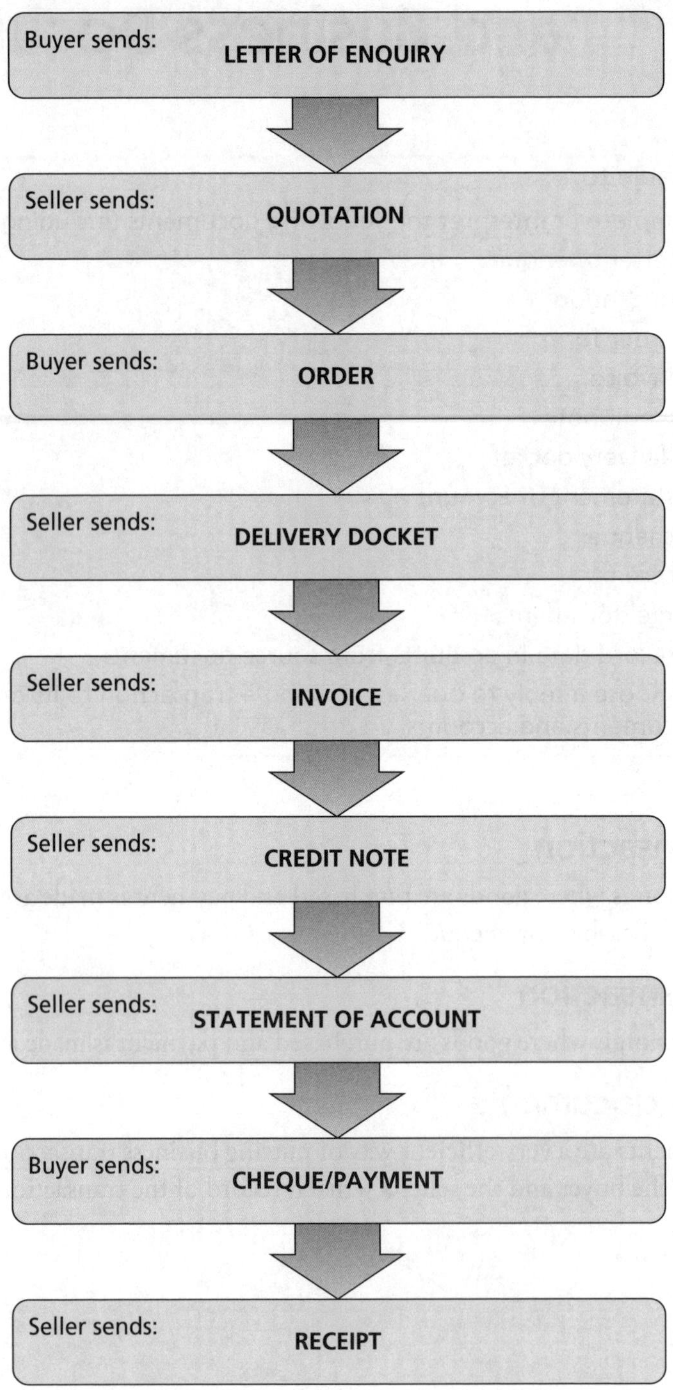
Buyer sends: LETTER OF ENQUIRY
Seller sends: QUOTATION
Buyer sends: ORDER
Seller sends: DELIVERY DOCKET
Seller sends: INVOICE
Seller sends: CREDIT NOTE
Seller sends: STATEMENT OF ACCOUNT
Buyer sends: CHEQUE/PAYMENT
Seller sends: RECEIPT

1. Letter of enquiry

A letter of enquiry is sent to a supplier enquiring about the prices, terms and conditions under which he is prepared to supply his goods.

Sample transaction

Murphy TV, Hi-Fi & Video Ltd wish to enquire about electrical equipment from Panasonic Ireland Ltd.

LETTER OF ENQUIRY

Tel (021) 639425
Fax (021) 639426

Murphy TV, Hi-Fi & Video Ltd
10 Princess Street – Cork

VAT Reg. No.: 258364X

Panasonic Ireland Ltd
Sandyford Industrial Est.
Dublin 18

10 May 2016

Dear Sir or Madam

Please send me a quotation for the following goods:

50 Panasonic 21" Nicam Stereo TVs
50 Panasonic HD Nicam Videos
50 Panasonic Mini Hi-Fi Systems

Yours sincerely

John Murphy

Purchasing Director

NB Murphy TV, Hi-Fi & Video Ltd may send letters of enquiry to a few different suppliers.

2. Quotation

A quotation is a document from a supplier giving advance information on prices and details of discounts, delivery and VAT. The following is the quotation sent by Panasonic Ireland Ltd.

QUOTATION No. 205

PANASONIC IRELAND LTD
Sandyford Industrial Est.
Dublin 18

Tel (01) 9986241
Fax (01) 9986242

Vat. Reg. No. 924651N

Murphy TV, Hi-Fi & Video Ltd
10 Princess Street
Cork

13 May 2016

Dear Sir

Thank you for your enquiry. Our quotation is as follows:

Quantity	Description	Unit Price	Delivery
50	Panasonic 21" Nicam Stereo TVs	€499	Ready
50	Panasonic HD Nicam Videos	€449	Ready
50	Panasonic Mini Hi-Fi Systems	€279	Ready

Yours sincerely

Gary Richards

Sales Director

TERMS OF SALE:
VAT 20% on all models. Trade Discount 10%. Carriage Paid.

(1) Procedure for processing quotations received.

- Compare with letter of enquiry, e.g. accuracy of details.
- Compare with other quotations.
- File the quotation.
- Check date the quotation is valid for.

(2) **The following procedures are recommended when preparing and processing quotations.**

- The quotation should be checked to ensure that the name and address of the buyer is correct.
- The quotation should be checked to ensure the accuracy of the prices quoted.
- Copies of quotations issued should be filed.
- Checks should be carried out to ensure the availability of goods.

(3) **Effective purchasing.**

Effective purchasing involves purchasing the right quantity and quality of goods at the right time and at the right price. It requires the purchasing managers to carry out research to know who the best suppliers are.

3. Order

An order is a document sent by the buyer ordering the goods required.

ORDER No. 648

Murphy TV, Hi-Fi & Video Ltd
10 Princess Street
Cork

Tel (021) 639425 **Vat Reg. No.: 258364X**
Fax (021) 639426

Panasonic Ireland Ltd
Sandyford Industrial Est.
Dublin 18

17 May 2016

Please supply the following goods:

Quantity	Description	Unit Price
50	Panasonic 21" Nicam Stereo TVs	€499
50	Panasonic HD Nicam Videos	€449
50	Panasonic Mini Hi-Fi Systems	€279

Signed: *John Murphy*
Purchasing Director

Treatment of incoming orders

(a) Date-stamp order.
(b) Get goods ready for delivery.
(c) Send order to office for preparation of invoice and delivery docket.
(d) File order.

4. Delivery note

When the goods are delivered, the buyer will sign the delivery docket. It gives a list of the goods delivered. If any goods are missing or damaged, it should be noted on the delivery docket. It is made out in **duplicate**, one copy given to the buyer and the second copy kept by seller as proof of delivery.

The goods were delivered to Murphy TV, Hi-Fi & Video Ltd on 20 May 2016.

DELIVERY NOTE **No. 74**

PANASONIC IRELAND LTD
Sandyford Industrial Est.
Dublin 18

Tel (01) 9986241 **VAT Reg. No.** 924651N
Fax (01) 9986242

Murphy TV, Hi-Fi & Video Ltd
10 Princess Street
Cork

20 May 2016

Quantity	Description
50	Panasonic 21" Nicam Stereo TVs
50	Panasonic HD Nicam Videos
50	Panasonic Mini Hi-Fi Systems

Received the above goods in perfect condition.

Signed: *John Murphy*
Purchasing Director

Treatment of incoming delivery dockets

(a) The **delivery note should be checked against the order** to ensure that the goods received were ordered.

(b) The delivery note should be **carefully filed** so that it can be checked against the invoice when it arrives.

Treatment of outgoing delivery dockets

(a) Check that the **name and address of the buyer are correct.**

(b) Check details **as per order or invoice.**

(c) **File copy** of delivery docket, or record on computer.

(d) Ensure that the delivery docket is **signed** by the recipient of the goods.

5. Invoice

An invoice is sent from the seller to the buyer. It is the bill for the goods. It shows the quantity, description and price of the goods, details of trade discount and VAT and the total due to the seller.

The invoice received will be checked against the delivery docket to make sure that the buyer received what he is being charged for.

key point

The invoice is the source document for recording credit sales and credit purchases.

(a) The **seller** writes up his **Sales Day Book** from **invoices sent.**

(b) The buyer writes up his **Purchases Day Book** from **invoices received.**

What Seller Should Do Before Sending Invoices/Treatment of Outgoing Invoices

(1) Compare prices with the quotation given.

(2) Check calculations for accuracy.

(3) Check address of customer.

(4) Write up sales day book.

(5) File a copy of invoice.

What Buyer Should Do on Receiving Invoices/Treatment of Incoming Invoices

(1) Compare with order and delivery docket.

(2) Check accuracy of prices and calculations.

(3) Write up purchases day book.

(4) Post to the creditors ledger.

(5) File invoice.

The following invoice was sent by Panasonic Ireland Ltd to Murphy TV, Hi-Fi & Video Ltd on 21 May 2016.

INVOICE **No. 61**

PANASONIC IRELAND LTD
Sandyford Industrial Est.
Dublin 18

Tel (01) 9986241
Fax (01) 9986242 **VAT Reg. No.** 924651N

21 May 2016

Murphy TV, Hi-Fi & Video Ltd
10 Princess Street
Cork

Quantity	Description	Unit Total	Price (Ex. VAT)
50	Panasonic 21" Nicam Stereo TVs	€499	€24,950
50	Panasonic HD Nicam Videos	€449	€22,450
50	Panasonic Mini Hi-Fi Systems	€279	€13,950
	Total (ex. VAT)		€61,350
	Less Trade Discount 10%		€6,135
			€55,215
	Add VAT 21%		€11,043
	Total Due		€66,258

Terms of Sale:
Carriage paid.

E & O E

Notes:

(i) The design and layout of invoices may vary.

(ii) E & O E means Errors and Omissions Excepted. This gives the seller the right to correct any errors discovered later.

(iii) On the invoice always deduct the trade discount before adding VAT.

(iv) If an **undercharge** occurs on an invoice a new corrected invoice is sent to the buyer.

(v) VAT is a tax imposed by the government on consumer spending. It is collected in stages as value is added to the good or service.

(vi) Trade discount is a reduction in the price of goods given by the manufacturer to the wholesaler/retailer to encourage them to sell the goods. It is the wholesaler's/retailer's profit.

Recording invoices sent in the sales day book of seller

Books of Panasonic Ireland Ltd (Seller)

SALES DAY BOOK

Date	Details	Inv. No.	Fo	Net	VAT	Total
21/5/16	Murphy TV, Hi-Fi & Video Ltd	61		€55,215	€11,043	€66,258

Recording invoices received in purchases day book of buyer

Books of Murphy TV, Hi-Fi & Video Ltd (Buyer)

PURCHASES DAY BOOK

Date	Details	Inv. No.	Fo	Net	VAT	Total
21/5/16	Panasonic Ireland Ltd	61		€55,215	€11,043	€66,258

6. Credit note

A credit note is sent from seller to buyer if:

(a) The buyer has been **overcharged** on the invoice.

(b) The **buyer returns goods** to the seller and the seller issues a credit note to the buyer.

Reasons for returning goods

- Goods damaged.
- The seller overcharged for the goods.
- The goods did not arrive on time.
- The amount of goods received was less than that stated on the invoice.

The credit note reduces the amount of money the buyer owes the seller.

Let us assume that Murphy TV, Hi-Fi & Video Ltd returned two Panasonic Mini Hi-Fi Systems because they were faulty.

A credit note is issued by Panasonic Ireland Ltd to the buyer as follows:

CREDIT NOTE **No. 140**

PANASONIC IRELAND LTD
Sandyford Industrial Est.
Dublin 18

Tel (01) 9986241 **VAT Reg. No. 924651N**
Fax (01) 9986242

24 May 2016

Murphy TV, Hi-Fi & Video Ltd
10 Princess Street
Cork

Quantity	Description	Unit Price	Total (Ex. VAT)
2	Panasonic Mini Hi-Fi Systems	€279	€558
	Total (Ex. VAT)		€558
	Less Trade Discount 10%		€55.80
			€502.20
	Add VAT 20%		€100.44
	Total		€602.64

Faulty Goods Ref. Inv. No. 61
E & O E

Notes:

(i) If trade discount was deducted on the original invoice, it must be **deducted on the credit note**.

(ii) If VAT was paid on the original invoice, it must be **added in the credit note**.

The credit note is the source document for recording Sales Returns and Purchases Returns.

(a) The seller writes up his **Sales Returns Day Book** from credit notes sent.

(b) The buyer writes up his **Purchases Returns Day Book** from credit notes received.

Recording credit notes sent in sales returns day book of seller

SALES RETURNS DAY BOOK – OF PANASONIC IRL. LTD (SELLER)

Date	Details	Credit Note No.	Fo	Net	VAT	Total
24/5/16	Murphy TV Hi-Fi & Video Ltd	140		€502.20	€100.44	€602.64

Recording credit notes received in purchases returns day book of buyer

PURCHASES RETURNS DAY BOOK – OF MURPHY TV, HI-FI & VIDEO LTD (BUYER)

Date	Details	Credit Note No.	Fo	Net	VAT	Total
24/5/16	Panasonic Ireland Ltd	140		€502.20	€100.44	€602.64

Treatment of credit notes issued

(1) Check figure and dates for accuracy.

(2) Check that the name and address is correct.

(3) Record the credit note in sales returns book.

(4) File a copy of the credit note.

7. Statement of account

A statement of account is a document sent from the seller to the buyer at the end of a period of time (usually one month).

It outlines the transactions that took place between the seller and the buyer and shows how much the buyer owes at the end of the period.

Let us assume that Panasonic Ireland Ltd sent a statement of account to Murphy TV, Hi-Fi & Video Ltd on 31 May 2016 as above.

Notes:

(i) The statement of accounts is presented on the continuous balance format – thus you get a new balance after each transaction.

(ii) Invoices are put into the debit column and are added to the balance figure, increasing the amount owed by the buyer.

(iii) Credit notes and payments (cash or cheque) are put into the credit column and are subtracted from the balance figure, reducing the amount owed by the buyer.

STATEMENT OF ACCOUNT **No. 210**

PANASONIC IRELAND LTD
Sandyford Industrial Est.
Dublin 18

Tel (01) 9986241 **VAT Reg. No.** 924651N
Fax (01) 9986242

31 May 2016

Murphy TV, Hi-Fi & Video Ltd
10 Princess Street
Cork

Date	Details	Debit	Credit	Balance
21/5/16	Invoice No. 61	€66,258		€66,258
24/5/16	Credit Note No. 140		€602.64	€65,655.36

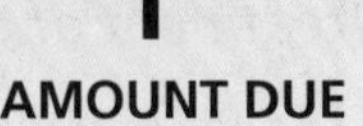

What Seller Should Do Before Sending Statements/Treatment of Outgoing Statements	What Buyer Should Do on Receiving Statements/Treatment of Incoming Statements
1. Check that the details are the same as in the accounts in the Debtors Ledger. 2. Check that all calculations are accurate. 3. Check that name and address of buyer are correct. 4. File copy of statement.	1. Compare statement transactions with relevant documents. 2. Compare statement with account of seller in creditors ledger. 3. Check all calculations. 4. Pay seller amount due. 5. File statement.

8. Payment

The buyer will usually pay the statement of account promptly by cheque.

Assume Murphy TV, Hi-Fi & Video Ltd pays Panasonic Ireland Ltd by cheque on 5 June 2016.

CHEQUE

5/6 2016		**AIB Bank**		5/6 2016
To *Panasonic*			PATRICK STREET CORK	99–66–33
For *Electrical goods*		Pay *Panasonic Ireland Ltd*		or order
Balance b/f	*€70,000 –*	Pay *Sixty five thousand six hundred and fifty*		€ *65,655.36*
this cheque	*€65,655.36*	*five euro and thirty six cent only*		Murphy TV, HI-FI & VIDEO Ltd
Bal. forwd	*€4,344.64*			*John Murphy*
				Purchasing Manager
0000168		0000168	396632	486176481

Treatment of cheques issued

(1) Check accuracy, i.e. that it is made out to correct person for correct amount.

(2) Complete stub.

(3) Record in Cash Book (credit side).

(4) Record in debit side of creditor's account in Creditors Ledger.

Balance B/f €70,000 – Assume Murphy TV, Hi-Fi & Video Ltd had €70,000 in its account before writing this cheque.

9. Receipt

When the seller receives the payment, it is usual to issue a receipt to the buyer. This acknowledges payment and when it is received by the buyer it should be filed as proof of payment.

Assume Panasonic Ireland Ltd issued a receipt on 10 June 2016.

RECEIPT	**No. 802**
PANASONIC IRELAND LTD **Sandyford Industrial Est.** **Dublin 18**	
	Date *10 June 2016*
Received with thanks, The sum of *sixty five thousand six hundred and fifty five Euro and thirty six cent only.*	IR£ *65,655.36*
FROM *Murphy TV, Hi-Fi & Video Ltd* *10 Princess Street – Cork.*	Signed *Jim Kelly* Accounts Dept

Procedure to be followed when preparing and processing receipts

Check amount received against invoice/credit note/statement.

Check accuracy of name, address of purchaser/debtor.

Insert correct date.
Insert amount in figures and words.
Sign receipt.
File copy of receipt.
Record amount received in Analysed Cash Book and Debtors Ledger (if appropriate).

10. Dealing with customers' complaints

Reasons why businesses try to have few complaints about their goods and services

(a) They do not want to lose customers.

(b) They do not want to lose profit.

(c) They do not want to incur extra expenses in dealing with complaints.

(d) They may gain a bad reputation.

Procedure for dealing with customers' complaints

(a) Listen to the complaint.

(b) Investigate the complaint.

(c) Take necessary action.

(d) Reply to the complaint.

(e) File and record the complaint for future reference.

The Business Documents Question usually requires students to complete two or three documents.

Question 1

This is an Integrated Document and Bookkeeping question. Answer ALL sections.

On 16 April 2011, COONEY FURNITURE Ltd, Athlone, Co. Westmeath sent an Order No. 3 to MUNSTER FURNITURE Ltd, Limerick, for the following goods:

20 Solid Pine Doors	@ €50 each excluding VAT
30 Bedroom Lockers	@ €20 each excluding VAT

The goods ordered are in stock and on 5 May 2011 are delivered by MUNSTER FURNITURE Ltd. An Invoice No. 55 accompanies the goods.

Trade discount is 25% and furniture is subject to VAT at 21%.

COONEY FURNITURE Ltd paid for the goods, by cheque, on 20 May 2011. The cheque was signed by Hilary Cooney.

(A) Outline how COONEY FURNITURE Ltd should treat incoming invoices and cheques issued. (12)

(B) From the above details complete the Invoice No. 55 and the Cheque No. 1. (15)

(C) Record the invoice received and the cheque issued in the Purchases and Analysed Cash Books of COONEY FURNITURE Ltd, provided. (13)

(40 marks)

Solution and marking scheme

(A) COONEY Ltd should treat incoming invoices as follows:

(i) Check calculations.
(ii) Record in the Purchases Book.
(iii) Post to credit Side of MUNSTER FURNITURE Ltd Account in Creditors Ledger.
(iv) File the invoice.
(v) Check that goods are per order/quotation.

Any two from the above @ 3 marks each.

COONEY Ltd should treat cheques issued as follows:

(i) Check accuracy – made out to the correct person for the correct amount.
(ii) Complete stub.
(iii) Record in Cash Book (Credit Side).
(iv) Record in Debit Side of MUNSTER FURNITURE Ltd Account in the Creditors Ledger.

On the invoice and credit note trade discount is deducted. VAT is added.

Any two from the above @ 3 marks each.

(B) Invoice

INVOICE NO. 55

MUNSTER FURNITURE LTD, LIMERICK

To: *COONEY FURNITURE Ltd*
Athlone,
Co. Westmeath. (1)

Tel. No. 061 212300
VAT:L IE 334231
Date: *5/5/11* (1)

Order No. 3 (1)

Quantity	Description	Unit Price €	Total (Ex. VAT) €
20	Solid Pine Doors	50	1,000
30 (1)	Bedroom Lockers (1)	20 (1)	600
		Total (Ex VAT)	1,600 (1)
		Trade Discount	400 (1)
			1,200
		VAT	252 (1)
E & OE		Total (Inc. VAT)	1,452 (1)

(B) Cheque (10 marks)

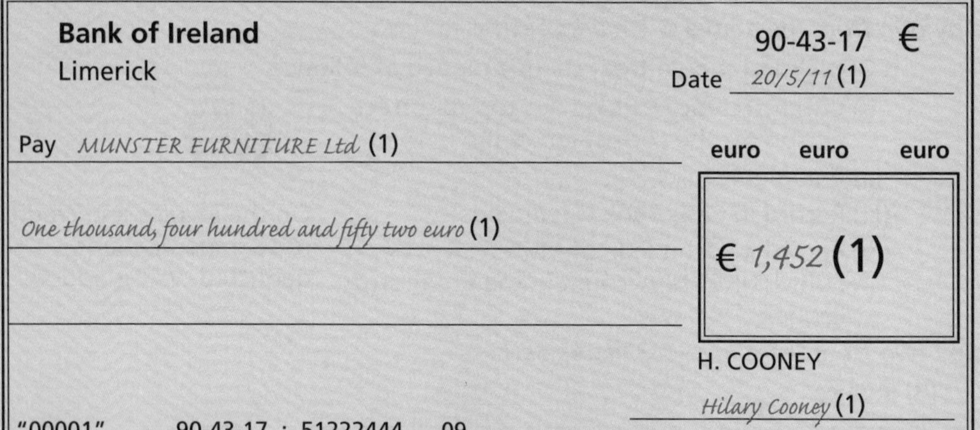

Bank of Ireland
Limerick

90-43-17 €

Date 20/5/11 (1)

Pay MUNSTER FURNITURE Ltd (1)

euro euro euro

One thousand, four hundred and fifty two euro (1)

€ 1,452 (1)

H. COONEY

Hilary Cooney (1)

"00001" 90-43-17 : 51222444 09

(5 marks)

(C) **PURCHASES BOOK page 1**

Date	Details	Invoice No.	Fo	Net €	VAT €	Total €
5/5/11 (1)	MUNSTER FURNITURE Ltd (1)	55 (1)	CL (1)	1,200 (1)	252 (1)	1,452 (1)

(7 marks)

ANALYSED CASH BOOK (CREDIT SIDE) page 1

Date	Details	Cheque No.	Fo	Bank	Creditor
20/5/11 (1)	MUNSTER FURNITURE Ltd (1)	1 (1)	CL (1)	1,452 (1)	1,452 (1)

(6 marks)

Question 2

Answer ALL sections. This is an Integrated document and Bookkeeping Question.

(A) On 5 May 2011 WEST Ltd, a clothing manufacturer, received a letter of complaint from one of its customers, LIFE Ltd, Top Street, Sligo. In the letter from LIFE Ltd it was stated that twenty shirts, which had just been delivered, were torn. The price per shirt was €20 excluding VAT.

WEST Ltd issued a Credit Note, No. 16, on 25 May 2011.

Trade discount was 25% and VAT was 20%

Complete this **credit note**. (11)

(B) Record the credit note issued in the **Sales Returns Book** and in the **Sales Returns, VAT** and **LIFE Ltd** accounts. (17) **(28 marks)**

You will probably be required to record the information from the documents to the books of First Entry and Ledger Accounts.

Suggested solution and marking scheme

(A)

CREDIT NOTE No. 16

WEST LTD

Joyce Street, Dublin

To: *LIFE Ltd*
Top Street
Sligo (1)

Tel. No. 01 23434565
VAT Reg. No. IE 234345
Date: *25/05/2011* (1)

Order No.: 71

Quantity	Description	Unit Price €	Total (Ex. VAT) €
20 (1)	*Shirts (shirts were torn)* (1)	*20* (1)	*400* (1)
		Total (Ex VAT)	*400* (1)
		Trade Discount	*100* (1)
			300 (1)
		VAT	*60* (1)
E & OE		Total	*360* (1)

(11 marks)

(B)

Sales Returns Book (Page 1)

Date	Details	Credit Note No.	Fo	Net €	VAT €	Total €
25/5/11 (1)	*LIFE Ltd* (1)	*16* (1)	*DLI* (1)	*300* (1) o/f	*60* (1) o/f	*360* (1) o/f

(7 marks)

Date	Details	Fo	Amount €	Date	Details	Fo	Amount €
			Sales Returns A/C (p. 1)				
25/5/11 (1)	*Total Sales Returns* (1)	*SRB*	*300* (1)				
			VAT A/C (p. 2)				
25/5/11 (1)	*Sales Returns* (1)	*SRB*	*60* (1) o/f				
			LIFE Ltd A/C (p. 3)				
				25/5/11 (1)	*Sales Returns* (1)	*SRB*	*360* (1)

Folios 1 mark

(10 marks)

Question 3

This is an Integrated Business Documents Question. Answer ALL sections.

The following details refer to the sale of goods on credit by HARRIS Ltd to MULLEN Ltd, 24 South Square, Tuam, Co. Galway, for the month of July 2011.

On 1 July 2011 there was a balance of €1,360 in MULLEN's account in the Debtors Ledger of HARRIS Ltd.

8/7/2011 HARRIS Ltd sent Invoice No. 50 to MULLEN Ltd €3,840
11/7/2011 HARRIS Ltd sent Invoice No. 64 to MULLEN Ltd €20,800
18/7/2011 HARRIS Ltd received a Cheque from MULLEN Ltd €13,600
22/7/2011 HARRIS Ltd sent Invoice No. 78 to MULLEN Ltd €10,720
26/7/2011 HARRIS Ltd sent Credit Note No. 94 to MULLEN Ltd €1,920 + VAT 20%
30/7/2011 HARRIS Ltd sent Invoice No. 89 to MULLEN Ltd €10,400

On 31 July 2011 HARRIS Ltd sent a Statement of Account to MULLEN Ltd. MULLEN Ltd paid the amount due on the statement by cheque. HARRIS Ltd sent Receipt No. 31 to MULLEN Ltd on 8 August 2011 signed by JAMIE HARRIS.

(A) Outline how HARRIS Ltd should treat outgoing statements of account. (6)

(B) Complete the Statement of Account No. 106 sent by HARRIS Ltd on 31 July 2011. (17)

(C) Complete Receipt No. 31 issued by HARRIS Ltd on 8 August 2011. (5)

(D) Record the issuing of Credit Note No. 94 in the Sales Returns Book and in the Sales Returns, VAT and MULLEN Ltd Accounts provided. (12)

(40 marks)

Suggested solution and marking scheme

(A) How Harris Ltd should treat outgoing Statements of Account

- Check that buyer's name and address is correct.
- Check that all calculations are accurate
- Check that the details are the same as in the accounts in the Debtors Ledger.
- Ensure that all transactions are included.
- File copy for own records.
- Ensure terms of trade are as agreed.

3 points × 2 marks
(6 marks)

(B)

		STATEMENT		**NO. 106**
		Harris Ltd **Eyre Business Park, Galway**		
To: Mullen Ltd 24 South Square Tuam Co. Galway (1)				Tel. 091 861253 VAT Reg. No. IE 326461 Account No. 4231 Date: 31/07/11 (1)
Date	**Details**	**Debit €**	**Credit €**	**Balance €**
1/7/11	Balance			1,360 (1)
8/7/11	Invoice No. 50	3,840 (1)		5,200 (1)
11/7/11	Invoice No. 64	20,800 (1)		26,000 (1)
18/7/11	Cheque		13,600 (1)	12,400 (1)
22/7/11	Invoice No. 78	10,720 (1)		23,120 (1)
26/7/11	Credit No. 94		2,304 (1)	20,816 (1) o/f
30/7/11	Invoice No. 89	10,400 (1)		31,216 (1) o/f
(1 mark)	**(1 mark)**			amount due ↑

o/f = own figure consistent with calculations

(C)

Receipt	No. 31
Harris Ltd Eyre Business Park Galway	
Date: **8 August 2011 (1)**	
Received from: **Mullen Ltd**	
24 South Square, Tuam, Co. Galway (1)	
The sum of: **Thirty one thousand two hundred and**	
sixteen euro (1) o/f	**€31,216 (1) o/f**
With thanks	**Signed: Jamie Harris (1)** Accounts Department

(D)

Sales Returns Book page 1

Date	Details	Credit Note No.	Fo	Net	VAT	Total
26/7/11	Mullen Ltd	94	DL	1,920	384	2,304
(1/2)	(1/2)	(1/2)	(1/2)	(1) o/f	(1) o/f	(1) o/f

Date	**Details**	**Fo**	**Amount €**	**Date**	**Details**	**Fo**	**Amount €**
			Sales Returns A/C (P1)				
25/7/11 (1/2)	Sales Returns (1/2)	SRB	1,920 (1) o/f				
			VAT A/C (P2)				
25/7/11 (1/2)	Sales Returns (1/2)	SRB	384 (1) o/f				
			Mullen Ltd A/C (P3)				
				26/7/11	Sales Returns	SRB	2,304 (1)
				(1/2)	(1/2)		o/f

Folios 1 mark

See:

Ordinary Level	**Ordinary Level**	**Higher Level**	**Higher Level**
Section A	Section B	Paper I	Paper II
2009 Q4	2009 Q5	Section A	2009 Q2
2008 Q8	2008 Q5	2009 Q9	2008 Q2
2007 Q2	2007 Q5	2007 Q17	2007 Q2
2007 Q8	2006 Q5	2007 Q18	2006 Q2
2006 Q14	2005 Q5	2006 Q8	2005 Q2bc
		2006 Q13	

Introduction to the operation of formal double-entry accounting.

Introduction to Double-entry Bookkeeping, Day Books and Ledger

To understand the following:

- Rule of double-entry bookkeeping
- Operating the ledger
- Day books
- Source documents for day books
- Trial balance
- Purpose of a trial balance

A. Bookkeeping

Bookkeeping is the art of recording business transactions in a systematic manner so that the business will have a permanent record.

B. Double-entry bookkeeping

Double-entry Principle: Every business transaction has a twofold aspect: **giving** and **receiving**.

C. Fundamental rule of double-entry bookkeeping

Debit – Receiver
Credit – Giver

D. An account in the ledger

An account is a space in the ledger set aside for a particular purpose, e.g. cash account, computer account.

Example I

On 1 May a firm spends €2,000 cash on the purchase of a computer.

- Money goes out of the business – cash account is giving – **Credit Giving Account**.
- Computer comes into the business – computer account is receiving – **Debit Receiving Account**.

Our two entries are:

(1) Debit computer account.

(2) Credit cash account.

Computer A/C (Debit | Credit)

Date	Details	Total	Date	Details	Total
1 May	Cash	€2,000			

Cash A/C

Date	Details	Total	Date	Details	Total
			1 May	Computer	€2,000

Example II

10 Jan. Purchased machinery on credit from John Keane €10,000.

- Two accounts are machinery and John Keane.

(1) Debit machinery account (machinery account – receiving).

(2) Credit John Keane account (John Keane account – giving).

Ledger

Machinery A/C (Debit | Credit)

Date	Details	Total	Date	Details	Total
10 Jan	John Keane	€10,000			

John Keane A/C

Date	Details	Total	Date	Details	Total
			10 Jan	Machinery	€10,000

E. Day books

(1) Purchases Day Book – for recording goods purchased on credit for resale.

(2) Purchases Returns Day Book – for recording goods returned by the purchaser.

(3) Sales Day Book – for recording goods sold on credit.

(4) Sales Returns Day Book – for recording goods returned to the seller.

(5) Cash Book – Cash receipts and bank lodgments are entered on the debit side. Cash payments and cheque payments are entered on the credit side.

(6) **General Journal** – used to record transactions which are not recorded in other books of first entry.

F. Source documents for day books

(1) Seller writes up his **sales day book** from **invoices sent**. Purchaser writes up his **purchases day book** from **invoices received**.

(2) Seller writes up his **sales returns day book** from details on **credit notes sent**. Purchaser writes up his **purchases returns day book** from **credit notes received**.

Source documents for cash book

Cash receipts – from cash register, tally roll, or copy of receipts given to cash customers.

Bank lodgments – written up from bank lodgments, counterfoils, bank statements showing receipts paid directly into bank.

Cash payments – written up from cash vouchers showing what the payment was for.

Cheque payments – written up from cheque counterfoils or from bank statements.

G. Layout of books of first entry

Layout of the Sales Day Book and Purchases Day Book

Date	Details	Inv. No.	Fo	Net	VAT	Total

Layout of cash book

Layout Number 1: Use analysed cash receipts and lodgments book and analysed cash and cheque payments book, combined with a cash account and a bank account in the ledger.

Layout Number 2: This layout combines the above two books into what is known as The Analysed Cash Book.

Exactly same layout for returns day books, except credit note number replaces invoice number.

H. The ledger

Every debit entry will have a corresponding credit entry. The ledger is divided into three sections:

(1) **Debtors Ledger** – accounts of people and firms that **owe us money**.

(2) **Creditors Ledger** – accounts of people and firms to whom we **owe money**.

(3) **General Ledger** – accounts of a **non-personal nature** such as expenses, gains, assets and liabilities.

I. Trial balance

A Trial Balance is a list of **all balances standing on the ledger accounts and cash books of a business at the end of the period**. Debit balances go to the debit column, credit balances go to the credit column. **When totalled, the debit total should correspond to the credit total**, thus the entries on the accounts are **arithmetically** correct.

STAGES IN FINANCIAL RECORDING

Steps	Details
Step 1 Complete Business Documents	Letter of enquiry, quotation, order invoice, credit note statement of account, cheque, receipt
Step 2 Record information in books of first entry	Sales book, sales returns book, purchases book, purchases returns book, cash book, general journal
Step 3 Post to ledger	General ledger, debtors ledger, creditors ledger,
Step 4 Extract a trial balance	Debit balances – debit column Credit balances – credit column
Step 5 Prepare final accounts and balance sheet	Trading account, profit and loss account, balance sheet

exam Q

See:

Higher Level

Paper I

Section A

2009 Q7

2008 Q5

2007 Q20

2006 Q20

2005 Q7

Ordinary Level

Section A

2009 Q16

2008 Q16

2007 Q13

2006 Q12

2005 Q20

30 Purchases Day Book and Purchases Returns Day Book

Note: Chapter 30 is for Higher Level students only.

To understand how to record transactions in:

- Purchases Day Book
- Purchases Returns Day Book
- The ledger
- The Trial Balance

A. Purchases day book (PDB)

The purchases day book is used to record goods bought on credit. When you purchase goods, you receive an invoice. The purchases day book is written up from invoices received.

B. Purchases returns day book (PRDB)

The purchases returns day book is used to record the return of goods purchased on credit by a business. When goods are returned, the buyer receives a credit note. The purchases returns day book is written up from the credit notes received.

C. Source documents for recording purchases day book and purchases returns day book

Invoices Received →	Purchases Day Book
Credit Notes Received →	Purchases Returns Day Book

Question

Write up the purchases day book, purchases returns day book, post to the ledger, balance the accounts, and extract a trial balance.

- 1 Feb. Purchased goods on credit from Motorola Ltd. Invoice No. 186 €2,000 + VAT @ 20%.
- 8 Feb. Returned goods to Motorola Ltd. Received credit note No. 41 €400 + VAT @ 20%.

- 15 Feb. Received invoice No. 149 from Kestrel Ltd €6,000 + VAT @ 20%.
- 24 Feb. Received credit note No. 201 from Kestrel Ltd €200 + VAT @ 20%.

Solution

Day Books

Purchases Day Book **Page 1**

Date	Details	Invoice No.	Fo	Net €	VAT €	Total €
2015						
1 Feb.	Motorola Ltd	186	CL/1	2,000	400	2,400
15 Feb.	Kestrel Ltd	149	CL/2	6,000	1,200	7,200
28 Feb.	Debit Purchases and VAT A/Cs			8,000	1,600	9,600
				GL/1	GL/2	

Purchases Returns Day Book **Page 2**

Date 2015	Details	Credit Note No.	Fo	Net €	VAT €	Total €
8 Feb.	Motorola Ltd	41	CL/1	400	80	480
24 Feb.	Kestrel Ltd	201	CL/2	200	40	240
28 Feb.	Credit Purchases Returns and VAT A/Cs			600	120	720
				GL/3	GL/2	

CL = Creditors Ledger **GL** = General Ledger

Rules for Posting to Ledger

Posting Purchases Day Book	Posting Purchases Returns Day Book
Debit Purchases account with net amount. **Debit** VAT account with VAT amount. **Credit** Personal accounts with total amount, **i.e.** Credit Motorola Ltd with €2,400. Credit Kestrel Ltd with €7,200.	**Debit** Personal accounts with total amount, **i.e.** Debit Motorola Ltd with €480. Debit Kestrel Ltd with €240. **Credit** Purchases returns account with net amount. **Credit** VAT account with VAT amount.

General Ledger

Debit — Purchases A/C No. 1 — Credit

Date	Details	Fo	Total €	Date	Details	Fo	Total €
2015 28 Feb.	Total PDB	PDB1	8,000				

Debit — VAT A/C No. 2 — Credit

Date	Details	Fo	Total €	Date	Details	Fo	Total €
2015 28 Feb.	Total PDB	PDB1	1,600	2015 28 Feb.	Total PRDB	PRDB2	120
				28 Feb.	Balance	C/d	1,480
			1,600				1,600
28 Feb.	Balance	B/d	1,480				

Debit — Purchases Returns A/C No. 3 — Credit

Date	Details	Fo	Total €	Date 2015	Details	Fo	Total €
				28 Feb.	Total PRDB	PRDB2	600

Creditors Ledger

Debit — Motorola Ltd A/C No. 1 — Credit

Date	Details	Fo	Total €	Date	Details	Fo	Total €
2015 8 Feb.	Purchases Returns	PRDB2	480	2015 1 Feb.	Purchases	PDB1	2,400
28 Feb.	Balance	C/d	1,920				
			2,400				2,400
				28 Feb.	Balance	B/d	1,920

Debit — Kestrel Ltd A/C No. 2 — Credit

Date	Details	Fo	Total €	Date	Details	Fo	Total €
2015 24 Feb.	Purchases Returns	PRDB2	240	2015 15 Feb.	Purchase	PDB1	7,200
28 Feb.	Balance	B/d	6,960				
			7,200				7,200
				28 Feb.	Balance	B/d	6,960

Balancing the accounts

All accounts with more than one entry must be balanced off. Balance in VAT account is €1,480. Balance in Motorola Ltd account is €1,920 and balance in Kestrel Ltd account is €6,960. If an account has only one entry, there is no need to balance it off.

The trial balance

- The trial balance is a list of balances from the ledger.
- Debit balances go into the Debit column.
- Credit balances go into the Credit column.

Trial Balance as on 28 February 2015

Date	Details	Fo	Debit €	Credit €
	Purchases	GL1	8,000	
	VAT	GL2	1,480	
	Purchases Returns	GL3		600
	Motorola Ltd	CL1		1,920
	Kestrel Ltd	CL2		6,960
			9,480	9,480

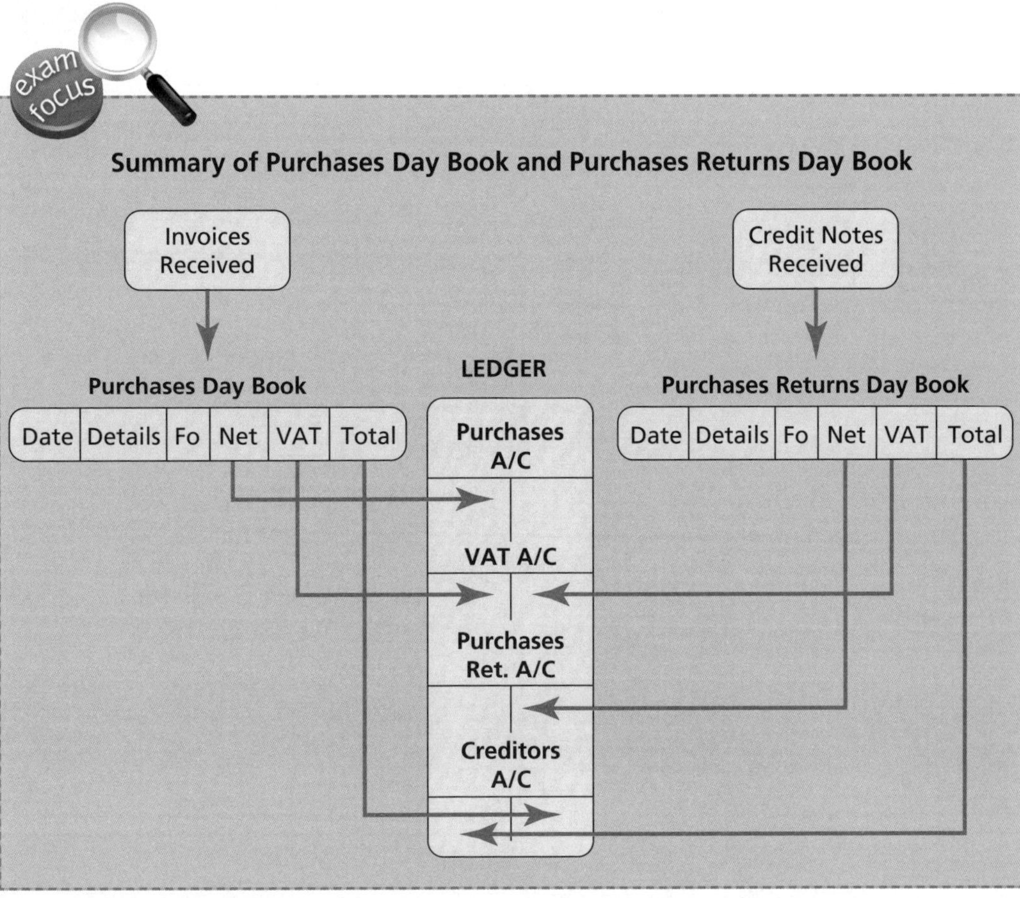

See:
Higher Level
Paper I
Section A
2009 Q18

31 Sales Day Book and Sales Returns Day Book

Note: Chapter 31 is for Higher Level students only.

To learn how to record transactions in:

- Sales Day Book
- Sales Returns Day Book
- Ledger
- Trial Balance

A. Sales day book (SDB)

The sales day book is used to **record goods sold on credit**. When a firm sells goods on credit, it sends an invoice to the buyer. The sales day book is written up from invoices sent.

B. Sales returns day book (SRDB)

The sales returns day book is used to **record goods returned to the business previously sold on credit**. When goods are returned, the seller issues a credit note.

The sales returns day book is written up from credit notes issued.

Reasons for sales returns

- Goods supplied faulty or damaged.
- Goods supplied were never ordered.
- Goods supplied were old stock.
- Goods did not arrive at agreed time/date.
- An excessive quantity were supplied.

C. Source documents for recording sales day book and sales returns day book

Invoices Sent ⟶	Sales Day Book
Credit Notes Sent ⟶	Sales Returns Day Book

Question

- Write up the sales day book and sales returns day book, post to the ledger, balance the accounts, and extract a trial balance.
- 1 Apr. Sold goods on credit to Sapphire Ltd. Invoice No. 238 €9,000 + VAT @ 20%.
- 6 Apr. Sent a credit note No. 412 to Sapphire Ltd for damaged goods €200 + VAT @ 20%.
- 15 Apr. Sent invoice No. 324 to Scott Ltd €6,000 + VAT @ 20%.
- 22 Apr. Sent credit note No. 202 to Scott Ltd for damaged goods €500 + VAT @ 20%.

Solution

Day Books

Sales Day Book **Page 1**

Date 2016	Particulars	Invoice No.	Fo	Net €	VAT €	Total €
1 Apr.	Sapphire Ltd	238	DL/1	9,000	1,800	10,800
15 Apr.	Scott Ltd	324	DL/2	6,000	1,200	7,200
30 Apr.	Credit Sales and VAT A/Cs			15,000	3,000	18,000
				GL/1	GL2	

Sales Returns Day Book **Page 2**

Date	Details	Credit Note No.	Fo	Net €	VAT €	Total €
2016						
6 Apr.	Sapphire Ltd	412	DL/1	200	40	240
22 Apr.	Scott Ltd	202	DL/2	500	100	600
30 Apr.	Debit Sales Returns and VAT A/Cs			700	140	840
				GL/3	GL/2	

Higher Level

DL = Debtors Ledger **GL** = General Ledger

Rules for Posting to Ledger

Posting Sales Day Book		Posting Sales Returns Day Book	
Debit	Personal accounts with total amount,	**Debit**	Sales Returns account with net amount.
i.e.	Debit Sapphire Ltd with €10,890.	**Debit**	VAT account with VAT amount.
	Debit Scott Ltd with €7,260.	**Credit**	Personal accounts with total amount,
Credit	Sales account with net amount.	**i.e.**	Credit Sapphire Ltd with €240.
Credit	VAT account with VAT amount.		Credit Scott Ltd with €600.

General ledger

Debit **Sales A/C No. 1** **Credit**

Date	Details	Fo	Total €	Date	Details	Fo	Total €
				2016			
				30 Apr.	Total as per SDB	SDB1	15,000

Debit **VAT A/C No. 2** **Credit**

Date	Details	Fo	Total €	Date	Details	Fo	Total €
2016				2016			
30 Apr.	Total as per SRDB	SRDB2	140	30 Apr.	Total as per SDB	SDB1	3,000
30 Apr.	Balance	C/d	2,860				
			3,000				3,000
				30 Apr.	Balance	B/d	2,860

Debit **Sales Returns A/C No. 3** **Credit**

Date	Details	Fo	Total €	Date	Details	Fo	Total €
2016							
30 Apr.	Total as per SRDB	SRDB2	700				

DEBTORS LEDGER

Debit **Sapphire Ltd A/C No. 1** **Credit**

Date	Details	Fo	Total €	Date	Details	Fo	Total €
2016				2016			
1 Apr.	Sales	SDB1	10,800	6 Apr.	Sales Returns	SRDB2	240
				30 Apr.	Balance	C/d	10,560
			10,800				10,800
30 Apr.	Balance	B/d	10,560				

Debit **Scott Ltd A/C No. 2** **Credit**

Date	Details	Fo	Total €	Date	Details	Fo	Total €
2016				2016			
15 Apr.	Sales	SDB1	7,200	22 Apr.	Sales Returns	SRDB2	600
				30 Apr.	Balance	B/d	6,600
			7,200				7,200
30 Apr.	Balance	B/d	6,600				

Balancing the accounts

All accounts with more than one entry must be balanced off. Balance in VAT account is €2,860. Balance in Sapphire Ltd account is €10,560 and balance in Scott Ltd account is €6,600. If an account has only one entry, there is no need to balance it off.

The Trial Balance

- The trial balance is a list of balances from the ledger.
- Debit balances go into the Debit column.
- Credit balances go into the Credit column.

Trial Balance as on 30 April 2016

Date	Details	Fo	Debit €	Credit €
	Sales	GL1		15,000
	VAT	GL2		2,860
	Sales Returns	GL3	700	
	Sapphire Ltd	DL1	10,560	
	Scott Ltd	DL2	6,600	
			17,860	17,860

exam focus

Summary of Sales Day Book and Sales Returns Day Book

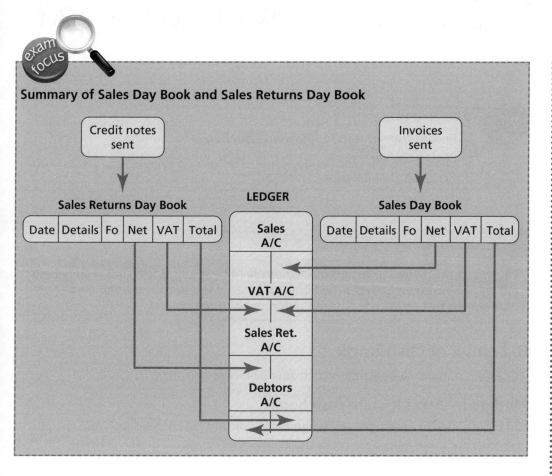

Credit notes sent

Sales Returns Day Book

Date	Details	Fo	Net	VAT	Total

Invoices sent

Sales Day Book

Date	Details	Fo	Net	VAT	Total

LEDGER

Sales A/C

VAT A/C

Sales Ret. A/C

Debtors A/C

See:

Higher Level

Paper I

Section A

2008 Q20

2008 Q4

2003 Q15

2000 Q17

32 Cash Book (Including VAT)

To be able to:

- Record transactions in Analysed Cash Book
- Post to Ledger
- Extract a Trial Balance

A. Cash book

The cash book is used to **record money received by the business and money paid out by the business**. Cash transactions are entered in the cash column, and transactions by cheque are entered in the bank column.

B. Format of cash book

The layout of the cash book may vary from one business to another.

Method I – Two separate cash books

Use (1) analysed cash receipts and lodgments book and (2) analysed cash and cheque payments book and bank account in the ledger.

OR

Method II – Analysed cash book

This combines the above two books.

(1) Information in the analysed cash receipts and lodgments book would appear on the debit side of the analysed cash book.

(2) Information in the analysed cash and cheque payment book would appear on the credit side of the analysed cash book.

No bank account is needed in the ledger, as the bank columns are balanced in the analysed cash book.

METHOD I – TWO SEPARATE CASH BOOKS

METHOD II – ANALYSED CASH BOOK

Either method will answer any question in Junior Certificate Business Studies.

Rules for writing up cash books

(1) Any money coming into the business goes into analysed cash receipts book, or debit side of analysed cash book.

(2) Any money going out of the business goes into the analysed cash and cheque payments book, or credit side of analysed cash book.

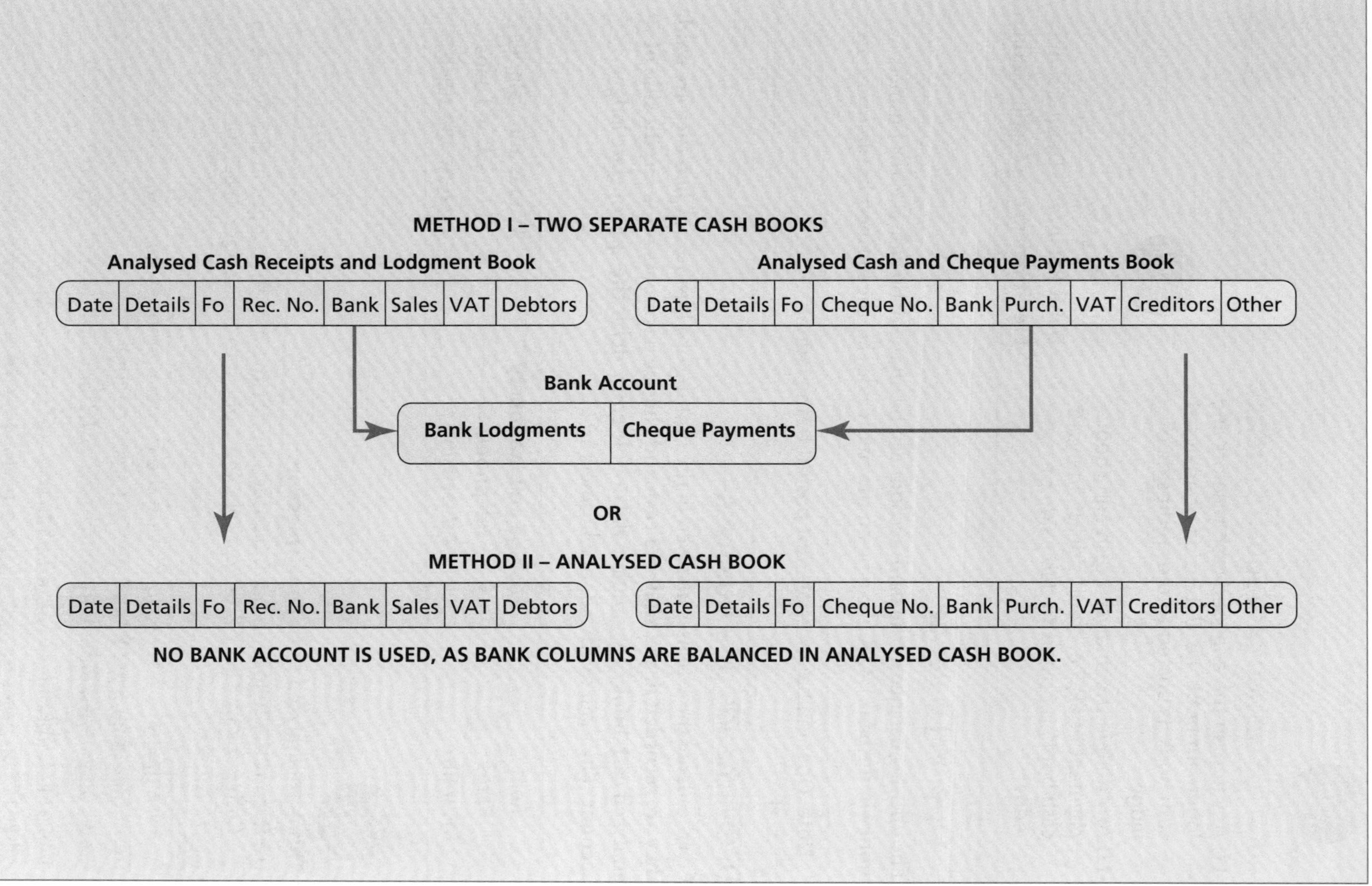
METHOD I – TWO SEPARATE CASH BOOKS
Analysed Cash Receipts and Lodgment Book
Date | Details | Fo | Rec. No. | Bank | Sales | VAT | Debtors
Analysed Cash and Cheque Payments Book
Date | Details | Fo | Cheque No. | Bank | Purch. | VAT | Creditors | Other
Bank Account
Bank Lodgments | Cheque Payments
OR
METHOD II – ANALYSED CASH BOOK
Date | Details | Fo | Rec. No. | Bank | Sales | VAT | Debtors
Date | Details | Fo | Cheque No. | Bank | Purch. | VAT | Creditors | Other
NO BANK ACCOUNT IS USED, AS BANK COLUMNS ARE BALANCED IN ANALYSED CASH BOOK.

RULES FOR POSTING CASH BOOK TO LEDGER

(1) Any item in the analysed cash receipts and lodgment book, i.e. debit side of analysed cash book, is posted to the credit side of ledger.

(2) Any item in the analysed cash and cheque payment book, i.e. credit side of analysed cash book, is posted to debit side of ledger.

TRIAL BALANCE

Debit Balance → Debit Column

Credit Balance → Credit Column

C. Opening balance

The opening balance in the bank account can be on the debit side (i.e. the business has money in the bank), **OR** it can be on the credit side (i.e. the business has an overdraft).

Note: Opening balances are not posted to the ledger.

D. Overheads of a business

Overheads are the expenses involved in the running of a business. **When they are paid, they are recorded in the analysed cash and cheque payments book/credit side of analysed cash book**. To complete the double entry, **debit the appropriate ledger account**. The main overheads of a business are:

Rent	**Postage and Stationery**	**Wages and Salaries**
Rates	**Telephone**	**Interest on Loans**
Insurance	**Advertising**	**Light and Heat**

This is an analysed Cash Book Question.

(A) Record the following bank transactions for the month of April in the Analysed Cash Book of KELLY Ltd. Post relevant figures to the Ledger Accounts.

Note:

Analyse the bank transactions using the following money headings:

Debit (Receipts) Side: Bank Sales VAT share Capital

Credit (Payments) Side: Bank Purchases VAT Light and Heat Creditors

1/4/2011 Shareholder invested €150,000 and this was lodged Receipt No. 24

2/4/2011 Purchases for reseal (Cheque No. 45) €70,000 + VAT 13.5%

13/4/2011 Paid electricity bill (Cheque No. 46) €1,700

19/4/2011 Cash Sales lodged €90,800 (€80,000 + VAT €10,800)

28/4/2011 Paid HAY Ltd (Cheque No. 47) €17,500

(B) Balance the accounts on 30 April 2011 and extract a Trial Balance as at that date. (22 marks)

Suggested solution and marking scheme

(A) **Analysed Cash Book (Debit Side) (page 1)**

Date	Details	Rec. No.	Fo	Bank €	Sales €	VAT €	Share Capital €
1/4/2011	Shareholder	24 (1)	GL	150,000 (½)			150,000 (½)
19/4/2011	Sales		GL	90,800 (½)	80,000 (½)	10,800 (½)	
				240,800	80,000	10,800	150,000
1/5/2011	Balance B/D			142,150			

Analysed Cash Book (Credit Side) (page 1)

Date	Details	Ch. No.	Fo	Bank €	Purchases €	VAT €	L & H €	Creditors €
2/4/2011	Purchases	45	GL	79,450 (½)	70,000 (½)	9,450 (½)		
13/4/2011	Electricity	46 (1)	GL	1,700 (½)			1,700 (½)	
28/4/2011	HAY Ltd	47	CL	17,500 (½)				17,500 (½)
				98,650	70,000	9,450	1,700	17,500
30/4/2011	Balance C/D			142,150 (1)				
				240,800				

12 entries @ ½ mark each = 6 marks. Closing Balance 1 mark, Rec. No. 1 mark. Cheque No. 1 mark.

(9 marks)

Alternative Bank Account in Ledger if separate cash books are used

Date	Details	Fo	Total €	Date	Details	Fo	Total €
			Bank A/C (P1)				
30/4/2011	Receipts	ACB	240,800	30/4/2011	Payments	ACB	98,650
				30/4/2011	Balance C/D		142,150
			240,800				240,800
1/5/2011	Balance B/D		142,150				

Ledger

Date	Details	Fo	Total €	Date	Details	Fo	Total €
2008				2008			
			Creditors Ledger				
			HAY Ltd A/C (p2)				
28/4/2011	Bank	ACB	17,500 (1)				
			General Ledger				
			Purchases A/C (p1)				
30/4/2011	Bank	ACB	70,000 (1)				
			VAT A/C (p3)				
30/4/2011	Cash Purchases	ACB	9,450 (1)	30/4/2011	Cash Sales	ACB	10,800 (1)
30/4/2011	Balance C/D		1,350 (1)				
			10,800				10,800
				1/5/2011	Balance B/D		1,350
			Share Capital A/C (p4)				
				1/4/2011	Bank	ACB	150,000 (1)
			Light and Heat A/C (p5)				
13/4/2011	Bank	ACB	1,700 (1)				
			Sales A/C (p6)				
				30/4/2011	Bank	ACB	80,000 (1)

8 entries @ 1 mark each = 8 marks

Dates with year 1 mark = 1 mark

(9 marks)

(B)

Trial Balance of KELLY Ltd as on 30 April 2008 (½)

	Dr €	Cr €
HAY Ltd	17,500 (½)	
Purchases	70,000 (½)	
VAT		1,350 (½)
Share Capital		150,000 (½)
Light and Heat	1,700 (½)	
Sales		80,000 (½)
Bank	142,150 (½)	
	231,350	231,350

Marking scheme

7 entries @ ½ mark = 3½

Heading with date = ½

4 marks

See:

Ordinary Level	**Higher Level**	**Higher Level**	**Higher Level**
Section B	Paper I	Paper I	Paper II
2006 Q6	Section A	Section B	2008 Q6
2001 Q6	2004 Q7	2000 Q1a	2004 Q6
	2001 Q12b		2000 Q6ab

33 Petty Cash Book

To be able to:

- Record transactions in the Petty Cash Book
- Understand the imprest system

A. Introduction

The petty cash book is **used to record small cash payments**, e.g. postage stamps, bus fares, envelopes. It has a debit side that records the petty cash float, and the credit side records payments. The credit side is analysed to give a breakdown of the payments.

B. Impress system

The petty cash book operates on the Imprest System, which works as follows:

(1) Chief cashier gives Petty cashier a sum of money called a **Float**, which it is estimated will cover petty cash expenses for the month. It is shown on the debit side of the petty cash book.

(2) During the month this float is used to pay small expenses. A petty cash voucher is completed by the person requiring the money. Payments are recorded on the credit side of petty cash book.

(3) At the end of month, the petty cash book is balanced, and amount spent is calculated.

(4) Chief cashier gives Petty cashier a sum equivalent to amount spent to restore imprest to original level so that Petty cashier can start next month with the same float. (Imprest: the same/fixed amount of cash with which the Petty cashier starts at the beginning of each month.)

C. Advantages of using the imprest system

(1) It saves on bank charges – fewer cheques used.

(2) It is a record of small payments.

(3) It sets an upper limit to small office expenses.

(4) It highlights excessive expenses.

(5) The voucher is proof of payment.

(6) It reduces entries in Bank A/C.

D. Petty cash voucher

If an employee needs money to purchase something small, he will complete a petty cash voucher giving:

(1) Date.

(2) Amount.

(3) Reason for money required.

(4) Signature of claimant.

(5) Signature of supervisor.

The payment is recorded in the credit side of the petty cash book.

This is a Petty Cash Question.

Complete and balance the Petty Cash Book of a business for the month of May 2011 from the data below.

Analyse the payments under the following headings:

Postage, Cleaning, Travel, Stationery, Tea Break.

2011		Voucher No.	€
1/5/11	Received a cheque for imprest		75.00
2/5/11	Purchased postage stamps	1	9.00
4/5/11	Paid for biscuits and milk	2	0.50
6/5/11	Paid for office cleaning	3	12.00
8/5/11	Purchased stapler and staples	4	9.50
12/5/11	Paid for taxi	5	7.50
14/5/11	Paid window cleaner	6	5.00
16/5/11	Paid for COD parcel	7	6.50
19/5/11	Paid milk bill	8	3.50
23/5/11	Paid for bus fare	9	10.50
28/5/11	Received a cheque to restore the imprest		

Solution

Petty Cash Book

Date	Details	Total	Date	Details	Voucher	Total	Post	Cleaning	Travel	Stat	Tea break
1/5/11	Bal b/d	5.00	2/5/11	Stamps	1	9.00	9.00				
			4/5/11	Biscuits, milk	2	0.50					0.50
			6/5/11	Cleaning	3	12.00		12.00			
			8/5/11	Stapler	4	9.50				9.50	
			12/5/11	Taxi	5	7.50			7.50		
			14/5/11	Cleaning	6	5.00		5.00			
			16/5/11	Postage	7	6.50	6.50				
			19/5/11	Milk bill	8	3.50					3.50
			23/5/11	Bus fare	9	10.50			10.50		
			28/5/11	Bal c/d		11.00					
		75.00				75.00	15.50	17.00	18.00	9.50	4.00
1/6/11	Bal b/d	11.00									
1/6/11	Bank	64.00									

34 General Journal

Note: Chapter 34 is for Higher Level students only.

To be able to understand:

- How to use the General Journal
- When to use the General Journal

A. Introduction

The General Journal is **used to record transactions that cannot be recorded in any other book of first entry**.

These transactions are:

(1) Opening entries.

(2) Purchase and sale of fixed assets on credit.

(3) Bad debts written off.

The General Journal is also posted to the Ledger.

B. Layout of General Journal

General Journal

Date	Details	Fo	Debit	Credit
	Names of Accounts and Narration (Explanation of Transaction)		A/C to be Debited	A/C to be Credited

1. Opening entries

A list of **Assets** and **Liabilities** at the start of the trading period.

Assets – Debit Column
Liabilities – Credit Column

The difference is called Share Capital and is entered in the Credit Column, i.e. money owed to owners/shareholders.

Assets − Liabilities = Share Capital

Narration – a brief explanation of the transaction.

Question

Kavanagh Ltd had the following Assets and Liabilities on 1 January. Enter these in the General Journal and post to the ledger.

Assets: Cash €10,000 Bank €20,000 Buildings €150,000

Debtor: Seamus McCarthy €6,000

Liabilities Creditor: Patrick Hennessey €3,000

Share Capital: €183,000

Solution

GENERAL JOURNAL **Page 1**

Date	Details	Fo	Debit €	Credit €
2014 1 Jan.	Assets			
	Cash	CB1	10,000	
	Bank	CB1	20,000	
	Buildings	GL1	150,000	
	Debtor: Seamus McCarthy	DL1	6,000	
	Liabilities			
	Creditor: Patrick Hennessey	CL1		3,000
	Share Capital	GL2		183,000
			186,000	186,000
	Assets, Liabilities and Share Capital of Kavanagh Ltd on 1 Jan.			

Posting opening entries to ledger.

- Assets that are in the Debit Column of the General Journal are Debit Balances in the Ledger.
- Liabilities and Share Capital that are in the Credit Column of the General Journal are Credit Balances in the Ledger.

General Ledger

Building Account **No. 1**

Date	Details	Fo	Total	Date	Details	Fo	Total
2014			€				
1 Jan.	Balance	GJ1	150,000				

Share Capital Account **No. 2**

Date	Details	Fo	Total	Date	Details	Fo	Total
				2014			€
				1 Jan.	Balance	GJ1	183,000

Debtors Ledger

Seamus McCarthy Account **No. 1**

Date	Details	Fo	Total	Date	Details	Fo	Total
2014			€				
1 Jan.	Balance	GJ1	6,000				

Creditors Ledger

Patrick Hennessey Account **No. 1**

Date	Details	Fo	Total	Date	Details	Fo	Total
				2014			€
				1 Jan.	Balance	GJ1	3,000

CASH BOOK

Date	Details	Fo	Cash €	Bank €	Date	Details	Fo	Cash	Bank
2014									
1 Jan.	Balance	GJ1	10,000	20,000					

2. Purchase and sale of fixed assets on credit

Question

- 2 Jan. Purchased office equipment on credit from Munster Business Equipment for €3,000 + VAT @ 20%
- 3 Jan. Sold office equipment on credit to Frank Boland for €500 + VAT @ 20%

Solution – Explanation

- 2 Jan. Debit office equipment account €3,000 – receiving account
  Debit VAT account €600
  Credit Munster Business Equipment – €3,600 – giving account
- 3 Jan. Debit Frank Boland account – €600 – receiving account
  Credit office equipment account – €500 – giving account
  Credit VAT account – €100

GENERAL JOURNAL **Page 1**

Date	Details	Fo	Debit €	Credit €
2015				
2 Jan.	Office Equipment A/C	GL1	3,000	
	VAT A/C	GL2	600	
	Munster Business Equipment A/C	CL1		3,600
	Purchase of Office Equipment on Credit			
3 Jan.	Frank Boland A/C	DL1	600	
	Office Equipment A/C	GL1		500
	VAT A/C	GL2		100
	Sale of Office Equipment on Credit			

General Ledger

Office Equipment Account

Date	Details	Fo	Total	Date	Details	Fo	Total
2015			€	2015			€
2 Jan.	Munster Business Equipment	GJ1	3,000	3 Jan.	Frank Boland	GJ1	500

VAT Account

Date 2015	Details	Fo	Total €	Date 2015	Details	Fo	Total €
2 Jan.	Munster Business Equipment	GJ1	600	3 Jan.	Frank Boland	GJ1	100

Debtors Ledger

Frank Boland Account

Date 2015	Details	Fo	Total €	Date	Details	Fo	Total €
3 Jan.	Office Equipment	GJ1	600				

Creditors Ledger

Munster Business Equipment Account

Date	Details	Fo	Total	Date 2015	Details	Fo	Total €
				2 Jan.	Office Equipment	GJ1	3,600

3. Bad debts written off

A bad debt arises when goods are sold on credit to a debtor and the debtor fails to pay the money owed. The business will then write the figure off as a bad debt.

Question

5 Feb. Jim Lawlor (debtor) owes €600 and has been declared bankrupt and can pay only €200. The remaining €400 is to be written off as a bad debt.

Solution

Debit bank account with €200 – amount received.
Debit bad debts account €400 – amount of bad debt.
Credit Jim Lawlor – €600 – to close his account.

GENERAL JOURNAL **Page 2**

Date	Details	Fo	Debit €	Credit €
2016				
5 Feb.	Bank A/C	CB1	200	
	Bad Debts A/C	GL1	400	
	Jim Lawlor A/C	DL1		600
	Jim Lawlor declared bankrupt. Paid €200, balance owed written off as a bad debt.			

CASH BOOK **Page 1**

Date	Details	Fo	Cash €	Bank €	Date	Details	Fo	Cash	Bank €
2016									
5 Feb.	Jim Lawlor	GJ2		200					

General Ledger

Bad Debts Account **No. 1**

Date	Details	Fo	Total	Date	Details	Fo	Total
2016			€				€
5 Feb.	Jim Lawlor	GJ2	400				

Debtors Ledger

Jim Lawlor Account **No. 1**

Date	Details	Fo	Total	Date	Details	Fo	Total
2016			€	2016			€
1 Feb.	Balance	GJ2	600	5 Feb.	Bank	GJ2	200
				5 Feb.	Bad Debts	GJ2	400
			600				600

See:

Higher Level

Paper I

Section A

2009 Q17

2008 Q18

2007 Q15

2006 Q15

2004 Q13

35 Bookkeeping Revision

Note: Chapter 35 is for Higher Level students only.

To be able to:

- Enter figures from source documents in the appropriate books
- Post to ledgers
- Prepare a Trial Balance
- Interpret a ledger entry
- The uses and limitations of a trial balance

In this chapter we will summarise briefly the **books of first entry** and work through a sample Junior Certificate Higher Level question.

Books of first entry – summary

Books of First Entry	Type of Transaction Book Is Used For	Source Documents	Rules for Posting to Ledger
Purchases day book	Goods purchased on credit	Invoices received	DR – Purchases A/C Net DR – VAT A/C – VAT CR – Personal A/C – Total
Purchases returns day book	Returns of goods purchased on credit	Credit notes received	DR Personal A/C – Total CR Purch. Ret. A/C – Net CR VAT A/C – VAT
Sales day book	Goods sold on credit	Invoices sent	DR Personal A/C – Total CR Sales A/C – Net CR Vat A/C – VAT
Sales returns day book	Return of goods previously sold on credit	Credit notes sent	DR Sales Ret. A/C – Net DR VAT A/C – VAT CR Personal A/C – Total

Cash book	Bank lodgments	Lodgment counterfoils/+ bank statements	Debit side of cash book ⟶ Credit side of ledger
	Cheque payments ⟶	Cheque counterfoils/+ bank statements	Credit side of cash book ⟶ Debit side of ledger
Petty cash book	Small items of expenditure ⟶	Petty cash vouchers	Total of each analysis column is posted to Debit side of ledger A/C
General journal	**(1)** Opening entries	Relevant invoices, etc.	**(1)** DR Assets – CR Liabilities
	(2) Purchase of assets on credit		**(2)** DR – Asset A/C DR – VAT A/C CR – Personal A/C
	(3) Sale of assets on credit		**(3)** DR – Personal A/C CR – Asset A/C CR – VAT A/C
	(4) Bad debts written off		**(4)** DR – Bank A/C DR – Bad Debts A/C CR – Personal A/C

Bookkeeping questions need regular practice – try to complete the questions under exam conditions.

This is a Book of First Entry, Ledger and Trial Balance Question.

Answer all parts of this question.

HARMON Ltd is a giftware store.

(A) Record the following Credit Transactions in the Purchases and Purchases Returns Books for the month of May 2011. Post relevant figures from the books to the Ledger Accounts.

7/5/2011	Purchased goods on credit from SIMMONDS Ltd	Invoice No. 54 €48,000 + VAT 13.5%
12/5/2011	Returned goods to SIMMONDS Ltd	Credit Note No. 20 €21,000 + VAT 13.5%
13/5/2011	Purchased goods on credit from HUTTON Ltd	Invoice No. 69 €67,500 + VAT 13.5%

(16)

(B) Record the following Bank Transactions for the month of May 2011 in the Analysed Cash Book of HARMON Ltd. Post relevant figures to the Ledger Accounts.

Note: Analyse the Bank Transactions using the following money headings:

Debit (Receipts) Side: Bank Sales VAT Share Capital

Credit (Payments) Side: Bank Purchases VAT Insurance Creditors

1/5/2011	Shareholders invested		€450,000 and this was lodged Receipt No. 15
6/5/2011	Paid Insurance	(Cheque No. 40)	€5,100
8/5/2011	Purchases for resale	(Cheque No. 41)	€210,000 + VAT 13.5%
18/5/2011	Cash sales Lodged		€272,400 (€240,000 + VAT €32,400)
30/5/2011	Paid HUTTON Ltd	(Cheque No. 42)	€52,500

(15)

(C) Balance the accounts on 31 May 2011 and extract a Trial Balance as at that date. (9)

(40 marks)

Solution and marking scheme

(A) **PURCHASES BOOK** (PAGE 1)

Date	Details	Invoice No.	Fo	Net €	VAT €	Total €
7/5/11	Simmonds Ltd	54 (1/2)	CL	48,000 (1/2)	6,480 (1/2)	54,480 (1/2)
13/5/11	Hutton Ltd	69 (1/2)	CL	67,800 (1/2)	9,153 (1/2)	76,953 (1/2)
				115,800	15,633	131,433
				GL	GL	

PURCHASES RETURNS BOOK (PAGE 1)

Date	Details	C/N No.	Fo	Net €	VAT €	Total €
12/5/11	Simmonds Ltd	20 (1)	CL	21,000 (1/2)	2,835 (1/2)	23,835 (1/2)
				GL	GL	

(B) ANALYSED CASH BOOK (DEBIT SIDE)

Page 1

Date	Details	Fo	Bank €	Sales €	VAT €	Share Capital €
1/5/11	Shareholder	GL	450,000 (1/2)	240,000 (1/2)	32,400 (1/2)	450,000 (1/2)
18/5/11	Sales	GL	272,400 (1/2)			
			722,400	240,000	32,400	450,000
	Balance b/d		426,450			
	Receipt No. 15 (1)					

ANALYSED CASH BOOK (CREDIT SIDE)

Page 1

Date	Details	Ch. No.	Fo	Bank €	Purchases €	VAT €	Insurance €	Creditors €
6/5/11	Insurance	40	GL	5,100 (1/2)	210,000 (1/2)	28,350 (1/2)	5,100 (1/2)	52,500 (1/2)
8/5/11	Purchases	41	GL	238,350 (1/2)				
30/5/11	Hutton Ltd	42	CL	52,500 (1/2)				
31/5/11	Balance c/d	(1)		295,950				
				426,450 (1)				
				722,400	210,000	28,350	5,100	52,500

Alternate Bank Account in Ledger if Separate Cash Books are Used

Date	Details	Fo	Total €	Bank A/c (P1)	Date	Details	Fo	Total €
31/5/11	Receipts	ACB		722,400	31/5/11	Payments	ACB	295,950
					31/5/11	Balance c/d		426,450
				722,400				722,400
1/6/11	Balance b/d			426,450 (1)				

Question 1 Ledger for (A, B and C)

Date	Details	Fo	Total €	Date	Details	Fo	Total €
2011				2011			

CREDITORS LEDGER

Simmonds Ltd A/C (P1)

Date	Details	Fo	Total €	Date	Details	Fo	Total €
12/5	Purchases Returns	PRB	23,835 (1)	7/5	Purchases	PB	54,480 (1)
31/5	Balance c/d		30,645 (1)				
			54,480				54,480
				1/6	Balance b/d		30,645

Hutton Ltd A/C (P2)

Date	Details	Fo	Total €	Date	Details	Fo	Total €
30/5	Bank	ACB	52,500 (1)	13/5	Purchases	PB	76,953 (1)
31/5	Balance c/d		24,453 (1)				
			76,953				76,953
				1/6	Balance b/d		24,453

GENERAL LEDGER

Purchases A/C (P1)

Date	Details	Fo	Total €	Date	Details	Fo	Total €
31/5	Total Net Purchases	PB	115,800 (1)				
8/5	Bank	ACB	210,000 (1)				
			325,800				

Purchases Returns A/C (P2)

Date	Details	Fo	Total €	Date	Details	Fo	Total €
				31/5	Total Net Purchases	PRB	21,000 (1)

VAT A/C (P3)

Date	Details	Fo	Total €	Date	Details	Fo	Total €
31/5	Credit Purchases	PB	15,633 (1)	31/5	Cash Sales	ACB	32,400 (1)
31/5	Cash Purchases	ACB	28,350 (1)	31/5	Purchases Returns	PRB	2,835 (1)
				31/5	Balance c/d		8,748 (1)
			43,983				43,983
1/6	Balance b/d		8,748				

Share Capital A/C (P4)

Date	Details	Fo	Total €	Date	Details	Fo	Total €
				1/5	Bank	ACB	450,000 (1)

Insurance A/C (P5)

Date	Details	Fo	Total €	Date	Details	Fo	Total €
6/5	Bank	ACB	5,100 (1)				

Sales A/C (P6)

Date	Details	Fo	Total €	Date	Details	Fo	Total €
				18/5	Bank	ACB	240,000 (1)

(C)

Trial Balance of Harmon Ltd as on 31 May 2011

Date	Details	Fo	DR €	CR €
	Simmonds Ltd			30,645 (1/2)
	Hutton Ltd			24,453 (1/2)
	Purchases		325,800 (1/2)	
	Purchases Returns			21,000 (1/2)
	VAT		8,748 (1/2)	
	Share Capital			450,000 (1/2)
	Insurance		5,100 (1/2)	
	Sales			240,000 (1/2)
	Bank		426,450 (1/2)	
			766,098	766,098

See:

Higher Level

Paper II

2009 Q1

2008 Q1

2007 Q1

2006 Q1

2005 Q1

36 Control Accounts

Note: Chapter 36 is for Higher Level students only.

To understand how to use:

- Simple Control Accounts
- Functions of Control Accounts – **Higher Level**

A. Principles of control accounts

We can check on the accuracy of the debtors and creditors ledger – by Control accounts (Total accounts).

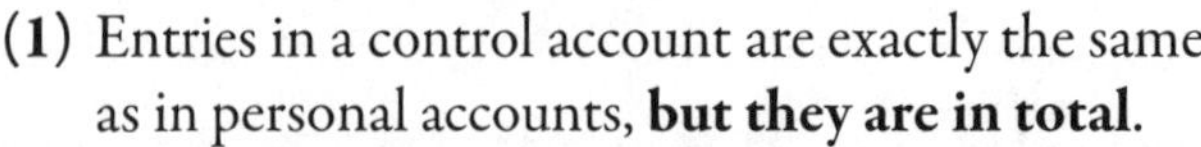

(1) Entries in a control account are exactly the same as in personal accounts, **but they are in total**.

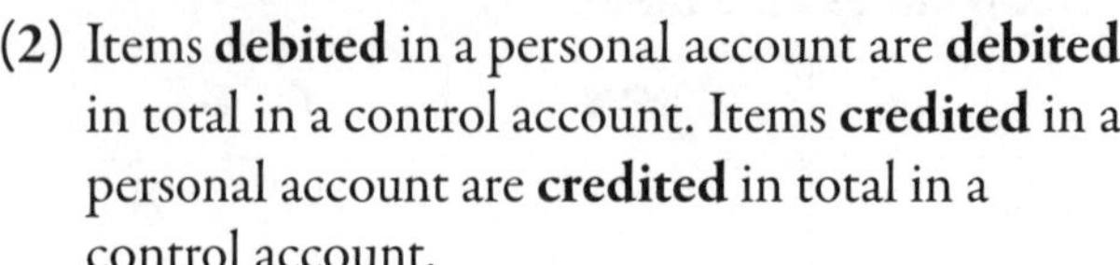

(2) Items **debited** in a personal account are **debited** in total in a control account. Items **credited** in a personal account are **credited** in total in a control account.

(3) The control account is prepared by taking the **totals from the day books**.

B. Types of control account

(1) Debtors Control Account	**(2)** Creditors Control Account
↓	↓
Checks Debtors (Sales) Ledger	Checks Creditors (Purchases) Ledger

There are two types:

1. Debtors control account

The debtors control account is a **total account** and is prepared by taking totals of sales day book, sales returns book and total cash/cheques received from debtors. The balance in the debtors control account should be equal to the total of the balances on **all** personal accounts in the debtors ledger, thus providing evidence of the accuracy of the debtors ledger.

Question

Complete and balance the debtors control account from the following data:

- Balance as on 1 June 2016 €2,000.
- Total cash received from debtors in June €10,000.
- Total sales on credit in June €15,000.
- Total sales returns in June €1,000.

Solution

'T' Account Format

Debtors Control Account

Date	Details	Fo	Total	Date	Details	Fo	Total
2016			€				€
1 June	Balance B/d	GJ	2,000	30 June	Cash rec. from debtors	CB	10,000
30 June	Credit sales	SB	15,000	30 June	Sales returns	SRB	1,000
				30 June	Balance	C/d	6,000
		B/d	17,000				17,000
			6,000				

OR

Continuous Balancing Format

Debtors Control A/C

Date	Details	Fo	Debit (€)	Credit (€)	Balance (€)
2016					
1 June	Balance B/d	GJ			2,000
30 June	Credit sales	SB			17,000
30 June	Cash received from debtors	CB	15,000	10,000	7,000
30 June	Sales returns	SRB		1,000	6,000

2. Creditors control account

The creditors control account is **also a total account** and is prepared by taking the totals of purchases day book, purchases returns book and total cash/cheques paid to creditors from the cash book. The balance in the creditors control account should be equal to the total of the balances on **all** personal accounts in the creditors ledger, thus providing evidence of the accuracy of the creditors ledger.

Question

Complete and balance the creditors control account from the following data:

- Balance as on 1 July 2016 €4,000.
- Total purchases on credit in July €20,000.
- Total payments (by cheque) during July to creditors €15,000.
- Total payments (by cash) during July to creditors €1,000.
- Total purchases returns during July €3,000.

Solution

'T' Account Format

Creditors Control Account

Date	Details	Fo	Total	Date	Details	Fo	Total
2016			€	2016			€
31 July	Payments to creditors – cheques	CB	15,000	1 July	Balance B/d	GJ	4,000
31 July	Payments to creditors – cash	CB	1,000	31 July	Total credit purchases	PB	20,000
31 July	Purchase returns	PRB	3,000	31 July			
31 July	Balance	C/d	5,000				
			24,000				24,000
					Balance B/d		5,000

Creditors Control A/C

Date	Details	Fo	Debit (€)	Credit (€)	Balance (€)
2016					
1 July	Balance	GJ			4,000
31 July	Credit purchases	PB		20,000	24,000
31 July	Payments to creditors – cheques	CB	15,000		9,000
	Payments to creditors – cash				
31 July	Purchases returns	CB	1,000		8,000
31 July		PRB	3,000		5,000

See: **Higher Level** Paper I Section A

2009 Q13

2008 Q13

2007 Q9

2006 Q9

2005 Q13

37 Continuous Presentation of Ledger Accounts

Note: Chapter 37 is for Higher Level students only.

To be able to:

- Convert accounts from 'T' account to continuous and vice versa
- Prepare accounts using a continuous presentation

A. Types of presentation

There are two ways of presenting ledger accounts.

1. 'T' account format

This has the debit side on the left and the credit side on the right.

2. Continuous balancing format

This has a debit column, a credit column and a balance column. The balance column is adjusted after each transaction so we can see immediately the balance on a particular day.

Students may opt to do ledger accounts using either the 'T' account format or the continuous balancing format. But Higher Level students must be able to convert from 'T' account format to continuous balancing format or vice versa.

Conversion of a Debtor's Account from 'T' Account Format to Continuous Balancing Format

Question

Convert the following account in the debtors ledger into continuous balancing format.

Debtors Ledger

Patrick Gallagher Account

DR ↑ CR ↓

Date	Details	Fo	Total €	Date	Details	Fo	Total €
2015				2015			
1 Jan.	Balance	GJ	2,000	15 Jan.	Cash	CB	2,000
10 Jan.	Sales	SB	15,000	18 Jan.	Bank	CB	9,000
22 Jan.	Sales	SB	11,000	22 Jan.	Sales returns	SRB	1,000
				25 Jan.	Balance	C/d	16,000
			28,000				28,000
31 Jan.		B/d	16,000				

Solution

Debtors Ledger

Patrick Gallagher A/C

Date	Details	Fo	Debit + (€)	Credit – (€)	Balance (€)
2015					
1 Jan.	Balance	GJ			2,000
10 Jan.	Sales	SB	15,000		17,000
15 Jan.	Cash	CB	—	2,000	15,000
18 Jan.	Bank	CB	—	9,000	6,000
22 Jan.	Sales	SB	11,000	—	17,000
25 Jan.	Sales Returns	SRB	—	1,000	16,000

In Debtors Ledger

Figures in Debit column increase the balance.
Figures in Credit column reduce the balance.

Conversion of a Creditor's Account from 'T' Account Format to Continuous Balancing Format

Question

Convert the following account in the creditors ledger into continuous balancing format.

Creditors Ledger

DR ↓ **John Molloy Account** CR ↑

Date	Details	Fo	Total €	Date	Details	Fo	Total €
2015				2015			
10 Feb.	Cash	CB	3,000	1 Feb.	Balance	GJ	10,000
15 Feb.	Bank	CB	6,000	6 Feb.	Purchases	PB	15,000
24 Feb.	Purchase returns	PRB	3,000	17 Feb.	Purchases	PB	2,000
28 Feb.	Balance	C/d	15,000				
			27,000				27,000
				28 Feb.	Balance	B/d	15,000

Solution

Creditors Ledger

John Molloy A/C

Date	Details	Fo	Debit – (€)	Credit + (€)	Balance (€)
2015					
1 Feb.	Balance	GJ			10,000
6 Feb.	Purchases	PB		15,000	25,000
10 Feb.	Cash	CB	3,000		22,000
15 Feb.	Bank	CB	6,000		16,000
17 Feb.	Purchases	PB		2,000	18,000
24 Feb.	Purchases returns	PRB	3,000		15,000

In Creditors Ledger

Figures in the Credit column increase the balance.
Figures in the Debit column reduce the balance.

See:
Higher Level
Paper I
Section A
2004 Q20
2002 Q15

Final Accounts of a Private Limited Company

Note: The stocktaking section is for Higher Level students only.

38 Trading Account

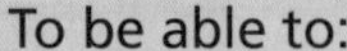

aims

To be able to:

- Present appropriate (simple) reports on stock and stocktaking
- Record stock in accounts
- Calculate closing stock as per accounts
- Operate the trading account in accordance with conventions of double entry
- Prepare a trading account from given data

- Interpret information presented in a trading account
- Calculate gross profit percentage

A. Purpose of a trading account

The purpose of a trading account is to find the gross profit or gross loss made by a business in the trading period.

B. Trading period

The trading period is the account period. It is usually twelve months (i.e. 1 January 2015–31 December 2015), but it could also be for six months.

C. Gross profit/gross loss

The gross profit/gross loss is the difference between sales and cost of sales.

D. Contents of a trading account

(1) **Sales** – Value of all sales during the year/turnover.

(2) **Sales Returns/Returns Inwards** – Goods returned to us by debtors.

(3) **Opening Stock** – Value of stock at start of year.

(4) **Purchases** – Goods bought for resale during the year.
(5) **Purchases Returns/Returns Outwards** – Goods returned to our suppliers.
(6) **Carriage Inwards** – Transport costs of purchases of goods for resale.
(7) **Customs Duty/Import Duty** – Tax on goods coming into the country.
(8) **Manufacturing Wages/Direct Wages** – Wages paid to manufacturing workers.
(9) **Closing Stock** – Value of stock at end of year.

Net Sales/Turnover = Sales − Sales Returns.

Net Purchases = Purchases − Purchases Returns.

Cost of Sales = Opening Stock + Purchases + Carriage Inwards
+ Customs Duty + Manufacturing Wages
− Closing Stock.

Gross Profit = Net Sales − Cost of Sales.

Question

From the following information, prepare the trading account of Platinum Ltd for year ending 31 December 2015.

- Sales €200,000
- Purchases €80,000
- Carriage inwards €6,000
- Manufacturing wages €3,000
- Sales returns €1,000
- Purchases returns €2,000
- Opening stock (1 January 2015) €10,000
- Closing stock (31 December 2015) €15,000
- Import duty €2,000

Solution

Trading Account of Platinum Ltd for Year Ending 31 December 2015				
			€	€
	Sales	200,000		
	Less sales returns		1,000	
	Net sales/turnover			199,000
	Deduct Cost of Sales			
	Stock 1/1/15		10,000	
	Purchases	80,000		
	Less purchases returns	2,000	78,000	
	Carriage inwards		6,000	
	Import duty		2,000	
	Manufacturing wages		3,000	
	Cost of goods available for sale		99,000	
	Less closing stock 31/12/15		15,000	
	Cost of Sales			84,000
	Gross Profit			115,000

E. Interpretation of information presented in a trading account

The trading account gives the owner(s) of a business a lot of valuable information. (Refer to trading account of Platinum Enterprises Ltd.)

1. Net sales/turnover

€199,000

2. Cost of sales

€84,000

3. Rate of stock turnover

This tells us how many times the stock is replaced in the business during the year.

$$\text{Formula} = \frac{\text{Cost of Sales}}{\text{Average Stock}} \qquad \frac{€84{,}000}{€12{,}500} = 6.72 \text{ Times}$$

$$\text{Average Stock} = \frac{\text{Opening Stock} + \text{Closing Stock}}{2}$$

$$\frac{€10{,}000 + €15{,}000}{2}$$

$$= \frac{€25{,}000}{2} = €12{,}500 = \text{Average Stock}$$

This business has a stock turnover of 6.72 times, which means that it replaces its stock every 54 days approx. (365 ÷ 6.72).

4. Gross profit margin/gross profit percentage

This rate shows how much gross profit was made on each €1.00 of sales.

key point

$$\text{Formula} = \frac{\text{Gross Profit} \times 100\%}{\text{Sales}} \qquad \frac{€115{,}000 \times 100\%}{€199{,}000} = 57.78\%$$

This firm is making a gross profit of 57.78c on every €1.00 of sales. The gross profit percentage can be compared with:

(a) Previous year's gross profit margin.

(b) Other firms in the same industry.

(c) The industry average.

F. Trading and non-trading stock

Trading stock is the stock of goods for resale to customers. Non-trading stock is stock of goods not for resale to customers, e.g. stock of heating, stock of stationery, stock of packing materials.

G. Stocktaking

The aim of stocktaking is to find out the value of goods in the business on a particular day. Stocktaking involves only trading stock.

1. Reasons for stocktaking

(a) To calculate the value of closing stock required for the trading account and balance sheet.

(b) To identify slow-moving items, damaged goods, and the condition of the stock.

(c) To find out whether goods have been stolen.

(d) To check stock records, and for stock control purposes.

(e) To identify goods that need to be ordered.

(f) To cross-check computer records.

2. Manual stocktaking procedure

(a) Close business on the day. Ensure that stock is low on the day.

(b) Divide store into sections. Arrange all stock in its correct place.

(c) Assign two stocktakers to each section: one will count the goods, the other will record the information on the stock sheets.

(d) Note all damaged or obsolete stock.

(e) On completion of task, stocksheets will be returned to the accounts department for valuation of stock on hand.

3. Valuation of stock

Stock is valued at the **lowest** of (a) cost price or (b) replacement price or (c) selling price.

exam Q

See:

Ordinary Level	**Higher Level**	**Higher Level**
Section A	Paper I	Paper II
2009 Q15	Section A	2005 Q2a
2004 Q10	2009 Q4	
2003 Q19	2008 Q11	
2000 Q19	2006 Q3a	
	2004 Q3b	
	2002 Q17	

39 Profit and Loss Account

Dealing with the main **overheads** incurred by business leading to the preparation of the profit and loss account.

To be able to:

- Operate the profit and loss account in accordance with conventions of double entry 
- Prepare a profit and loss account from given data
- Interpret data presented in profit and loss account form
- Calculate net profit percentage 
- Record overheads in accounts 

A. Purpose of a profit and loss account

The purpose of a profit and loss account is to **find the net profit or net loss made** by a business in the trading period – profit after all expenses are deducted.

B. Gains

Gains are income other than trading income received by a business, e.g. rent received, discount received, interest received, insurance received, bad debt recovered.

Net Profit/Net Loss = Gross Profit + Gains − Expenses

C. Expenses/overheads

Overheads are the expenses involved in the running of a business on a daily basis, e.g. rent, insurance, wages, telephone, carriage outwards (delivery costs of goods sold).

D. Finding net profit/net loss

(1) Add gains to gross profit.

(2) Subtract total expenses.

E. Monitoring overheads

Procedures to be in place to monitor overheads include:

- Prepare Budgets/Targets for each overhead.
- Record Actual overheads in Accounts/Analysed Cash Book.
- Compare the Actual overhead with the Budgeted overhead to see if they differ.
- Find out reasons for any difference found and take necessary action.

This is a Monitoring of Overheads (Expenses) Question. Answer all sections.

(A) Give **two** reasons why it is important for a business to monitor its overheads.

(B) The following table shows the Budget and Actual figures for a business's overheads for 2015.

(i) List the overheads whose actual figures are **greater than** the budgeted figures, and give one possible reason per overhead, for the difference.

(ii) List the overheads whose actual figures are **less than** the budgeted figures, and give one possible reason, per overhead, for the difference. (15)

Business overheads for 2015

Overheads	Budgeted €	Actual €
Rent	40,000	65,000
Advertising	20,000	15,000
Light and Heat	6,000	8,500
Insurance	8,000	10,000
Bank loan interest	7,000	5,000

Source: Junior Certificate Higher Level.

Solution

(A) (i) To identify the main overheads of a business, i.e. to see what the money is spent on.

(ii) To help in the planning process. Accurate figures are needed to make projections.

(iii) To compare the actual figures with budgeted figures to make sure the business is on target.

(iv) To identify areas where overruns take place.

(v) To make any necessary changes as soon as possible.

(B) (i) *Rent* – the landlord increased the rent.

Light and Heat – the winter was colder than expected.

Insurance – the premium was increased.

(ii) *Advertising* – in order to save, the business reduced its advertising expenditure.

Bank loan interest – the rate of interest fell.

F. Recording overheads

All overheads when paid are entered in the analysed cash book **credit side**. The relevant account is **debited** in the ledger.

Example

10 Jan. Paid insurance €2,000 by cheque.

Analysed Cash Book

Date	Details	Fo	Bank €	Date	Details	Fo	Bank €
				2014 10 Jan.	Insurance		2,000

Insurance A/C

Date	Details	Fo	Bank €	Date	Details	Fo	Bank €
2014 10 Jan.	Bank		2,000	2014 31 Jan.	P + L A/C		2,000

At end of year all overheads are closed off to the profit and loss account.

Debit P + L A/C (show under expenses).
Credit Overhead A/C (Insurance in above example).

Profit and Loss Account for year ending 31/1/2014

	<u>Expenses</u> Insurance		2,000

G. Difference between a trading A/C and a profit and loss A/C

Trading A/C shows	Profit and Loss A/C shows
(1) Sales (2) Opening stock, purchases and closing stock (3) Purchasing expenses (4) Gross profit/gross loss	(1) Gains (2) All expenses (3) Net profit/net loss

H. Capital expenditure and revenue expenditure

Capital Expenditure – Purchasing fixed assets which will last a number of years, e.g. equipment, machinery, premises, motor vehicles. These assets are recorded in the **balance sheet** and not in the profit and loss account.

Revenue Expenditure – Expenses involved in the day-to-day running of the business, e.g. wages, rent, insurance, advertising, telephone. These expenses are recorded in the **profit and loss account**.

Question

From the following, prepare a profit and loss account of Platinum Ltd for year ending 31 December 2015.

Gross profit	€115,000	Advertising	€1,600
Postage and telephone	€8,150	Audit fees	€4,000
Rent received	€6,800	Insurance received	€4,600
Bank charges	€200	Marketing expenses	€1,500
Loan interest	€6,500	Carriage outwards	€900
Bad debts w/o	€2,000	Sales staff's salaries	€10,400
Packing materials	€8,000	Travelling expenses	€9,000
Rent	€200	Showroom expenses	€2,500
Insurance	€2,500		

Solution

Profit and Loss Account of Platinum Ltd for Year Ending 31 December 2015

		€	€
	Gross Profit		115,000
	Add Gains		
	Insurance received	4,600	
	Rent received	6,800	11,400
			126,400
	Less Expenses		
	Postage and telephone	8,150	
	Bank charges	200	
	Loan interest	6,500	
	Bad debts W/o	2,000	
	Packing materials	8,000	
	Rent	200	
	Insurance	2,500	
	Advertising	1,600	
	Audit fees	4,000	
	Marketing expenses	1,500	
	Carriage outwards	900	
	Sales staff's salaries	10,400	
	Travelling expenses	9,000	
	Showroom expenses	2,500	57,450
	Net Profit		68,950

I. Interpretation of information presented in a profit and loss account

The profit and loss account gives the owner(s) of a business a lot of valuable information. (Refer to profit and loss account of Platinum Ltd.)

1. Total expenses

€57,450

2. Net profit

€68,950

3. Net profit margin/net profit percentage

This ratio shows how much net profit was made on each €1.00 of sales.

$$\text{Formula} = \frac{\text{Net Profit}}{\text{Sales}} \times 100\%$$

$$\frac{€68{,}950}{€199{,}000} \times 100\% = 34.64\%$$

This firm is making a net profit of 34.64c on every €1.00 of sales. The net profit percentage can be compared with:

(a) Previous year's net profit margin.

(b) Other firms in the same industry.

(c) The industry average.

See:

Higher Level

Paper I

Section A

2006 Q3b

2004 Q16

2003 Q7

2003 Q1

2002 Q4

2002 Q6

2001 Q5

40 Profit and Loss Appropriation Account

To be able to:

- Calculate dividends from given data 
- Prepare a profit and loss appropriation account
- Interpret data presented in a profit and loss appropriation account 

A. Purpose of profit and loss appropriation account

The purpose of the profit and loss appropriation account is to **show how the profit made is distributed** (shared out). The board of directors will recommend to the shareholders how the profit should be shared.

B. Ordinary share dividend

Profit made in a company belongs to the shareholders. Profit distributed to shareholders is called ordinary share dividend.

At the Annual General Meeting (AGM) it is decided how much of the profit should be paid out to the shareholders.

C. Retained earnings

It is normal practice to retain some profit for future use in the business. This is called retained earnings.

Ordinary Share Dividend is the amount of profit given to shareholders.

Retained Earnings is the amount of profit retained by the company for future use.

D. Calculation of ordinary share dividend

The dividend is calculated as a percentage of the issued share capital of the company.

Question

Platinum Ltd has an issued capital of €100,000 ordinary shares @ €1 each. Net profit for year ending 31 December 2015 was €68,950. The directors declared a dividend of 10%.

(A) Calculate the ordinary share dividend.

(B) Prepare the profit and loss appropriation account.

Solution

(A) Calculation of ordinary share dividend

Dividend = 10% of €100,000 (issued share capital) = €10,000.

Each shareholder will get 10c per share owned, e.g. John, who owns 2,000 shares, will get a dividend cheque of (2,000 × 10c) = €200.

The balance of the profit, i.e. €58,950, is retained by the company for future use.

(B) Profit and Loss Appropriation Account of Platinum Ltd for Year Ending 31 December 2015.

	Net profit			68,950
	Ordinary share dividend			10,000
	Retained earnings			58,950

E. Ledger account to record ordinary share dividend and retained earnings

Ordinary Share Dividend Account

Date	Details	Fo	Total	Date	Details	Fo	Total €
				31/12/15	Profit and Loss App. A/C		10,000

Retained Earnings Account

Date	Details	Fo	Total	Date	Details	Fo	Total €
				31/12/15	Profit and Loss App. A/C		58,950

(1) The ordinary share dividend is a **liability** of the business until it is paid – it will be entered in the balance sheet under current liabilities.

> **When the dividend is paid**
> **Debit** ordinary share dividend account.
> **Credit** bank account.

When the dividend is paid, there is no liability – thus there will be no entry in the balance sheet.

(2) The retained earnings will be entered in the balance sheet in the 'financed by' section under the heading 'Reserves'.

F. Why would a company retain profits at the end of a financial year?

(1) To finance expansion.
(2) To finance the purchase of fixed assets.
(3) To be able to pay dividends in years when losses are made.
(4) To save for the future.
(5) Repay any outstanding debt.

See:
Higher Level
Paper I
Section A
2009 Q5
2008 Q2
2007 Q11
2004 Q1
2004 Q18

41 Balance Sheet

To be able to:

- Differentiate between assets and liabilities
- Construct a simple company balance sheet
- Interpret information presented in balance sheet form

A. Balance sheet

A balance sheet is a statement of assets, liabilities and share capital of a business on a particular day.

Assets – Property or things that a business owns.
Liabilities – Debts that a business owes.
Share Capital – Money invested in the company by its owners/shareholders (money owed to shareholders).

B.

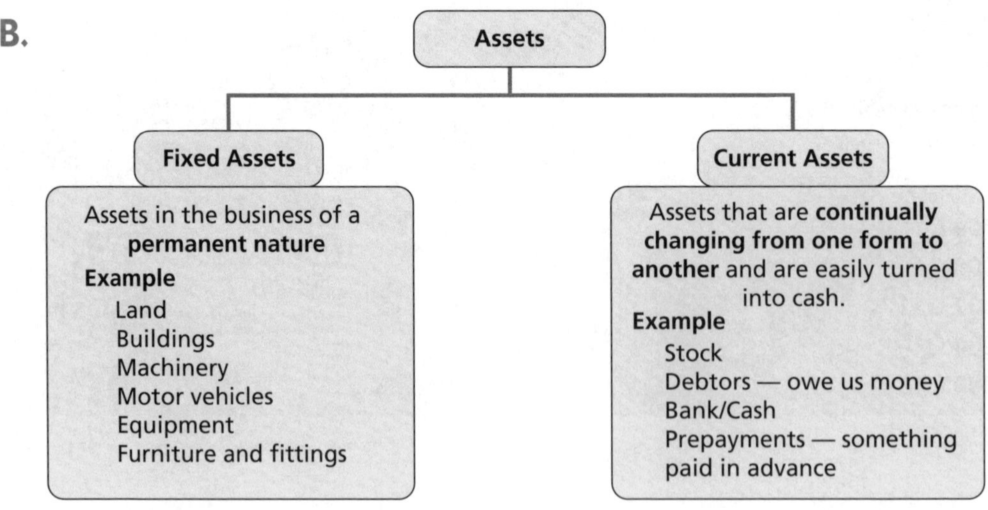

C.

Liabilities

Current Liabilities
(Creditors: **Amount falling due within one year**)

Debts that have to be paid back within one year.

Example
- Creditors
- Bank overdraft
- Dividends due and other expenses accrued (due)

Long-term Liabilities
(Creditors: **Amounts falling due after more than one year**)

Debts that will be repaid in the long term, usually between five years and twenty years.

Example
- Mortgage
- Long-term loan

D.

Share Capital

Money invested in the company by the shareholders (i.e. money is owed to shareholders)

Authorised Share Capital

Maximum amount of capital that company can raise through the issue of shares.

Issued Share Capital

This is the amount of finance that a limited company has raised to date from issuing shares to its shareholders (owners).

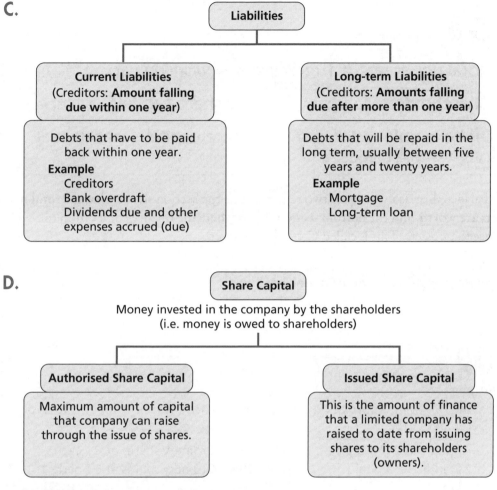

E. Reserves/retained earnings

Amount set aside out of profits and retained by the company for future use (balance in profit and loss appropriation account). This money is owed to shareholders.

F. Working capital

Working capital is the money available for the day-to-day running of the business.

Current assets – Current Liabilities = Working Capital

It shows whether the business can pay its debts as they fall due. If current assets are greater than current liabilities, the working capital is **positive** and the firm is said to be **liquid**. If current liabilities are greater than current assets, the working capital is **negative** and the firm is said to have a **liquidity problem** and to be **overtrading** (i.e. it cannot pay its debts as they arise).

G. Total net assets = fixed assets + working capital

H. Shareholders' funds = ordinary share capital + reserves

I. Capital employed = ordinary share capital + reserves + long-term liabilities

The balance sheet is made up of two sections. The top section shows what the **total net assets are worth**, and the bottom section shows where the finance comes from to finance these assets. This is called **Capital Employed**.

Total Net Assets must equal Capital Employed.

Question

From the following information prepare the balance sheet of Platinum Ltd as on 31 December 2015.

FB	Authorised share capital	€200,000	Ordinary shares at €1 each
FB	Issued share capital	€100,000	Ordinary shares at €1 each
FA	Land	€115,950	
CA	Closing stock	€15,000	
CL	Bank overdraft	€6,000	
CA	Debtors	€18,000	
FA	Buildings	€60,000	
FA	Machinery	€20,000	
RES	Retained earnings	€58,950	
CA	Bank	€6,000	
CL	Creditors	€10,000	
CA	Cash	€2,000	
CA	Prepayments	€1,000	
FA	Motor vehicles	€10,000	
CL	Dividends due	€10,000	
CL	Wages due	€3,000	
LTL	Long-term loan	€60,000	

Key

FB = Financed By

FA = Fixed Asset

CA = Current Asset

CL = Current Liability

RES = Reserves

LTL = Long-term Liability

Solution

Balance Sheet of Platinum Ltd as on 31 December 2015

		Cost €	Depreciation €	Value €
	Fixed Assets			
	Land	115,950		115,950
	Buildings	60,000		60,000
	Machinery	20,000		20,000
	Motor vehicles	10,000		10,000
		205,950		205,950
	Current Assets			
	Closing stock	15,000		
	Debtors	18,000		
	Bank	6,000		
	Cash	2,000		
	Prepayments	1,000	42,000	
	Less Current Liabilities (Creditors: Amounts falling due within one year)			
	Bank overdraft	6,000		
	Creditors	10,000		
	Dividends due	10,000		
	Wages due	3,000	29,000	
	Working capital			+ 13,000
	Total net assets			218,950
	FINANCED BY			
	Share capital and Reserves			
	(Authorised Issued)			
	200,000 ordinary shares @ €1 each			200,000
				100,000
	Reserves			
	Retained earnings			58,950
				158,950
	Long-term Liabilities (Creditors: Amounts falling due after more than one year)			
	Long-term loan			60,000
	Capital employed			218,950

Revision Trading, Profit and Loss Account, Appropriation Account and Balance Sheet (Without Adjustments)

To be able to:

- Prepare final accounts and balance sheet from a given date

Type of Question on Final Accounts at Ordinary Level

This question on the Junior Certificate examination requires the preparation of a **full set of final accounts** from information presented in a trial balance with closing stock listed underneath the trial balance. There also may be one or two other **theory** questions included.

PROCEDURE

(1) Examine each item in the trial balance, and establish where it will go in the accounts.

> **NB** Debit column contains Assets and Expenses.
> Credit column contains Liabilities and Gains.

(2) Write down on the question where each item goes, i.e. T (Trading A/C), P & L (Profit and Loss A/C), App. (Appropriation A/C), B/S (Balance Sheet).

(3) Tick off each item as you enter it in the accounts.

This is a question on Final Accounts and Balance Sheet (Ordinary Level).

Answer all parts of this question:

The following Trial Balance was taken from the books of Morgan Ltd on 31 December 2011, the end of its financial year. The Authorised Share Capital is 300,000 Ordinary Shares at €1 each.

Trial Balance as at 31 December 2011

		Dr €	Cr €
T	Cash Sales		204,000
T	Cash Purchases	137,460	
T	Carriage Inwards	2,160	
T	Opening Stock at 1 January 2011	28,500	
P+L	Rent	14,580	
P+L	Wages	39,900	
P+L	Insurance	8,940	
P+L	Advertising	1,500	
P+L	Heating and Lighting	11,760	
APP	Dividend Paid	2,640	
B/S	Cash in Hand	4,260	
B/S	Bank Overdraft		26,100
B/S	Issued Share Capital in €1 Shares		240,000
B/S	Premises	182,400	
B/S	Furniture and Fittings	36,000	
		470,100	470,100

T, B/S Closing Stock at 31 December 2011 was €51,000.

(A) From the above figures, prepare:

(i) A **Trading, Profit and Loss Appropriation Account** of Morgan Ltd for the year ended 31 December 2011. (45)

(ii) A **Balance Sheet** as at 31 December 2011.

(B) Explain what is meant by **'Bank Overdraft'**. (5)

(C) Find what percentage of the Cash Sales is the Net Profit. Show your answer and workings. (10)

(60 marks)

Suggested solution and marking scheme

(A)(i) Trading, Profit and Loss Appropriation Account of Morgan Ltd for the year ended 31 December 2011

	Sales			204,000 (1)
	COST OF SALES			
	Opening stock		28,500 (1)	
	Purchases		137,460 (1)	
	Carriage Inwards		2,160 (1)	139,620 (1)
			168,120 (1)	
	Closing Stock		51,000 (1)	117,120 (1)
	Gross Profit(2)			86,880 (1)
	Less Expenditure			
	Rent		14,580 (1)	
	Wages		39,900 (1)	
	Insurance		8,940 (1)	
	Advertising		1,500 (1)	
	Heating and Lighting		11,760 (1)	76,680 (1)
	Net Profit(2)			10,200 (2)
	Less Dividends			2,640 (2)
	Reserves			7,560 (2)

Marking Scheme – Final Accounts and Balance Sheet Question

Trading and Profit & Loss	**14 figures @ 1 mark each**	**= 14 marks**
Gross Profit 4 marks	**(2 figure, 2 words)**	**= 4 marks**
Net Profit 4 marks	**(2 figure, 2 words)**	**= 4 marks**
Dividends figure		**= 2 marks**
Reserves figure		**= 2 marks**
		26 marks

(ii) Balance Sheet of Morgan Ltd as at 31 December 2011 (2)

		COST	DEP	NBV
	FIXED ASSETS (1)			
	Premises			182,400 (1)
	Furniture and Fittings			36,000 (1)
				218,400 (1)
	CURRENT ASSETS (1)			
	Closing Stock	51,000 (1)		
	Cash in hand	4,260 (1)	55,260 (1)	
	Less Current Liabilities (1)			
	Bank Overdraft		26,100 (1)	
	Working Capital			29,160 (1)
	TOTAL NET ASSETS			247,560 (1)
	Financed by (1)			
	Ordinary Share Capital			300,000 (1)
	Authorised			
	Issued			240,000 (1)
	Reserves			7,560 (1)
	CAPITAL EMPLOYED			247,560 (1)

Marking Scheme

Balance sheet

Date	**2 marks**
Balance sheet subtitles 4 @ 1 mark	**4 marks**
13 figures @ 1 mark each	**13 marks**
	19 marks

(B) A Bank Overdraft means that a **bank allows a customer to write cheques or withdraw money (1) from his or her current account (1) up to a stated limit. Interest must be paid on the overdrawn balance. (1)** An overdraft is a short-term loan (1) which must be repaid within a year.

(5 marks)

(C) Percentage of the Cash Sales which is the Net Profit:

Answer: 5% (5 marks)

Workings: $\frac{10{,}200(1) \times 100(1)}{204{,}000(1) \times (1)} = 5(1)$

Marking Scheme

Correct Net Profit Percentage 5 marks

Workings (essential) 5 marks

(10 marks)

43 Adjustments to Final Accounts

Note: Chapter 43 is for Higher Level students only.

To be able to:

- Calculate adjustments
- Calculate depreciation using straight line method
- Record adjustments in accounts

The aim of final accounts is to **give a 'true and fair picture' of the business**, i.e. finding true figures for gross profit and net profit. To do this, certain adjustments must be made.

- Accruals (amounts due).
- Prepayments (amounts paid in advance).
- Bad debts written off.
- Depreciation – straight line.
- Dividends.
- Closing stocks.

Because these adjustments are not in the trial balance, they are not therefore in the books of account and must be included in the accounts twice, once debit/once credit.
One entry will be in the **trading or profit and loss account**.
The second entry will be in the **balance sheet**.

A. Accruals (Amounts due)

1. Accrued expenses (Expenses due by a firm)

All expenses relating to the trading period must be included in the accounts, whether paid or not.

Question

O'Flynn Ltd paid €10,000 insurance by cheque on 1 January 2016, but on 31 December there was still €1,000 due for the year 2016.

Solution

Entries in the Profit and Loss Account and Balance Sheet

RULES

(i) Add amount due on to amount paid in profit and loss account.

(ii) Show amount due as a **current liability** in balance sheet.

Profit and Loss Account (Extract) for Year Ending 31 December 2016

	Expenses				
	Insurance		10,000		
	Add insurance due		1,000	11,000	

Balance Sheet (Extract) as on 31 December 2016

	Current Liabilities				
	Insurance due		1,000		

2. Accrued income (Expenses due to the firm)

This is income for the period in question but not yet received, e.g.

- Rent receivable due.
- Commission receivable due.
- Insurance receivable due.

RULES

(i) Add amount due to the amount received in the gains section of the profit and loss account.

(ii) Show amount due as a **current asset** in balance sheet.

Question

Insurance Receivable €15,000 for year ending 31 December 2017.

Insurance Receivable due €2,000 at the end of December 2017.

Solution

Profit and Loss Account (Extract) for Year Ending 31 December 2017

	Gains				
	Insurance Receivable			15,000	
	Add insurance Receivable due			2,000	17,000

Balance Sheet (Extract) as on 31 December 2017

	Current Assets Insurance Receivable due		2,000		

B. Prepayments (amounts paid in advance)

1. Prepayment made by our business

This occurs when an amount is paid in this trading period, but it is for the next trading period (i.e. paid in advance). Since we can put only expenses that belong to a trading period into the profit and loss account, prepayments must be deducted.

RULES

(i) Deduct amount prepaid from expense figure in profit and loss account.

(ii) Show amount prepaid as a **current asset** in Balance Sheet.

Question

O'Callaghan Ltd rented a warehouse on 1 February 2016 for €500 per month. It paid €6,000 rent for the year ended 31 January 2017 (twelve months).

We can charge only eleven months rent to the profit and loss account for 2016 because one month's rent is paid for January 2017.

Solution

Profit and Loss Account (Extract) for Year Ending 31 December 2016

	Expenses				
	Rent		6,000		
	Less rent prepaid		500	5,500	

Balance Sheet (Extract) as on 31 December 2016

	Current Assets				
	Rent prepaid		500		

2. Prepayments made to our business

If a business has surplus storage space, it may (sublet) rent some of it to another business. The rent we get is called rent receivable. Sometimes this rent receivable is prepaid to us (i.e. it is received before it is due).

RULES

(i) Subtract amount prepaid from amount received in the gains in profit and loss account.

(ii) Show amount prepaid as a **current liability** in balance sheet.

Question

Rent received €1,000 for year ending 31 December 2017.

Rent receivable prepaid €100 at end of December 2017.

Solution

Profit and Loss Account (Extract) for Year Ending 31 December 2017

	Gains				
	Rent received			1,000	
	Subtract rent receivable prepaid			100	900

Balance Sheet (Extract) as on 31 December 2017

	Current Liabilities				
	Rent receivable prepaid			100	

C. Bad debts written off

A bad debt arises when a debtor is declared bankrupt and cannot pay what is owed. The business must then write the amount off as a bad debt (loss to the business).

Question

1/1/16 Debtors €10,000.

Adjustment 31.12.16 Bad debts to be written off €1,000.

Solution

Writing up Profit and Loss Account and Balance Sheet

RULES

(i) Show bad debts written off as **an expense** in the profit and loss account.
(ii) Deduct bad debts from debtors in the balance sheet.

Profit and Loss Account (Extract) for year ending 31/12/2016

	Expenses Bad debts		1,000		

Balance Sheet (Extract) as on 31/12/2016

	Current Assets Debtors Less bad debts written off		10,000 1,000	9,000	

NB Bad debts figure in trial balance – show as expense in P & L A/C. Do not deduct from debtors in balance sheet. (It is already deducted.)

Methods by which a business could reduce its bad debts

- Ask customer to supply a bank reference or trade reference before selling goods on credit.
- Limit the amount of credit given to the customer.
- Give cash discounts to encourage prompt payment.
- Charge interest on overdue accounts.

D. Depreciation – straight line

Depreciation is the reduction in the value of an asset due to usage, wear and tear, and age.

Depreciation is calculated by getting a percentage of the cost of the asset – the figure will be the same every year. This is called straight line depreciation.

RULES

(i) Show depreciation as **an expense** in the profit and loss account.

(ii) Deduct depreciation from the cost of the asset in the fixed assets section of the balance sheet.

Question

Machinery 1 January 2017 €10,000.

Adjustment Depreciate machinery by 20%.

Solution

Machinery Account

Date	Details	Fo	Total €	Date	Details	Fo	Total €
1/1/17	Balance		10,000	31/12/17	Depreciation		2,000
				31/12/17	Balance	B/d	8,000
			10,000				10,000
31/12/17	Balance	C/d	8,000				

Depreciation Account

Date	Details	Fo	Total €	Date	Details	Fo	Total €
31/12/17			2,000	31/12/17	Profit and Loss A/C		2,000

Profit and Loss Account (Extract) for Year Ending 31 December 2017

	Expenses Depreciation of machinery			2,000	

Balance Sheet (Extract) as on 31 December 2017

	Fixed Assets		Cost €	Deprec. €	Net Bk Val. €
	Machinery		10,000	2,000	8,000

E. Dividends

Dividends can be paid or proposed.

1. Dividends paid

Dividends paid will appear in the debit column of the trial balance. Since they are paid, there is no liability in the balance sheet. **Dividends paid are entered in the profit and loss appropriation account only.**

2. Dividends proposed

Dividends proposed will appear as an adjustment. Dividends proposed are calculated as a percentage of the issued share capital of the company.

RULES

(i) Calculate the dividend, and enter it as a **deduction from net profit in the profit and loss appropriation account.**

(ii) Show dividend due as a **current liability** in the balance sheet.

F. Closing stocks

1. Closing stocks of goods

Closing stock is entered in the **trading account** and as a **current asset** in the balance sheet.

2. Closing stocks of oil and stationery etc., i.e. non-trading stocks

RULES

(i) **Subtract** closing stock from **appropriate expenses** in the profit and loss account.

(ii) Show closing stock as a **current asset** in the balance sheet.

See:

Higher Level

Paper I

Section A

2009 Q11

2001 Q18

Revision Final Accounts and Balance Sheet (Including Adjustments)

Note: Chapter 44 is for Higher Level students only.

To be able to:

- Prepare final accounts and balance sheet (including adjustments) from given data

A. Type of exam question

This question is given in the form of a trial balance, i.e. figures in the debit column and credit column.

Debit Column Assets/Expenses	Credit Column Liabilities/Gains

B. Adjustments

Adjustments will be given under the totals of the trial balance, and items in the trial balance that must be adjusted should be marked with '*'.

Adjustments must be entered twice: once in the Trading, Profit & Loss account and once in the Balance Sheet.

C. Summary of adjustments

Adjustment	How Adjustment Is Treated in Profit and Loss Account	How Adjustment Is Treated in Balance Sheet
(1) Accruals (a) Due by firm (b) Due to firm	 Add to amount paid Add to amount received	 Current liability Current asset
(2) Prepayments (a) Made by us (b) Made to us	 Deduct from expense Deduct from amount received	 Current asset Current liability
(3) Bad debt written off	Show as expense	Deduct from debtors
(4) Depreciation	Show as expense	Deduct from fixed asset
(5) Dividends (a) Paid (b) Proposed	Enter in profit and loss appropriation account Enter in profit and loss appropriation account	No entry Current liability
(6) Closing Stock (a) Goods (b) Non-trading stock	 Trading account Deduct from expense	 Current asset Current asset

This is a Final Accounts and Balance Sheet Question.

The following Trial Balance was extracted from the books of RUDDY Ltd on 31 August 2011. The Authorised Share Capital is 560,000 €1 Ordinary Shares.

		DR	CR
		€	€
T	Purchases and Sales T	208,000	560,000
T	Sales Returns	16,000	
T	Opening Stock 01/09/2010	28,800	
CA	Debtors and Creditors CL	24,000	28,800
T	Carriage Inwards	4,800	
FA	Buildings	392,000	
LTL	15 Year Loan		32,000
GAIN	Rent Receivable		12,800
EXP	Insurance	3,200	
FA	Delivery Vans	124,800	
EXP	Wages	83,200	
CA	Cash	6,400	
EXP	Repairs	8,000	
APP	Reserves (Profit and Loss Balance)		41,600
FA	Equipment	176,000	
FB	Issued Share Capital: 400,000 €1 shares		400,000
		1,075,200	1,075,200

(A) You are required to prepare the Company's **Trading, Profit and Loss and Appropriation** Account for the year ending 31 August 2011 and a **Balance Sheet** as on that date.

You are given the following information as on 31 August 2011.

1. Closing Stock €33,000 [T + CA]

2. Wages Due €8,000 [EXP + CL]

3. Rent Receivable Prepaid €3,200 [GAIN + CL]

4. Dividends Declared 20% [APP + CL]

5. Depreciation: Delivery Vans 12% [EXP + FA]

Equipment 15% [EXP + FA] (35)

(B) Calculate the average stock for the year. (5)

(40 marks)

Suggested solution and marking scheme

(A) Trading and profit and loss (1)/ and appropriation account of Ruddy (1/2) Ltd for year ended 31/8/2011 (1½)

	Sales		560,000 (1/2)	
	Less Sales Returns		16,000 (1/2)	544,000 (1/2)
	Less Cost of Sales			
	Opening Stock 1/9/2010		28,800 (1/2)	
	Purchases	208,000 (1/2)		
	Carriage Inwards		4,800 (1/2)	
	Less Closing Stock 31/8/11		33,600 (1/2)	
	Cost of Sales			208,000 (1/2)
	Gross Profit			336,000 (1/2)
	Add Gains			
	Rent Receivable		12,800 (1/2)	
	Less Rent Receivable Prepaid		3,200 (1/2)	9,600 (1/2)
				345,600 (1/2)
	Less Expenses			
	Insurance		3,200 (1/2)	
	Wages	83,200 (1/2)		
	Add Wages Due	8,000 (1/2)	91,200 (1/2)	
	Repairs		8,000 (1/2)	
	Depreciation: Delivery Vans	14,976 (1/2)		
	: Equipment	26,400 (1/2)	41,376 (1/2)	143,776 (1/2)
	Net Profit			201,824 (1/2)
	Less Dividends			80,000 (1)
				121,824 (1/2)
	Add Opening Balance			41,600 (1)
	Reserves			163,424 (1/2)

(18 marks)

Alternative presentation of figures where expenses are deducted before adding gains and where opening Profit and Loss Account is added back before deducting dividends

Gross Profit	336,000
Less Expenses	143,776
	192,224
Add Gains	9,600
Net Profit	201,824
Add Opening Profit and Loss Balance	41,600
	243,424
Less Dividends	80,000
Reserves	163,424

Balance Sheet of Ruddy Ltd (1/2) as on 31/8/2011 (1/2)

		€	€	€
	Fixed Assets	Cost	Deprec.	NBV
	Buildings	392,000 (1/2)		392,000 (1/2)
	Delivery Vans	124,800 (1/2)	14,976 (1/2)	109,824 (1/2)
	Equipment	176,000 (1/2)	26,400 (1/2)	149,600 (1/2)
		692,800 (1/2)	41,376 (1/2)	651,424 (1/2)
	Current Assets			
	Closing Stock	33,600 (1/2)		
	Debtors	24,000 (1/2)		
	Cash	6,400 (1/2)	64,000 (1/2)	
	Less Current Liabilities			
	Wages due	8,000 (1/2)		
	Creditors	28,800 (1/2)		
	Dividends	80,000 (1)		
	Rent Receivable Prepaid	3,200 (1/2)	120,000 (1/2)	
	Total Net Assets			595,424 (1/2)
	Financed by	Authorised	Issued	
	560,000 € ordinary shares	560,000 (1)	400,000 (1)	
	Add Reserves		163,424 (1/2)	563,424 (1/2)
	Long-term Liabilities			
	15-year loan			15,000 (1)
	Capital employed			595,424 (1/2)

(17 marks)

Alternative presentation of 'financed by' section of Balance Sheet if Opening Profit and Loss balance was not added in the TPLA Account.

Financed by	
Issued Share Capital	400,000
Add Opening Profit & Loss Balance	41,600
Add Profit and Loss Balance after dividends	121,824
	563,424
Add 15 year loan	32,000
	595,424

(B) Average Stock Calculation

Formula

$$\frac{\text{Opening Stock} + \text{Closing Stock (2)}}{2}$$

$$= \frac{28{,}800 + 33{,}600\ (2)}{2}$$

$= 31{,}200(1)$

(5 marks)

(Total 40 marks)

See:

Higher Level	**Higher Level**
Paper I	Paper II
Section A	2009 Q4
2008 Q16	2008 Q4
2005 Q6	2007 Q4
	2006 Q4
	2005 Q4

Reporting on Accounts

Having completed the preparation of final accounts you are now introduced to the **analysis** of this information and the **compiling of reports** thereon.

45 Assessing a Business

Note: Chapter 45 is for Higher Level students only.

To be able to:

- Interpret and compare final accounts
- Interpret and compare ratios
- Select and calculate relevant ratios
- Compile a report (in simple form) on final accounts and balance sheet together with valid recommendations

A. Introduction

It is important that accounts are interpreted or made clear for the benefit of interested parties.

This is done by the use of **ratios** that show the relationships between figures.

These figures are then compared with

(1) Previous year's figures.

(2) Other firms in the same industry.

B. Parties interested in the accounts of a company

(1) **Banker** – Can loans and overdrafts be repaid?

(2) **Creditors** – Can business pay for goods supplied on credit?

(3) **Shareholders** – How much profit does the company make, and what will the dividend per share be?

(4) **Employees** – Is employment secure?

(5) **Investors** – Is company a good investment?

(6) **Management** – Is company performing better or worse than last year?

(7) **Revenue Commissioners** – How much profit is company making for tax purposes?

C. Interpretation of accounts using ratios

A company can be assessed by using the following headings or areas:

- Profitability
- Liquidity
- Efficiency
- Solvency
- Dividend Policy

1. Profitability

The profitability ratios show how successful the management of the business was in making profit for the company.

Importance of profitability ratios for business are:

- To compare the return from the business with the return of a risk-free investment.
- To compare the return with that of a similar business.
- To compare the returns with the previous year.
- To help management in decision-making.
- Positive returns make it easier to raise funds.
- Positive returns boost share price.

The profitability ratios are as follows:

Ratio	Formula	Ans.	Information Given by Ratio
(a) Return on capital employed	$\frac{\text{Net Profit}}{\text{Capital Employed}} \times 100$	Percentage %	Shows return on total amount invested in company and should be compared with return from banks or other firms.
(b) Gross profit percentage/ margin	$\frac{\text{Gross Profit}}{\text{Sales}} \times 100$	Percentage %	Tells us how much gross profit was made on each €1.00 of sales. Compare with last year or other firms.
(c) Net profit percentage/ margin	$\frac{\text{Net Profit}}{\text{Sales}} \times 100$	Percentage %	Tells us how much net profit was made on each €1.00 of sales. Compare with last year or other firms.

2. Liquidity

Liquidity is the ability of the company to pay its debts as they fall due. Liquidity is measured by subtracting current liabilities from current assets. This is called **working capital**.

Working Capital = Current Assets − Current Liabilities

If the working capital is positive, the firm is said to be liquid. If the working capital is negative, the firm is said to be **overtrading**.

Overtrading: This is where a company has a negative working capital , i.e. current liabilities are greater than current assets.

The Liquidity Ratios are:

Ratio	Formula	Ans.	Information Given by Ratio
(a) Current ratio or working capital ratio	Current Assets: Current Liabilities	Ratio	Tells us if the company has enough current assets to pay its current liabilities. A company should have a current ratio of 2:1, i.e. current assets should be double current liabilities.
(b) Quick asset ratio or acid test ratio	Current Assets – Closing Stock: Current Liabilities	Ratio	Omits closing stock, as stock may not be quickly turned into cash. The recommended ratio is 1:1, i.e. a healthy firm should be able to pay its current liabilities out of liquid assets (i.e. CA – stock).

3. Efficiency

Efficiency ratios measure how well the assets of a business are used. The main ratio is the rate of stock turnover.

Ratio	Formula	Ans.	Information Given by Ratio
(a) Rate of stock turnover	$\frac{\text{Cost of Sales}}{\text{Average Stock}}$	Times	Tells us how many times the stock is replaced in the business during the year.

4. Solvency

This is the ability of a company to pay all its debts as they fall due for payment. A firm is **solvent** if total assets (Current and Fixed) are greater than its liabilities (Current and Long-term).

Total Assets = Fixed Assets + Current Assets

Outside Liabilities = Current Liabilities + Long-term Liabilities

If outside liabilities are greater than total assets, the firm is said to be **insolvent** or **bankrupt**. (Firm cannot continue in business.)

Ratio	Formula	Ans.	Information Given by Ratio
Solvency	Total Assets: Outside Liabilities	Ratio	Tells us whether business is solvent or insolvent.

5. Dividend policy

Dividend is the amount of profit given to shareholders. It is the board of directors which decides how much of a dividend will be paid to shareholders. The rate of dividend ratio tells us how much dividend is paid to shareholders.

Ratio	Formula	Ans.	Information Given by Ratio
Rate of dividend	$\frac{\text{Dividend Paid}}{\text{Issued Share Capital}} \times 100$	Percentage %	Rate of dividend paid to shareholders.

Question

Scott Ltd has an authorised share capital of 400,000 €1 ordinary shares. Its accounts for year ended 31 December 2016 are as follows.

Trading and Profit and Loss Account for Year Ending 31 December 2016

	Sales		100,000
	Deduct Cost of Sales		
	Opening stock	6,000	
	Purchases	44,000	
	Cost of goods available	50,000	
	Less closing stock	10,000	
	Cost of Sales		40,000
	Gross Profit		60,000
	Less expenses		10,000
	Net Profit		50,000
	Less dividend 10%		20,000
	Retained earnings		30,000

Balance Sheet as on 31 December 2016

	FIXED ASSETS			260,000
	Current Assets			
	Closing stock	10,000		
	Debtors	10,000		
	Bank	60,000	80,000	
	Current Liabilities			
	(Creditors: Amounts falling due within one year)			
	Creditors	8,000		
	Dividend due	20,000		
	Accruals	12,000	40,000	
	Working capital			40,000
	Total Net Assets			**300,000**
	FINANCED BY			
	Authorised Share Capital			400,000
	Issued share capital			200,000
	Retained Earnings			30,000
	Long-term Liabilities			
	(Creditors: Amounts falling due after more than one year)			
	Long-term loan			70,000
	Capital Employed			**300,000**

Calculate and comment on:

(1) Return on capital employed.

(2) Gross profit margin.

(3) Net profit margin.

(4) Working capital ratio.

(5) Acid test ratio.

(6) Rate of stock turnover.

(7) Solvency ratio.

(8) Rate of dividend.

Solution

Ratio	Formula	Figures	Answer	Comment
1. Return on capital employed	$\frac{\text{Net Profit}}{\text{Capital Employed}} \times 100$	$\frac{50,000}{300,000} \times 100$	16.66%	Satisfactory when compared with rates of return from bank or building society.
2. Gross profit margin	$\frac{\text{Gross Profit}}{\text{Sales}} \times 100$	$\frac{60,000}{100,000} \times 100$	60%	This business is making a gross profit of 60c on every €1.00 of sales.
3. Net profit margin	$\frac{\text{Net Profit}}{\text{Sales}} \times 100$	$\frac{50,000}{100,000} \times 100$	50%	This business is making a net profit of 50c on each €1.00 of sales.
4. Working capital ratio	Current Assets : Current Liabilities	80,000 : 40,000	2 : 1	This ratio is ideal because the recommended working capital ratio is 2 : 1. Firm can pay debts as they fall due from current assets. Firm has no liquidity problem.
5. Acid test ratio	CA – Closing Stock : CL	80,000 –10,000 : 40,000 70,000 : 40,000	1.75 : 1	This ratio is very satisfactory as the recommended acid test ratio is 1 : 1. Firm can pay current liabilities from liquid assets.
6. Rate of stock turnover	$\frac{\text{Cost of Sales}}{\text{Average Stock}}$	$\frac{40,000}{8,000}$	5 times	Stock is being replaced 5 times a year in business. (New stock is purchased every 10.5 weeks.)
7. Solvency ratio	Total Assets : Outside Liabilities	340,000 : 110,000	3.09 : 1	This business is solvent, as total assets are greater than outside liabilities.
8. Rate of dividend	$\frac{\text{Dividend Paid}}{\text{Issued Share Capital}} \times 100$	$\frac{20,000}{200,000} \times 100$	10%	Firm paid a 10% dividend to shareholders.

Comparison of Accounts and Balance Sheet and Preparation of a Report

To get an accurate picture of any business, it is necessary to compare the accounts and balance sheets of a number of trading periods. Once the accounts have been assessed and the ratios prepared, a report on the performance of the company is compiled for interested parties.

This is a question on Report Writing and Assessing a Business.

Answer all parts of this question:

(A) The following information was supplied by the Directors of ROSS Ltd, Bridge Street, Kildare, for the year 2009.

	€
Sales	300,000
Capital Employed	450,000
Issued Share Capital	200,000
Current Assets	80,000
Net Profit	45,000
Current Liabilities	40,000
Dividend paid	40,000

The following **four** ratios are used by ROSS Ltd to assess the performance of its business.

1. Net Profit Percentage.
2. Current Ratio.
3. Return on Capital employed.
4. Rate of Dividend.

Using the information supplied, calculate the four ratios for **2009**. (16)

(B) The relevant figures for **2008** were:

Net Profit Percentage	18%
Current Ratio	1.6 : 1
Return on Capital Employed	7%
Rate of Dividend	10%

Assume you are BRIAN PETERS, Financial Consultant, Riverview, Newbridge, Co. Kildare. Prepare a report, dated 10 January 2010 for the directors of ROSS Ltd, comparing and commenting on the performance of the company for 2008 and 2009. (24)

(40 marks)

Solution and marking scheme

Assessing a business and report writing

(A) Ratio Calculations for 2009

Ratio	Formula	Workings	Answer
Net Profit Percentage	$\frac{\text{Net Profit}}{\text{Sales}} \times 100$	$\frac{€45{,}000}{€300{,}000} \times 100$	15% (4)
Current Ratio	Current Assets : Current Liabilities	80,000 : 40,000	2 : 1 (4)
Return on Capital Employed	$\frac{\text{Net Profit}}{\text{Capital Employed}} \times 100$	$\frac{€45{,}000}{€450{,}000} \times 100$	10% (4)
Rate of Dividend	$\frac{\text{Dividend paid}}{\text{Issued Share Capital}} \times 100$	$\frac{€40{,}000}{€200{,}000} \times 100$	20% (4)

4 correct answers @ 4 marks each

(B) REPORT ON ROSS LTD

*Riverview
Newbridge
Co. Kildare **(2 marks)**

*10 January 2010 **(2 marks)**

*Report on the performance of Ross Ltd for years 2008 and 2009 **(2 marks)**

The following are my main findings.

Main Findings:

Ratio	2009	2008
Net Profit Percentage	15%	18%

Comment: The net profit percentage has fallen by 3%. **(2 marks)**

Ratio	2009	2008
Current Ratio	2 : 1	1.6 : 1

Comment: The liquidity situation is improving. (1)

The ratio is now at the recommended level in 2009. (1)

(2 marks)

	2009	2008
Return on Capital employed	10%	7%

Comment: The return on capital employed has improved by 3%. (1)

In both years it was better than what would be received on a Bank Deposit Account. (1)

(2 marks)

	2009	2008
Rate of Dividend	20%	10%

Comment: In 2009 the shareholders received double the amount of dividends that they got in 2008. **(2 marks)**

*I am available to discuss this Report if required **(2 marks)**

*Brian Peters **(2 marks)**

*Financial Consultant **(2 marks)**

Reasons why a business would use ratio analysis

(1) To **assess its performance** against:
- Previous years.
- Other enterprises.
- Other forms of investment.

(2) To calculate its **level of profitability** through:
- Gross profit margin.
- Net profit margin.
- Return on capital employed.

(3) To calculate its **level of liquidity** through:
- Working capital ratio.
- Acid test ratio.

(4) To help management make **informed decisions**.

(5) To present additional information about itself in reports for interested parties.

Limitations of final accounts in assessing a business

The final accounts of a business give us financial information only. The following are not taken into account.

(1) **Experienced and efficient staff. Management/staff relationships**. Loyal staff and customers.

(2) **Balance sheet holds only for a particular day.**

(3) Assets may not be shown at their current values – some assets may have appreciated over the years, e.g. premises.

(4) The accounts of a business are a record of **past transactions** and can be used only as an estimate of future performance.

(5) Final accounts only give information about a **particular year**.

46 Club Accounts

To be able to:

- Prepare and analyse receipts and payments account
- HL Prepare an income and expenditure account (incorporating adjustments which are Higher Level only)
- Prepare a balance sheet
- Present a simple treasurer's report

A. Introduction

A club is an organisation set up for the benefit of its members. Members elect officers at its AGM to run the club.

All clubs must keep a record of their financial activities during the year. They are non-profit-making organisations.

B. Functions of club officers

Chairperson	Secretary	Treasurer
1. Runs club.	1. Calls meetings.	1. Collects subscriptions. 2. Issues receipts for all money received.
2. Chairs meetings.	2. Sends agenda to members.	3. Lodges money received to bank account.
3. Keeps order at meetings.	3. Arranges the meetings.	4. Makes all club payments.
4. Follows agenda. 5. Puts motions to a vote.	4. Takes notes at meetings and writes up minutes.	5. Keeps records. 6. Prepares annual accounts. 7. Prepares a financial report for AGM.

C. Annual general meeting (AGM)

Members attend, speak and vote on various items on the agenda (programme for meeting).

The treasurer presents his report to the members at the AGM.

1. Purpose of treasurer's report

(a) To inform members of the club's cash position at the end of the year.
(b) To inform members if the club had a surplus or deficit for the year.
(c) To give details of the club's assets and liabilities.
(d) To provide a basis for future financial decisions, i.e. subscriptions, borrowings, fundraising, expansion, etc.
(e) To state the main items of capital expenditure.

2. Agenda

The agenda is the programme for the meeting sent by the secretary to all members, outlining the items to be discussed at the meeting.

Agenda for AGM of a Club

The AGM of Masters Tennis Club will be held on 10 March 2015 at 8 p.m. at the Clubhouse.

The agenda is as follows:

(a) Minutes of last AGM
(b) Matters arising from minutes
(c) Chairperson's Report
(d) Secretary's Report
(e) Treasurer's Report
(f) Election of Officers
(g) AOB.

Mary Green
Secretary

3. Minutes of meetings

Minutes are a written record of discussions and decisions taken at meetings. They are prepared by the secretary of the club.

D. Accounts kept by a club

The following accounts are usually kept by the treasurer of a club.

- Analysed cash book/analysed receipts and payments book, usually written up on a monthly basis.
- Receipts and payments account for the year.
- Income and expenditure account for the year.
- Balance sheet on the last day of the year.

1. Analysed cash book/analysed receipts and payments book

- It is the same as a cash book for business.
- Receipts on the debit side.
- Payments on the credit side.
- It is analysed into suitable columns to meet the requirements of the club.

2. Receipts and payments account (cash book)

A receipts and payments account is prepared at the end of the year using totals from analysis columns.

It shows:

(a) Cash balance at **start** of year.

(b) **Receipts** – on the debit side.

(c) **Payments** – on the credit side.

(d) Cash balance at **end** of year.

Rule for Receipts and Payments Account

Debit – Receipts

Credit – Payments

This is a question on Club Accounts.

Answer ALL sections.

The Hibernian Hurling Club kept a record of its finances in an analysed Cash Book. On 1 January 2011, it had an overdraft of €781 in the bank. The following transactions took place during 2011.

8 Jan	Paid Caledonian Ltd for insurance.	Chq. No. 70	€1,648
15 Feb	Lodged membership fees.		€1,500
7 Mar	Paid Sportswear Ltd for jerseys.	Chq. No. 71	€ 700
19 Mar	Deposited gate receipts of St Patrick's Day game.		€ 516
13 Apr	Paid caretaker's wages.	Chq, No. 72	€ 240
9 May	Paid Bus Éireann for bus hire.	Chq. No. 73	€ 325
21 Jun	Lodged proceeds of church gate collection.		€2,347
4 Jul	Purchased hurley sticks.	Chq. No. 74	€ 470
15 Aug	Lodged membership fees.		€ 500
3 Sep	Paid cleaner's wages.	Chq. No. 75	€ 160
19 Oct	Lodged gate receipts of game.		€1,200
6 Nov	Paid Bus Éireann.	Chq. No. 76	€1,700
10 Dec	Lodged proceeds of flag day collection.		€ 849

(A) Record the above transactions for the year in the Club's Analysed Cash Book using the following money column headings:

Debit (Receipts) side: Total, Membership fees, Game receipts, Collections.

Credit (Payments) side: Total, Travel, Insurance, Equipment, Wages

Complete and balance the Analysed Cash Book on 31 December 2011. (22)

(B) Prepare a Summary Receipts and Payments Account for the year from the figures you compiled in the Analysed Cash Book. (12)

(C) (i) Name the club official whose duty it is to keep the financial records. (2)

(ii) Name the final accounts which this official should present to the Club's AGM. (4)

(40 marks)

Source: Junior Certificate Higher Level

Solution and marking Scheme

(A)

Debit **Analysed Cash Book(1)** **Credit**

Date (1/2) 2011	Details (1/2)	Total €	Members Fees €	Game Receipts €	Collection €	Date (1/2) 2011	Details (1/2)	Chq. No.	Total €	Travel €	Insurance €	Games Equip. €	Wages €
15 Feb	Membership Fees	1,500(1/2)	1,500(1/2)			1 Jan	Balance		781(1/2)				
19 Feb	Gate Receipts	516(1/2)		516(1/2)		8 Jan	Calidonian Ltd	70	1,648(1/2)		1,648(1/2)		
21 June	Church Collection	2,347(1/2)			2,347(1/2)	7 Mar	Sportswear Ltd	71	700(1/2)			700(1/2)	
15 Aug	Membership Fees	500(1/2)	500(1/2)			13 Apr	Caretaker	72	240(1/2)				240(1/2)
1 Dec	Gate Receipts	1,200(1/2)		1,200(1/2)		9 May	Bus Éireann	73	325(1/2)	325(1/2)			
10 Dec	Flag Day	849(1/2)			849(1/2)	4 Jul	Hurleys	74	470(1/2)			470(1/2)	
						3 Sep	Cleaner	75	160(1/2)				160(1/2)
						6 Nov	Bus Éireann	76	1,700(1/2)	1,700(1/2)			
		6,912(1/2)	2,000(1/2)	1,716(1/2)	3,196(1/2)				6024(1/2)	2,025(1/2)	1,648(1/2)	1,170(1/2)	400(1/2)
						31 Dec	Balance c/d	(1/2)	888(1/2)				
		6,912(1/2)							6,912(1/2)				

Marking scheme

Heading 1 mark

Date column 2 × 1/2

Details column 2 × 1/2

37 figures × 1/2 mark **(22 marks)**

(B) Receipts & Payments(1) Account for year ending(2) 31/12/11

	Membership	2,000(1)	1 Jan.	Balance b/d	781(1)
	Game Receipts	1,716(1)		Travel	2,025(1)
	Collection	3,196(1)		Insurance	1,648(1)
				Equipment	1,170(1)
				Wages	400(1)
				Balance c/d	888(1)
		6,912			6,912
	Balance b/d	888			

Marking scheme

9 figures × 1 mark

Date 2 marks

Two details columns × 1/2 mark each **(12 marks)**

(C) (i) Treasurer **(2 marks)**

(ii) Receipts & Payments A/C

Income & Expenditure A/C

Balance Sheet

Any two × 2 marks **(4 marks)**

(6 marks)

3. Income and expenditure account

An income and expenditure account for a club is the same as a profit and loss account used in business. It shows all the club's **income** and all the club's **expenditure** for the year.

Expenditure	Income
Cleaning	Subscriptions
Repairs	Bar profit
Insurance	Catering profit
Light and heat	Competition receipts
Depreciation of assets	Dance receipts
Telephone and stationery	Raffle profit
Secretarial expenses	
Wages	

If income is greater than expenditure, it is called excess of income over expenditure. If expenditure is greater than income, it is called excess of expenditure over income.

How to prepare an income and expenditure account

From a given receipts and payments account with adjustments included:

(i) Exclude opening and closing balances.

(ii) Exclude purchase or sale of assets.

(iii) Include adjustments.

4. Balance sheet

The balance sheet of a club is exactly the same as the balance sheet of a business. It shows assets and liabilities as usual.

There are two differences in the 'Financed By' section:

Capital is called **Accumulated Fund.**

Net Profit is called **Excess of Income over Expenditure**, which is added to accumulated fund.

E. Adjustments in club accounts

HL

1. Bar trading account

If the club operates a bar, it will be necessary to prepare a bar trading account. The profit or loss on the bar is transferred to the income and expenditure account.

Example

	€
Bar sales	10,000
Bar purchases	6,000
Bar stock at start	2,000
Bar stock at end	1,800

Bar Trading Account

		€	€
	Bar sales		10,000
	Deduct Cost of Sales		
	Opening stock	2,000	
	Bar purchases	6,000	
	Cost of goods available for sale	8,000	
	Less closing stock	1,800	
	Cost of Sales		6,200
	Bar profit		3,800

2. Functions

Profit → Income
Loss → Expenditure

Most clubs run functions such as dances, dinners, concerts, competitions. A profit or loss must be worked out on these functions and entered in the income and expenditure account.

Example

Dance receipts	€2,000
Dance expenses	€1,200
Profit on dance	€800 → Income

3. Subscriptions

Clubs get their finance mainly from members' subscriptions. We must include in the income and expenditure account only subscriptions for the period of account we are dealing with. Thus subscriptions will need to be adjusted.

Rule for Adjusting Subscriptions
- Start with subscriptions received.
- Add subscriptions due at end.
- Deduct subscriptions prepaid at end.

Balance Sheet

Subscriptions due at end → **Current Assets**

Subscriptions prepaid at end → **Current Liability**

Example

Subscriptions received €2,000

Subscriptions due at end €100

Subscriptions prepaid at end €300

Solution

Subscriptions received	€2,000
Add subscriptions due end	€100
	€2,100
Less subscriptions prepaid end	€300
Income and expenditure account	€1,800

Balance Sheet

Subscriptions due	€100 → CA
Subscriptions prepaid	€300 → CL

4. Depreciation of fixed assets

(a) Calculate percentage depreciation on the cost figure at end of year. Enter figure in **expenditure** section.

(b) **Deduct depreciation from cost of asset** in the fixed assets section of balance sheet.

5. Accruals at end of year (amounts due)

(a) **Add** to expenditure figure in income and expenditure account.

(b) Show amount due as **current liability** in balance sheet.

6. Amounts paid in advance at end of year

(a) **Deduct** prepaid amount from expenditure in income and expenditure account.

(b) Show prepaid amount as **current asset** in balance sheet.

7. Calculation of accumulated fund if not given

Add up all assets in club at start of year. Add up all liabilities in club at start of year. Subtract liabilities from assets. Difference is accumulated fund.

This is a Club Account Question.

Answer all parts of this question:

The Country Golf Club had the following Assets and Liabilities on 1 January 2011.

Clubhouse €216,000 Bar Stock €6,720 Cash €2,040 Term Loan €16,800

The following is a summary of the Club's financial transactions for the year ended 31 December 2011.

Receipts:	€	Payments:	€
Bar Receipts	42,480	Light and Heat	6,960
Dance Receipts	13,560	Bar Purchases	20,040
Subscriptions	23,640	Wages	7,680
		Insurance	14,580
		Equipment	42,000

Additional information on 31 December 2011.

(i) Bar Stock €7,380

(ii) Light and Heat due €300

(iii) Insurance prepaid €408

(iv) Subscriptions due €960

(v) Equipment to be depreciated by 20% each year.

(A) Prepare a statement calculating the club's Accumulated Fund on 1 January 2011. (3)

(B) From the information above prepare:

(i) Receipts and Payments Account for the year ending 31/12/2011 (6)

(ii) A Bar Trading Account for the year ending 31/12/2011. (6)

(iii) An Income and Expenditure Account for the year ending 31/12/2011. (13)

(iv) A Balance Sheet as at 31/12/2011. (12)

(40 marks)

Suggested solution and marking scheme

CLUB ACCOUNT QUESTION

(A) Statement Club's Accumulated Fund

Statement of Accumulated Fund on 1/1/2011

ASSETS		
Clubhouse	216,000(1/2)	
Bar Stock	6,720(1/2)	
Cash	2,040(1/2)	224,760
LIABILITIES		
Term Loan		16,800(1/2)
Accumulated Fund 1/1/11		207,960(1)

(3 marks)

(B) (i) Receipts and Payments Account for year ending 31/12/2011

1 mark complete heading (must have date)

1/1/11	Balance	2,040(1/2)	Light and Heat	6,960(1/2)
	Bar Receipts	42,480(1/2)	Bar Purchases	20,040(1/2)
	Dance Receipts	13,560(1/2)	Wages	7,680(1/2)
	Subscriptions	23,640(1/2)	Insurance	14,580(1/2)
	Balance c/d	9,540(1/2)	Equipment	42,000(1/2)
		91,260		91,260
			Balance b/d	9,540

(6 marks)

(ii) Bar Trading Account for year ending 31/12/2011

1 mark complete heading (must have date)

Sales		42,480(1/2)
Opening Stock	6,720(1/2)	
Purchases	20,040(1/2)	
	26,760(1/2)	
Less Closing Stock	7,380(1/2)	
Cost of Sales		19,380(1/2)
Bar Profit		23,100(1/2)

(6 marks)

(iii) Income and Expenditure Account for year ending 31/12/2011

1 mark complete heading (must have date)

	INCOME			
	Bar Profit		23,100(1)	
	Dance Receipts		13,560(1)	
	Subscriptions	23,640(1)		
	Add subscriptions Due	960	24,600(1)	61,260
	EXPENDITURE			
	Light and Heat	6,960(1)		
	Add Light and Heat due	300	7,260(1)	
	Wages		7,680(1)	
	Insurance	14,580(1)		
	Less Insurance Prepaid	408	14,172(1)	
	Depreciation Equipment		8,400(1)	37,512
	Excess of Income over Expenditure(1)			23,748(1)

(13 marks)

(iv) Balance Sheet as at 31/12/2011

1 mark complete heading (must have date)

		Cost	Deprec.	NBV
	<u>Fixed Assets</u>			
	Clubhouse	216,000(1/2)		216,000
	Equipment	42,000(1/2)	8,400(1/2)	33,600(1/2)
		258,000(1/2)	8,400	249,600(1/2)
	<u>Current Assets</u>			
	Closing Stock	7,380(1/2)		
	Subscriptions Due	960(1/2)		
	Insurance Prepaid	408(1/2)	8,748(1/2)	
	<u>Less Current Liabilities</u> (Creditors: amounts falling due within one year)			
	Bank Overdraft	9,540(1/2)		
	Light and Heat Due	300(1/2)	9,840(1/2)	
	Working Capital			(1,092) (1)
	Total net Assets			248,508(1/2)
	<u>Financed by</u>			
	Accumulated Fund		207,960(1/2)	
	Add Surplus of Income over Expenditure		23,748(1/2)	231,708(1/2)
	<u>Long-term Liabilities</u> (Creditors: Amounts falling due after one year)			
	Term Loan			16,800(1)
	Capital Employed			248,508(1/2)

(12 marks)

8. Treasurer's Report

The treasurer will present the treasurer's report at the AGM. It informs the members of the financial situation of the club.

Treasurer's Report on Country Golf Club – Refer to Accounts and Solution above (Higher Level Question)

COUNTRY GOLF CLUB

Treasurer's Report

To All Club Members 31 December 2011
From Rob Clarke, Treasurer

Please find attached with this report the final accounts and the balance sheet of the club.

Body of Report

1. Bar profit was €23,100 as shown in bar trading account.
2. The income and expenditure shows that the club had a surplus of €23,748 for the year.
3. There is €960 owing in subscriptions at end of the year.
4. To improve facilities for members for the future I recommend that members' subscriptions be increased by 10%.

I am available to discuss this report if required.

Signed

Rob Clarke
Treasurer

See:

Ordinary Level	**Ordinary Level**	**Higher Level**
Section A	Section B	Paper I
2006 Q5	2007 Q6	Section B
2005 Q13	2006 Q3	2009 Q2
2004 Q19	2000 Q6	2008 Q2
2001 Q2		2007 Q2
		2006 Q2
		2005 Q2

47 Farm Accounts

To be able to:

- Prepare simple accounts from given data
- Prepare a simple report on farm accounts

A. Introduction

Farming in Ireland is a big and important business. Farmers, like any other business, must keep proper accounts.

B. Purpose of farm accounts

(1) To find out whether the farm made a **profit** or **loss**.
(2) To find out **which sections** of farming are most profitable.
(3) For submission to **Revenue Commissioners** for tax liability.
(4) To provide information to **bank manager** when making a loan application.
(5) To provide information if applying for **government** or **EU grants**.
(6) To calculate net worth/value of the farm.

C. Farm accounts

(1) Most farmers will keep an **analysed cash book** to record daily receipts and payments.
(2) At the end of the year an **income and expenditure account** is prepared to find profit or loss made.
(3) A **balance sheet** is also prepared to show the farmer's assets, liabilities and capital.

Analysed cash book

This book is used to record the daily receipts and payments of the farmer.

Receipts – Debit side. **Payments – Credit side.**

This is an Analysed Cash Book question.

(A) Roland and Sheena Winters own a farm in Kerry and have a balance of €3,500 in the bank on 1 May 2011. They ask you to help them write up their Analysed Cash Book (Analysed Receipts and Payments Book) for the month of May 2011 from the data below:

Use the following money column headings:

Debit (Receipts) side: Bank, Sheep, Cattle, Grants, Other.

Credit (Payments) side: Bank, Feed, Fertiliser, Cattle, Vet, Expenses.

2/5/2011	Paid the vet	(cheque no. 11)	€ 130
5/5/2011	Sale of sheep	(receipt no. 2)	€ 1,600
8/5/2011	Purchased calves	(cheque no. 12)	€ 1,500
12/5/2011	Received EU Grant		€ 2,000
13/5/2011	Purchased fertiliser	(cheque no. 13)	€ 400
16/5/2011	Purchased feed	(cheque no. 14)	€ 200
19/5/2011	Paid ESB	(cheque no. 15)	€ 165
21/5/2011	Sold cattle	(receipt no. 3)	€ 3,000
24/5/2011	Paid insurance	(cheque no. 16)	€ 460
27/5/2011	Received a loan		€ 12,000
28/5/2011	Paid contractor	(cheque no. 17)	€ 18,500
30/5/2011	Purchased tractor	(cheque no. 18)	€ 5,700
31/5/2011	Sold cattle	(receipt no. 4)	€ 6,900
31/5/2011	Sale of vegetables	(receipt no. 5)	€ 145

(23)

(B) List **four** reasons why farmers should keep accounts. (8)

(31 marks)

Solution and marking scheme

(A) Farm Accounts

Analysed Cash Book (Analysed Receipts and Payments Book)
Debit (Receipts) Side

Date (1/2) 2011	Details	Rec. No.	Fo	Bank	Sheep	Cattle	Grants	Other
1/5/	Balance	(2)	b/d	3,500 (2)				
5/5/	Sales	2		1,600 (1/2)	1,600 (1/2)			
12/5/	Grant			2,000 (1/2)			2,000 (1/2)	
21/5/	Sales	3		3,000 (1/2)		3,000 (1/2)		
27/5/	Loan			12,000 (1/2)				12,000 (1/2)
31/5/	Sales	4		6,900 (1/2)		6,900 (1/2)		
31/5/	Sales	5		145 (1/2)				145 (1/2)
				29,145 (1/2)				
1/6/	Balance		b/d	2,090 (1)	1,600	9,900	2,000	12,145

Credit (Payments) Side

Date (1/2) 2011	Details	Ch. No. (2)	Fo	Bank	Feed	Fertil.	Cattle	Vet	Expen.
2/5/	Vet	11		130 (1/2)				130 (1/2)	
8/5/	Purchases	12		1,500 (1/2)			15,00 (1/2)		
13/5/	Purchases	13		400 (1/2)		400 (1/2)			
16/5/	Purchases	14		200 (1/2)	200 (1/2)				
19/5/	ESB	15		165 (1/2)					165 (1/2)
24/5/	Insurance	16		460 (1/2)					460 (1/2)
28/5/	Contractor	17		18,500 (1/2)					18,500 (1/2)
30/5/	Tractor	18		5,700 (1/2)					5,700 (1/2)
				27,055	200	400	15,00	130	24,825
				2,090 (1)					
31/5/	Balance		c/d	29,145					

(23 marks)

(B) Any four good reasons why farmers should keep accounts from the list below are acceptable:

- To find out if the farm made a profit or a loss for a given period.
- To identify which section of the farm is performing well/poorly.
- To find out how much the farm is worth.
- Accounts are needed when applying for loans.
- Accounts are needed to obtain EU/government grants.
- Required by the Revenue if above a certain size.

4 reasons @ 2 marks each

This is a Farm Accounts question.

Frank and Victoria Mills carry on a farming business. The following figures were extracted from their books for year ended 31/12/2016.

	€	€
Income – Potatoes		32,000
– Fruit		28,000
Land and Buildings	300,000	
Debtors	16,000	
Creditors		5,300
Long-term Loan		56,000
Interest on Loan	3,000	
Wages	9,000	
Light and Heat	1,400	
Rent	1,100	
Seeds and Plants	7,400	
Telephone	3,800	
Insurance	1,300	
Fertiliser	3,240	
Diesel and Oil	2,800	
Tractors and Equipment	60,000	
Bank	7,200	
Capital		300,000
Drawings	5,060	
	421,300	421,300

The following additional information is available on 31/12/2016.

Light and Heat due €100

Rent Prepaid €200

Depreciate Tractors and Equipment by 10% of Cost.

Prepare (A) Income and Expenditure account for year ending 31/12/2016

(B) Balance Sheet as at 31/12/2016.

Solution

(A) Income and Expenditure Account for Year Ending 31 December 2016

		€	€	€
	Income			
	Potatoes		32,000	
	Fruit		28,000	60,000
	Less Expenditure			
	Interest on loan		3,000	
	Wages		9,000	
	Light and heat	1,400		
	Add light and heat due	100	1,500	
	Rent	1,100		
	Less rent prepaid	200	900	
	Seeds and Plants		7,400	
	Telephone		3,800	
	Insurance		1,300	
	Diesel and Oil		2,800	
	Fertiliser		3,240	
	Depreciation of tractors and Equipment		6,000	38,940
	Farm net profit/excess income over expenditure			21,060

(B) Balance Sheet as at 31 December 2016

	Cost	Deprec.	NBV
Fixed Assets			
Land and Buildings	300,000	–	300,000
Tractors and Equipment	60,000	6,000	54,000
Equipment	10,000	–	10,000
	360,000	6,000	354,000
Current Assets			
Debtors	16,000		
Bank	7,200		
Rent prepaid	200	23,400	
Less Current Liabilities (Creditors: Amounts falling due within one year)			
Creditors	5,300		
Light and heat due	100	5,400	
Working capital			18,000
Total net assets			372,000
Financed By			
Capital	300,000		
Add farm profit	21,060	321,060	
Less drawings		(5,060)	316,000
Long-term Liabilities (Creditors: Amounts falling due after more than one year)			
ACC loan			56,000
Capital employed			372,000

exam Q

See:

Ordinary Level	**Ordinary Level**	**Higher Level**
Section A	Section B	Paper I
2007 Q4	2009 Q6	Section A
2006 Q9	2004 Q6	2008 Q10
		2006 Q7

48 Service Firms

To be able to:

- Prepare accounts from given data

A. Introduction

Service firms supply and sell a service rather than a product.

Examples: Travel agencies, hairdressing, accounting, banking, insurance, cleaning, secretarial, horse training.

B. Accounts prepared by service firms

- **Analysed cash book** to record daily receipts and payments.
- **Operating statement** (profit and loss account) for year.
- **Balance sheet** as at last day of the year.

1. Analysed cash book

Most service firms will keep an analysed cash book as their main financial record.

2. Final accounts of service firms

(a) Service firms will prepare an **operating statement** (profit and loss account) to find out whether the firm made a profit or a loss.

(b) Service firms will also prepare a **balance sheet** and it is the same as any other balance sheet.

This is an Integrated Services Firm question.

Answer (A) and (B).

(A) List **three** reasons why service firms should keep accounts. (6)

(B) (i) Write up the Analysed Cash Book (Analysed Receipts and Payments Book) of Decorate Ltd, a decorating firm, for the month of May 2011 from the data below:

1/5/2011	Bank Overdraft		2,500
1/5/2011	Received from Smith Ltd	Receipt No. 1	1,500
3/5/2011	Received from M. Kelly	Receipt No. 2	1,200

4/5/2011	Paid wages	Cheque No. 1	600
6/5/2011	Paid ESB	Cheque No. 2	200
7/5/2011	Paid Telecom	Cheque No. 3	350
9/5/2011	Paid for advertising	Cheque No. 4	400
10/5/2011	Received from St Mary's National School	Receipt No. 3	2,800
10/5/2011	Received from M. Walshe	Receipt No. 4	1,400
16/5/2011	Received loan from AIB	Receipt No. 5	15,000
17/5/2011	Purchased a van	Cheque No. 5	22,000
18/5/2011	Owner withdrew for own use	Cheque No. 6	300
23/5/2011	Paid rent	Cheque No. 7	500
26/5/2011	Paid for van insurance	Cheque No. 8	1,100
27/5/2011	Paid wages	Cheque No. 9	600
28/5/2011	Received from Lyle Ltd	Receipt No. 6	3,600
30/5/2011	Owners invested in firm	Receipt No. 7	10,000

Use the following money column headings:

Debit (Receipts) side: Bank, Business, Domestic, Other.

Credit (Payments) side: Bank, Light, Wages, Telephone, Advertising, Other.

(ii) Name **four entries** in the Analysed Cash Book you have written up which **should not** be included in the firm's Operating Statement (Income and Expenditure Account). (34)

(40 marks)

Suggested solution and marking scheme

Integrated Service Firm Account

(A) Reasons why service firms keep accounts.

(i) To find out if the service firm made a profit or loss.

(ii) To identify which section of the firm is performing well or poorly.

(iii) To find out how much the firm is worth.

(iv) Accounts are needed when applying for loans or grants.

(v) Required by the Revenue.

3 reasons @ 2 marks **(6 marks)**

(B) (i)

ANALYSED CASH BOOK (DEBIT SIDE)

Date (1/2) 2011	Details	Fo	Receipt No. (1)	Bank €	Business (1) €	Domestic (1) €	Other (1) €
1/5	Smith Ltd	DL	1	1,500 (1/2)	1,500 (2)		
3/5	Ms Kelly	DL	2	1,200 (1/2)		1,200 (1/2)	
10/5	St Mary's NS	DL	3	2,800 (1/2)			2,800 (1/2)
10/5	Mr Walshe	DL	4	1,400 (1/2)		1,400 (1/2)	
16/5	AIB Loan	GL	5	15,000 (1/2)	1,500 (1/2)		15,000 (1/2)
28/5	Lyle Ltd	DL	6	3,600 (1/2)	3,600 (1/2)		
30/5	Owners	GL	7	10,000 (1/2)			10,000 (1/2)
				35,500 (1/2)	5,100	2,600	27,800
1/6	Balance	B/d		6,950 (1/2)			

ANALYSED CASH BOOK (CREDIT SIDE)

Date (1/2) 2011	Details	Fo	Cheque No. (1)	Bank €	Light €	Wages €	Tel. €	Adv. €	Other €
1/5	Balance	B/d		2,500 (2)					
4/5	Wages	GL	1	600 (1/2)		600 (1/2)			
6/5	ESB	GL	2	200 (1/2)	200 (1/2)				
7/5	Telecom	GL	3	350 (1/2)			350 (1/2)		
9/5	Advert	GL	4	400 (1/2)				400 (1/2)	
17/5	Van	GL	5	22,000 (1/2)					22,000 (1/2)
18/5	Drawings	GL	6	300 (1/2)					300 (1/2)
23/5	Rent	GL	7	500 (1/2)					500 (1/2)
26/5	Insurance	GL	8	1,100 (1/2)					1,100 (1/2)
27/5	Wages	GL	9	600 (1/2)		600 (1/2)			
				28,550	200	1,200	350	400	23,900
31/5	Balance	C/d		6,950 (1)					
				35,500					

(26 marks)

(B) (ii) Four entries that **should not be included** in the Operating Statement. Any **four** from the following:

Opening Balance, AIB Loan, Owners investment, Purchase of Van, Drawings, Closing Balance.

4 @ 2 marks **(8 marks)**

SECTION 4
Information Technology

49 Modern Information Technology

To be able to:

- Identify parts of a computer
- Explain computer and IT terms
- Identify uses of computers in
  - Business
  - Homes
  - Banks

A. Introduction

Information Technology (IT) is a modern term applied to the processing of knowledge and data using computers and other electronic advances.
Data Processing (DP) is the operation of collecting, storing, processing and transmitting data.

B. Computers

A computer is a device capable of solving problems by accepting data, performing mathematical operations on the data, and giving out results.

C. Hardware and software

Hardware

Physical part of a computer system, e.g. monitor, keyboard, disk drive, printer.

Software

Programs which provide the instructions to the computer . Examples include spreadsheet, word processing, database, CAD, CAM.

D. Hardware/computer equipment

A computer is made up of many parts called hardware, and includes monitor, keyboard and system unit. The system unit holds the computer's processor (CPU), memory and disk drives.

E. Parts of a computer

The **Keyboard** is used to get the information into the computer.
The **CPU** is used to process the information, i.e. do calculations.
The **Visual Display Unit** is a screen on which we see information that is output from the computer.

The **Printer** produces a hard copy of this display.

The **Disk Drive** makes it possible for the information to be stored on disk for use in the future.

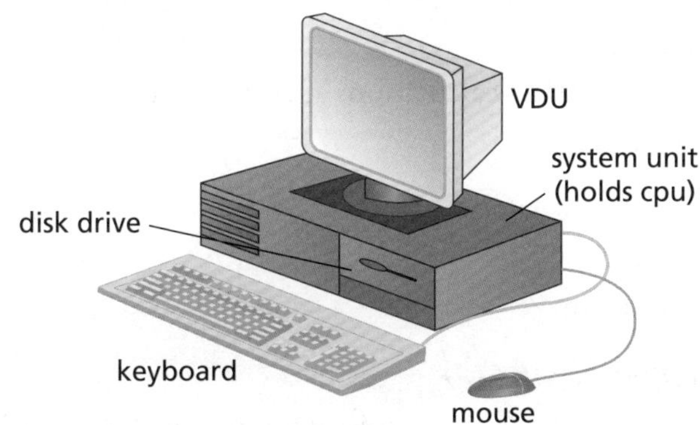

F. Main components of a computer

(1) **Input devices** – hardware used to enter data.

(2) **Processor** – hardware that produces results.

(3) **Output devices** – hardware that displays results.

(4) **Storage** – hardware used to store information.

G. Input devices

1. Keyboard

A device for entering data and programs into the computer. It is a display of keys that produce characters on the VDU when pressed.

2. Mouse

A hand-held electronic device which allows the cursor to move on the screen.

3. Digital camera

A digital camera can be linked to a computer allowing photographs to be uploaded, viewed, modified and printed.

4. Scanner

A scanner is used to copy text, pictures, drawings, etc., into the computer.

5. Modem

This is a device that links a computer to the telephone system. It is used to transfer information from one computer to another.

H. Processing hardware

Central processing unit (CPU)

This is the brain of the computer, where all calculations on the data are carried out. It is the place where the computer interprets and processes information. The speed of processors is measured in Gigahertz (GHz).

There are three main areas in the CPU.

(1) The Control Unit

Controls all computer operations.

(2) The Arithmetic Unit

The part where the mathematical calculations are carried out.

(3) Storage/Memory Unit

Stores data and programs.

Memory and storage

There are two types of memory.

(i) Random access memory (RAM)

The instructions your computer gets and information it processes are kept in RAM during your work session. RAM is not a permanent storage place for information, as it is active only while your computer is on. When you turn off your computer, information is deleted from RAM, so it must be saved before switching off your computer. This can be done internally on the hard drive or externally on CD ROM (Compact Disc Read Only Memory) or on a memory stick.

(ii) Read only memory (ROM)

This memory holds the data and instructions permanently needed by the computer, e.g. the instructions needed for the operation of the computer. This information is entered at the time of manufacture and cannot be altered by the user. When the computer is turned off, this information is not lost.

Size of memory

Computer memory is measured in Kilobytes (KB), Megabytes (MB) and Gigabytes (GB).

I. Output hardware

Output devices allow you to see the information entered and processed.

1. Monitor/VDU

A monitor (Visual Display Unit) is the most common method of displaying information.

2. Printer

A printer is a device that allows you to put the information on paper. This is a permanent copy, sometimes called a 'printout' or 'hard copy'. The most popular are laser or inkjet printers.

J. Computer software/packages

Software is the set of instructions that enables the computer to perform its functions. There are two types of software.

1. Operating system

The operating system gets your computer running and controls the operation of its activities. It looks after the internal running of the computer, i.e. reading disks, listing contents of disks, saving and loading programs, etc. A common operating system used with IBM-compatible computers is Microsoft Windows.

2. Programs

A program is a coded set of instructions that interprets the information you give the computer. A wide variety of programs are used for different tasks, including word processing, e.g. Microsoft Word, and spreadsheets, e.g. Microsoft Excel.

K. Software programs used in business

1. Word processing

A software system that allows you to write sentences and paragraphs. You can produce letters, documents and reports. Text can be moved, copied, replaced and checked for spelling, print sizes can be changed, and when finished, it can all be printed on paper.

2. Database

A database is a filing system on the computer. It can be used in business for names and addresses of customers, in schools for students and class lists, in hospitals for patients, etc.

3. Spreadsheet

A computer program which allows the operator to do accounts, budgets, etc. It performs calculations. Any change to a figure will have a knock-on effect on all other figures.

4. Mail merge

This program allows you to produce personalised letters, i.e. they look as if they were written specially for a particular person. To do this you type out a letter on the word processor and merge with a name and address from the database. The same letter can be addressed to a number of people.

5. Payroll

A program used by business to calculate wages.

6. Computerised accounts

Used to prepare accounts in business.

7. Computer-aided design (CAD)

Used in the design of products.

8. Computer-aided manufacture (CAM)

A package used to assist in the manufacture of goods.

9. Desktop publishing (DTP)

This program is used to produce professional-quality reports, booklets, magazines, brochures and other publications on computer. A high-quality printer is essential.

L. Use of information technology

1. In business

(a) For **word processing**.

(b) For **filing**, e.g. names and addresses of customers using database.

(c) For **doing accounts, payroll and wages slip, stock records** using spreadsheet.

(d) For **reading bar codes** in shops and controlling stock.

(e) Some firms use computers for **designing products** (CAD), and in **manufacturing** (CAM).

(f) For **communicating** with other firms and customers. e.g. email, Internet.

(g) For **selling goods and services** on the Internet.

2. In communications

(a) Through **satellite TV** we can get immediate coverage of all major events throughout the world, e.g. World Cup soccer.

(b) **Mobile phones** can be used by reporters to send information back to radio or TV headquarters.

(c) **A modem** can be used to transfer information from one computer to another over a telephone line, e.g. foreign journalists can send information back to headquarters using a PC and modem.

(d) **Fax machine** can be used to transmit information; this is made up of a scanner, modem and printer.

(e) **Eircom** provides a wide range of services that are computer-based, e.g. videoconferencing.

(f) **Email** is used extensively to communicate, and many businesses have **Internet websites** for advertising their products and services worldwide.

3. In the home

There are many uses of information technology in the home.

(a) Internet access – reservations/online banking/research.

(b) Email for communications.

(c) Word processing – writing a letter.

(d) Spreadsheets/budgets/accounts.

(e) Database/filing/storing information.

(f) Security/remote control/sensors, e.g. fire alarms, burglar alarms.

(g) Timers in household appliances, e.g. central heating systems.

(h) Texting/email/Internet access via mobile phone.

4. In banking

(a) All **deposit** accounts, **current** accounts, **loan accounts** and **overdrafts** are recorded on computer.

(b) **All information processed** through banks is done on computer – direct debits, standing orders, credit transfers and PayPath.

(c) **Bank statements** are prepared through a computer.
(d) All **bank information** is kept on computer, e.g. interest rates on mortgages and term loans, deposit account rates of interest, rates of exchange of foreign currency.
(e) All **ATMs** are linked to computer and allow customers to withdraw, lodge, check balance, order a cheque book, order a statement twenty-four hours a day.
(f) **Electronic Funds Transfer at Point of Sale (EFTPOS):** the customer is given a plastic card, and when she/he comes to a shop checkout, the card is inserted into an electronic device, the PIN is keyed in and the amount of the bill is deducted from the customer's bank account and put into the shop's bank account, e.g. Laser.

M. Computerised accounts

Computers have many uses in accounting.

(1) Day books, debtors, creditors and nominal ledger, cash book, and preparing trial balance.
(2) Business documents – invoicing, credit notes, etc. and printing statements for customers.
(3) VAT analysis.
(4) Trading and profit and loss account and balance sheet.
(5) Wages/payroll/wages slips.
(6) Stock control/stock records.

N. Keyboarding

A keyboard is used for entering information into a computer by typing. Efficient keyboarding involves being able to type properly, i.e. resting fingers on home keys ASDF JKL, and moving around the keyboard without looking at keyboard. Here are some of the keys on a computer keyboard and their use.

(1) **QWERTY** – First six letters on the second row.
(2) **Home Keys** – ASDF JKL.
(3) **Space Bar** – To move on one space, i.e. between words.

(4) **Shift Key** – To make capital letters.
(5) **Caps Lock Key** – To make a line of capital letters.
(6) **Enter/Return Key** – Moves cursor to next line, or when using a program, tells the computer to carry out instruction.
(7) **Function Keys** – To perform special functions within a program, e.g. F1 – Help.
(8) **Del (Delete)** – To eliminate data from screen.
(9) **Ins (Insert)** – To insert a character omitted.
(10) **Tab Key** – To set margins.
(11) **Esc (Escape)** – To cancel an operation.

O. Proofreading

Proofreading is checking your work for errors and making the necessary corrections before making a printout.

P. Factors to be considered before purchasing a computer system

(1) How much will the system cost and how will it be financed?
(2) Is a computer system required, and how will firm benefit from owning a computer?
(3) Size of system required and availability of software.
(4) Will employees have to be trained? How much will training cost? Will there be staff lay-offs?
(5) Where will computer system be located, and is the location suitable?

Q. Recording purchase of a computer in the books of a company

1. Purchase of computer by cheque

Rule
Debit Computer Account
Credit Bank Account

2. Purchase of computer on credit

The purchase of an asset on credit is recorded in the **general journal** then posted to **ledger**.

Rule
Debit Computer Account
Credit Supplier's Account

Example

1 January 2016 Purchased computer system on credit from Lotus Ltd for €5,000.

General Journal **Page 1**

Date	Particulars	Fo	Debit €	Credit €
1/1/16	Computer A/C	GL1	5,000	
	Lotus Ltd			5,000
	Purchase of computer system on credit			

Ledger

Computer A/C

Date	Particulars	Fo	Total €	Date	Particulars	Fo	Total €
1/1/16	Lotus Ltd	GJ	5,000				

Lotus Ltd

Date	Particulars	Fo	Total	Date	Particulars	Fo	Total €
				1/1/16	Computer	GJ1	5,000

R. Dictionary of information technology terms

Broadband Internet Access Broadband offers 'high speed always on' Internet access. It is currently the fastest Internet access available, fifteen times faster than dial-up, allowing downloading and other transactions to be completed more efficiently for Internet users.

Central Processing Unit (CPU) Part of computer system which interprets and carries out instructions.

Computer-aided Design (CAD) A program that converts rough sketches into a finished form.

Computer-aided Manufacture (CAM) Using computers in manufacturing.

E-commerce Buying or selling on the Internet or making payment on the Internet.

Electronic Mail (Email) A way of sending typed messages and computer files directly from one computer to another over the Internet.

Facsimile/Fax Scanning of a document and transmission of it via wires. Copy is produced at destination.

Internet An international network linking millions of computers in different countries through the telephone system. It is a means of communication and a source of information on supplies or services. It can also be used for banking, email, reservations and ordering.

Internet Service Provider (ISP) A company that allows you access the Internet. e.g. Eircom, Indigo, Ireland on Line (IOL).

Network Where many computers within an organisation are linked together, so that all of them can access information from the same source.

Software Package A pre-written program that can be purchased for specific use, e.g. word processing package.

World Wide Web (WWW) A vast collection of linked documents available over the Internet.

This is an Information Technology question.

Answer all sections.

The directors of P.J. Ltd, manufacturers and suppliers of household furniture, were very impressed with the quotation from Hiteck Computers. Hiteck Ltd were offering an 'all-in' package, which included the computer system and a selection of business software, at a special price of €10,000.

(A) What are the three main hardware parts of a computer system? (6)

(B) Give three types of computer software suitable for the business. (6)

(C) State three ways in which P.J. Ltd may benefit from purchasing a computer system. (9)

(D) P.J. Ltd purchased the computer system from Hiteck Ltd on credit, on 25/5/15. Record this purchase in the appropriate book of first entry of P.J. Ltd and post the relevant figures to the ledger. (12)

(E) State two suitable outside sources of finance that P.J. Ltd could use to finance the computer system.

Give a brief explanation of any **one** of these **two** sources. (7)

Source: Junior Certificate Higher Level. **(40 marks)**

Suggested solution

(A) Visual display unit, keyboard, disk drive, printer, mouse.

(B) Since P.J. Limited manufacture and supply household furniture, the main type of software would be Computer-aided Design (CAD), Computer-aided Manufacture (CAM) plus any of the following: word processing, spreadsheet, database, payroll, accounts, stock control.

(C) (i) Reduction in number of staff required.
(ii) Speed in production.
(iii) Letter designs.
(iv) More accurate work.

(D) **General Journal**

			€	€
25/5/15	Computer A/C Hiteck Ltd A/C Purchase of computer system on credit	GL1 GL1	10,000	 10,000

LEDGER

Computer A/C

			€				
25/5/15	Hiteck Ltd	GJ1	10,000				

Hiteck Ltd A/C

							€
				25/5/15	Computer	GJ1	10,000

(E) Leasing, Term Loan, Hire Purchase.

Leasing – This is a form of renting where you obtain the use but never the ownership.

Term Loan – P.J. Ltd could get a loan from the bank of €10,000 and repay it over three to five years.

Hire Purchase – This is a system where you pay a deposit and the balance over an agreed number of instalments. P.J. Ltd would get immediate possession of the computer system but become the legal owner only when the last instalment was paid.

exam Q

See:

Higher Level
Paper I
Section A
2009 Q1
2008 Q1
2005 Q1
2004 Q19
2003 Q2

Higher Level
Paper I
Section B
2001 Q6

Ordinary Level
Section A
2009 Q20
2008 Q5
2008 Q12
2006 Q10

Ordinary Level
Section B
2005 Q3
2002 Q3
2000 Q8

Index